STORYTELLING: HOW TO WRITE A NOVEL

JONATHAN MOELLER

DESCRIPTION

Want to learn to write a novel? This is the book for you!

The key to writing a good novel is to tell a good story, and this book will show you how to tell a good story in novel form. We'll look at all the important parts of a satisfying story structure:

-The introduction. How to set the stage for your book.

-The conflict and the inciting incident. All stories revolve around conflict, and the more emotionally significant the conflict, the better.

-Rising action. Your characters need to take action to resolve their conflict, and they will experience setbacks and failures.

-The climax. The more significant the conflict, the more powerful its climax and resolution.

-The resolution. We see how the conflict and its resolution have changed the characters.

Finally, this book contains a complete annotated copy of the author's novel SILENT ORDER: IRON HAND to provide an example of a novel that follows the rules of story structure.

From the introduction to the resolution, STORY-TELLING: HOW TO WRITE A NOVEL will show you how to write a compelling novel of your own!

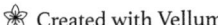

INTRODUCTION: WHY WRITE THIS BOOK?

Welcome to STORYTELLING: HOW TO WRITE A NOVEL!

In this book, I will show you how to use story structure to write a novel with a compelling and thrilling plot. You don't need a college degree or advanced training to write a novel, just persistence and an understanding of how an interesting story is put together.

In the pages to come, I will explain story structure and how you can apply that to a novel to create a riveting plot and fascinating characters.

WHY WRITE THIS BOOK?

My name's Jonathan Moeller, and sometimes people ask me for writing advice.

I thought that odd, but then I thought about it some more, and it made sense. I've been self-publishing my books for almost ten years. As of this writing (March 2021), I have self-published one hundred and eighteen novels and sold 1.7 million copies of my books. There are quite a few writers who have written more books and sold more copies than I have, but thanks to my readers, I've been fortunate enough to do pretty well with self-publishing. Given that, it does make sense that people would ask me for writing advice.

Additionally, the question itself is a gracious compliment. People liked my books well enough to ask for advice about how to write their own.

With all that in mind, I decided to write this book for three reasons.

First, I can't answer every question someone might have about writing a novel. But if I wrote this book and published it at an affordable price, I could direct people to this book to answer their questions. Additionally, a book can reach far more people than I could on my own. There's only so much time in the day to answer email.

Second, I have written a lot of books. I would like to share my experience with people who might benefit from it, but in a way that is neither pushy nor arrogant. By putting together my advice for writing a novel here, I'm not pushing it on anyone, and it is available for anyone who wants to read it.

Third, since I'm self-published, I hold all the rights to most of my books. This means I can include one of my novels in this book with annotations explaining the various points about story structure I will make. Specifically, at the end of this book, you will find one of my shorter science fiction novels, SILENT ORDER: IRON HAND, the first book of my SILENT ORDER science fiction series. I will use this novel to provide an example of the various explanations for story structure I will make.

WHAT TO EXPECT IN THIS BOOK

First, we'll go through basic story structure. I will explain how to put together a proper story, one that will hold readers' attention and not leave them disappointed. We'll examine the various components of a complete story.

Next, we'll go into more detail in some of the other elements of storytelling. We'll discuss how to make interesting and compelling characters, how to write intriguing descriptions, and how to create a conflict that must be resolved at the heart of the story.

WHAT DO I MEAN BY PULP WRITER?

For the past ten years, the header on my website has been "Jonathan Moeller, Pulp Writer," my podcast is titled "The Pulp Writer Show" (listen at https://thepulpwritershow. libsyn.com/), and this book is the first of a planned "Pulp Writer Guides" series. But what do I mean by the term?

"Pulp Writer" originally referred to someone who wrote for the old pulp magazines, which were extremely popular in the United States during the first half of the 20th century. The magazines were called "pulps" because they used cheap paper to help keep printing costs down, which helped the pulps rise to new heights of popularity during the Great Depression. Most of the pulp magazines published genre fiction – mystery stories, detective stories, science fiction, fantasy, horror, occult fiction, and adventure tales.

The mission of the pulps was to sell copies. To do that, the editors needed to fill the pages with interesting stories. Writers for the pulps put an emphasis on writing quickly – some of the pulp writers of the era occasionally wrote entire editions of magazines under multiple pen names. The writers, therefore, needed to focus on giving the readers what they wanted – a good, solid, entertaining story. Several prominent science fiction, fantasy, horror, and mystery writers wrote for the pulps – Raymond Chandler, Dashiel Hammett, Poul Anderson, Robert E. Howard, Robert Bloch, Leigh Brackett, Ray Bradbury, and numerous others. Eventually, the pulp magazines died out, replaced by television, comic books, and novels, but they had a lasting impact. Most of us have heard of Conan the Barbarian or the trope of the cynical private eye in a trench coat and a fedora, and they and numerous other story tropes originated in the pulp magazines.

I chose "Pulp Writer" for my website title because it reflected the kind of writer I wanted (and continue to want) to be. I don't want to be a writer who writes tedious "literary" fiction or the kind of writer who writes dreary "deconstructions" of popular genre conventions. You can see books, TV shows, and movies like that everywhere – stories that deconstruct the idea of heroes and heroism, of good vs. evil, of people overcoming challenges both internal and external through struggle and sacrifice. I don't like the idea of deconstruction on a philosophical level – if we look at the state of the world, is heroism something we should discourage?

Additionally, some people think that the purpose of fiction is to educate people to a particular political or religious viewpoint and that fiction that doesn't support a particular viewpoint is dangerous or regressive. I strongly disagree with that. The purpose of fiction, in my opinion, is to tell a good story, not to preach a sermon. If you want to listen to a sermon, whether religious, secular, or political, there are many people who preach one to you for free. This isn't to say that a story cannot have a political or religious viewpoint or plot, but if delivering that message becomes the main point of the story, the lecture usurps the story and will almost certainly ruin it.

Instead, I want to be the kind of writer who writes stories that people enjoy, that take them out of their troubles for a little while. To paraphrase sentiments from the letters of J.R.R. Tolkien and C.S. Lewis (not, admittedly, pulp writers), the only people opposed to escapism are the jailors. I want to write stories that aren't a chore to read, that aren't dreary diatribes, and that people look forward to reading. I view my job as an entertainer, which means, logically enough, that my job is to entertain the readers, not to lecture them. The world is often a grim place, and if I can write a book that will distract and entertain people for a few hours, then I will have done my job.

If that's the kind of writer you want to be, then this is the book for you!

1

STORY STRUCTURE

We can all think of books, TV shows, and movies that had disappointing endings. To cite a few examples, a premium cable fantasy series about knights and dragons that completely fell apart in its final season. Or a popular space opera movie franchise that chose in its eighth installment to make its hero into a cowardly recluse who spends his time drinking blue space milk. Or a show about an organized crime boss that cut abruptly to black while the protagonist ate dinner, ending so abruptly that some viewers called their cable companies to complain about an interruption of service during the series finale.

No doubt you can think of similar disappointing stories. But why did they fail to deliver?

We can trace the cause to one of two (or potentially both) problems.

Either these shows, movies, and books failed to follow proper story structure, or they didn't deliver on promises made during the plot. And failing to deliver on the promises of the plot is also a failure of proper story structure.

There are many, many different kinds of stories. No doubt you have seen books that argue there are only seven different basic plots. But, of course, these plots can be combined and altered and played within a million different ways.

That said, I believe that all stories have a basic structure to them. A skeleton, as it were, a foundation upon which the story is built. In both humans and animals, skeletal problems can result in serious health difficulties. In stories, if the skeleton of basic story structure isn't followed, the story likewise will not work, or will not make sense, or will fail to satisfy readers.

What, then, is basic story structure? I believe that every successful story contains five elements.

-The introduction.

-The conflict.

-Rising action.

-Climax.

-Resolution.

We'll take a look at each of these five parts now.

THE INTRODUCTION

As you might expect, the introduction introduces the reader to the story and sets the stage for what comes next. By this, I don't mean a prologue or a section before the book proper called "the introduction." No, I mean the opening of the story, the way you introduce the reader to the characters and prepare the story's conflict.

The sentence "it was a dark and stormy night" is probably one of the best-known and most cliched opening sentences in the English language, but it's cliched for a reason. It sets a tone and a mood right away, which is one of the roles of the introduction. The introduction to a story has three basic functions.

-Capture the reader's interest.

-Set the mood and the tone.

-Lay the ground for the introduction of the conflict.

None of these three things must be particularly long. Indeed, some books manage to do all three with only a few sentences. Other books take a long time to set up the story. For example, a murder mystery might not kill the victim until forty percent of the way through the book, but the author spent the introduction building the web of tangled personal relationships that caused the murder. Agatha Christie did this in many of her novels. Or in another example, in The Lord Of The Rings, the nature of the One Ring and the book's central conflict isn't revealed until several chapters into The Fellowship Of The Ring.

We will have an entire chapter on introductions later in this book, and we'll look at three different ways to introduce the story. You can use a technique called "in media res," which will start in the middle of the action. This can be a good way to immediately capture the reader's interest. Alternatively, you can slowly introduce all the characters and build up to the conflict, much like the Agatha Christie novels mentioned above. Or you can use a short prologue to set the stage for the story and the conflict, though it's best to use this technique sparingly since some readers do not care for prologues at all.

And, of course, you can combine all three techniques! One of the realities about writing fiction is that you can break any writing "rules" so long as the result isn't boring and improves the story. Nevertheless, to break the rules, you must first successfully understand them.

THE CONFLICT

ONCE YOU HAVE SET the stage with your introduction, it's time to bring in the conflict.

"Conflict" is a broad term in the context of storytelling, but it just means the central problem around which the events of the story revolve. For The Lord of the Rings, it's the quest to destroy the One Ring. For a mystery novel, it's the hunt for the killer or to find a missing person. For a thriller novel, it's the mission to capture the terrorists or defeat the hostage-takers or to stop a plot of international intrigue.

Even for a genre with a less violent plot, such as sweet romance, the conflict will revolve around the heroine and her love interest and whatever obstacles are keeping them apart – for example, the heroine could inherit a business from her late father, only for her love interest to own a rival company.

And, of course, it's common for the conflict to revolve entirely around an antagonist. Villains hold a special place in the popular imagination. Darth Vader, Emperor Palpatine, Hans Gruber, Hannibal Lecter, Lord Voldemort, Lex Luthor, Professor Moriarty, Thanos, the Joker, and other popular villains are so widely known that they've become sort of a cultural shorthand. Think of how many memes you've seen on social media comparing politicians and CEOs to Emperor Palpatine and other fictional villains. A charismatic villain who poses a genuine and serious challenge to your protagonist can be the chief ingredient for a memorable story.

That said, it isn't necessary for a story to have an actual villain. It's entirely possible for the conflict to be internal without any sort of villain or antagonist. One of my favorite examples of a story with an entirely internal conflict is the movie The King's Speech, which was about the efforts of Britain's King George VI to overcome his speech impediment. At no point is George in physical danger during the movie, he is wealthy and powerful, and his wife and children love and respect him. Yet his speech impediment, and the internal conflict that produced it, are a crippling hindrance in his duties.

You can also have a story with an external conflict that doesn't require a villain. Think of a survival story where someone is lost in the woods and needs to survive, or where a natural disaster strikes at a town and the characters need to cope with it. There's no villain making threats, but the conflict comes from the dangers of the situation. It's possible to have secondary conflicts and villains arise from the central conflict – the protagonist might have to turn his attention from dealing with the natural disaster in order to confront opportunistic looters attacking his town.

Either way, the protagonist needs to attempt to resolve the conflict in some way, which leads to the next part of story structure.

RISING ACTION

THIS SECTION WILL LIKELY FORM the bulk of your story. The "rising action" phase of your novel will begin when the protagonist attempts to deal with the conflict, whether internal, external, or caused by a villainous antagonist.

However, whatever the nature of the story's conflict, it is important to remember one thing above all else.

The protagonist absolutely MUST take action to attempt to resolve the conflict!

This is one of the biggest storytelling failures that can sink a novel, with the possible exception of messing up the ending. Readers absolutely hate a passive protagonist that does nothing to resolve his or her difficulties. Granted, the protagonist's actions might make the conflict worse or exacerbate the conflict, but at least the protagonist is still taking action. A hero who takes no action, who is a passive observer to the plot without actually doing anything to resolve conflict, will quickly draw the annoyance of the reader.

One of the common worries of someone writing a novel for the first time is to wonder whether or not it will be long enough. The "rising action" phase is where the writer solves that problem because when your protagonist sets out to achieve his or her goals, these efforts will inevitably be met with complications and setbacks. The number and intensity of the complications that your protagonist faces will do a major part to determine your novel's length.

To use a simple example from real life, let's say you needed to drive to the post office to put the gas bill in the mail. This simple task is a story in miniature – you have a problem (the gas bill needs to be paid) and are taking action (driving to the post office) to resolve that problem. But let's say you go to your car and find that it won't start. That is a complication that you need to deal with before you can resolve the main conflict of paying the gas bill. And further complications could ensue – you could fix your car and set out for the post office only to find that the road is closed, or that the police have surrounded the post office, or bad weather causes your car to go off the road and into a ditch. (After all this, paying the bill online seems like a good idea!)

With a little imagination, you can see how this technique applies to writing novels. Consider the classic fantasy story of a farm boy setting off with a magic sword to kill the dark lord. Complications ensue along the way – the farm boy is taken captive by orcs, or the magic sword is broken, or there is a traitor among the farm boy's companions.

Murder mysteries likewise thrive on complications. The detective could go to interview her chief suspect, only to find that he's been killed or committed suicide. A necessary witness could go into hiding, or the detective's superior officer could pull her off the case.

In the past, I have joked that it's easy to think of story plots. Just imagine all the things that could go wrong in real life and apply them to your story, and you'll have your plot! This is particularly useful when it comes to the Rising Action phase of the story.

THE CLIMAX

THE CLIMAX IS the peak of the story, the point when the protagonist and the other characters resolve the conflict that kicked off the events of the plot.

Every part of the story is important, but the climax and

the following resolution are arguably the most important part of story structure.

Why? Because it validates what came before as worthy of the reader's time and attention. Reading a novel is a significant investment of time for many people. If you're reading this book, you might be the sort of person who reads a book a week or even every few days. Think how annoying it is to read a book and find that you don't like the ending. Now imagine that it takes you a month to read a novel, and think how annoyed you would be if you didn't like the ending after all that effort!

If you recall books, TV shows, and movies that you did not like, it is likely that for a significant number of them, the reason for the dislike boiled down to a bad ending.

What constitutes a successful climax in story structure? Basically, the climax needs to do two things. First, the protagonist must confront the conflict or act to resolve it, and second, the conflict raised in the story must be resolved in an emotionally satisfying manner. Note that "emotionally satisfying" doesn't mean that the ending has to be happy. A sad or bittersweet ending, depending upon the story, can be just as emotionally satisfying as an ending where everyone lives happily ever after.

The ideal climax is one that comes as a surprise to the reader but nonetheless makes perfect sense in hindsight.

The worst climaxes are ones that fail to resolve the conflicts raised within the story. A "deus ex machina" ending where the conflict is resolved through no effort from the protagonists is also to be avoided because it will leave the reader unsatisfied and possibly annoyed. A deconstructive ending that invalidates the struggle of the characters' journey to reach the climax will also irritate the reader.

It is important not to screw up the ending because while

readers will forgive many things in a writer, they will never forgive a bad ending.

RESOLUTION

FINALLY, the resolution is the last phase of story structure. Here we see the effects of the resolved conflict upon the characters.

Some writers like to end the story almost immediately after the climax. The bad guy gets shot or falls off the top of a skyscraper, and then the story ends a few sentences or a few seconds of screen time later. That does always seem a little abrupt, so I think it's a good idea to at least include some resolution, to show the effects of the resolved conflict on the characters and how they've changed.

The resolution can be as long or as short as you like, but too long and you will start to bore readers. Good examples of concise resolutions can be found in Sir Arthur Conan Doyle's Sherlock Holmes stories. At the end of the stories, there were usually scenes where Holmes and Watson discussed the case that Holmes just solved, with Holmes filling in a few details that Watson missed and thereby providing a resolution to the storyline. Alternatively, since the frame of the Holmes stories was that Dr. Watson was writing Holmes's cases, Watson would do the "wrapping up" at the end of the story, usually in a few paragraphs or so.

By contrast, The Lord of the Rings (both in the book and the Peter Jackson movies) have a long resolution after the One Ring is destroyed. In fact, the resolution in the books is even longer since the conflicts of the Scouring of the Shire have to be resolved, a sequence which was omitted from the movies. However, a longer resolution was necessary for The Lord of the Rings due to the epic scope and scale of the story.

The resolution is also a good place to embed a sequel hook if you intend to write a sequel to your novel.

FROM SKELETON TO MUSCLE

TO RETURN to our earlier metaphor, basic story structure gives you a skeleton. In the next chapter, we'll show you how to put some meat on the bones of your story's skeleton.

2

THE FIVE IRON LAWS OF STORYTELLING

Understanding basic story structure gives you an excellent foundation upon which to write your novel. But going from understanding the structure of a story to actually telling a good story can be something of a challenging leap.

In this chapter, we'll discuss five rules for telling an interesting and compelling story. You will note that most of these rules revolve around the conflict and the climax, which are the most important parts of the story. I'm sure you can remember a book, a movie, or a TV show where the dialogue was clunky or some of the characters were annoying, but you kept reading or watching because the story was sufficiently interesting to hold your attention.

The last chapter showed you story structure. This chapter will describe how to tell an interesting story within that structure using five rules. I originally thought up these five rules for a blog post I wrote back in 2014, and I jokingly called them "iron laws" to make fun of how intellectuals frequently think up "iron laws" for politics or economics or whatever. Storytelling is a much less dour affair than politics and economics (thankfully!), but as we've discussed previously in this book, the closer you follow story structure, the better your book will be.

These five "iron laws" will help you put strong muscle on the skeleton of your story.

ONE: THE PROTAGONIST MUST HAVE A PROBLEM THAT RESULTS IN A CONFLICT

BECAUSE IF THERE is no problem, there is no story. Conflict and problems are the engines that drive stories. A happy existence with minimal conflicts and problems might be ideal for real life, but it makes an exceedingly dull story. The main character of a story needs to have a problem that results in a conflict.

The protagonist battling a villain is the most popular way to generate a conflict. There are countless different kinds of villains you can use. A mystery novel would have the murderer or the instigator of the crime the detective wants to solve. A thriller novel might have a terrorist group plotting a large-scale attack. A fantasy novel could have an evil wizard or a dark lord. Science fiction often has malevolent artificial intelligence, alien empires, or the space navy of a rival human nation. Romance novels can have a variety of villains – a rival who threatens to steal the heroine's love interest, or the heroine's evil boss, or someone else who stands in the way of the heroine having a Happily Ever After with her love interest.

The point of having a villain is to create an obstacle that the protagonist must overcome or a conflict that the protagonist must resolve. It's not even necessary for the antagonist to be a "villain" as such. You can have a story where two protagonists are having a strong disagreement. Lawyers on the opposite sides of a major court case, for example. Neither one of them is the villain or may not even be in the wrong, but the conflict between them drives the story.

Note that the story doesn't necessarily have to have an actual villain – it just needs a problem. Disaster movies are a good example of this kind of storytelling. The chief conflict is not against another character, but the natural disaster that threatens the characters and their town or city. Think of the movie Apollo 13, a dramatization of NASA's ill-fated Apollo 13 launch to the moon. The movie doesn't have a lot of interpersonal conflicts because the chief problem is so overwhelming and huge – how to get the astronauts back home to Earth after their spacecraft suffers a dangerous mechanical failure.

Speaking of another "space survival" genre movie, the film Gravity starring Sandra Bulloch is another excellent example of a movie without a villain. The movie has no villain – the conflict results when bad luck destroys the space shuttle in orbit and the heroine is trapped in space. Her efforts to survive and get back to Earth make up the plot, all while struggling to find the will to keep fighting after her child's death several years ago.

To sum up, your story's protagonist absolutely must have a conflict to resolve or a problem to face.

TWO: THE PROTAGONIST'S PROBLEM AND
CONFLICT MUST BE CONSEQUENTIAL AND HAVE
REAL STAKES

THE PROBLEM MUST BE serious because if it is not, there are no real stakes, and the reader will get bored and cease to care about the character. The worst of all worlds is an unlikeable character with a trivial problem. Then you wind up with your reader rooting for bad things to happen to the protagonist if the reader doesn't abandon the book entirely.

A "high stakes" problem doesn't necessarily mean physical danger, though it can. Nor does it mean that the problem has to be something apocalyptic like stopping terrorists from detonating a nuclear bomb in a major city. While that obviously is a high-stakes problem, it's not something that can happen in every book. A common difficulty writers of long series face is the escalation problem. The hero saves a city in the first book, the country in the second, and the world in the third. What's after that?

A good way to avoid that problem and to write a conflict is to have the problem be high stakes for the protagonist personally, especially in an emotional sense. The hero doesn't have to save the world, or the country, or even his town. In a thriller, it might be about rescuing one person or saving a group of hostages from bank robbers. Or in a mystery, it could be about solving the murder of one person. Sadly, people are murdered every day, and the world at large rarely takes notice of one murder. But if the protagonist is emotionally invested in finding the killer, that will create a compelling story.

As I mentioned above, physical danger doesn't necessarily have to be part of an emotionally significant plot. The classic novel Pride & Prejudice by Jane Austen is a good example of a novel without much physical danger. The protagonist Elizabeth Bennett is in no physical danger throughout the book, save for when Elizabeth gets caught in a rainstorm and falls sick afterward. Nonetheless, the stakes of her problem – her feelings for Mr. Darcy – are consequential. If she does not secure a good marriage, when her father dies there is the very real possibility Elizabeth will be impoverished. Or if she marries an unsuitable man like Mr. Wickham, her life will be miserable. While a young woman dealing with her feelings seems like a trivial problem, Elizabeth will nonetheless face potentially dire consequences if she chooses wrongly.

That said, the problem must be something the protagonist can conceivably deal with and handle, albeit with difficulty. Too vague of a problem, or too intractable of a problem, and the story goes off the rails. It is possible to write a story where the central conflict arises from social injustice or class divisions. Indeed, many classic novels and movies deal with these themes – much of the work of Charles Dickens, for example. Nevertheless, it is a good idea to keep those themes contained in a conflict between characters in a way that can actually be resolved at the end of the story. Sadly, no human society has yet solved the problems of social injustice and class divisions, and it is unlikely that one ever will. If you have a story where your protagonist is essentially fighting human nature itself rather than trying to resolve a conflict or problem that can actually be resolved, you will leave your reader unsatisfied at the end.

That leads us to the third iron law of storytelling.

THREE: THE PROTAGONIST MUST TAKE ACTION AND STRUGGLE TO RESOLVE HIS OR HER CONFLICT AND PROBLEM.

A COMMON FAILURE in storytelling is a protagonist who has a serious problem but does nothing about it. We've all read stories with a passive protagonist, or worse, a protagonist who does nothing but whine about his difficulties or thinks that by feeling bad about his problems, they will somehow magically get better. Worst of all is when a protagonist does nothing but complain for two hours or 300 pages and somehow does solve all of his or her problems. Not to pick on a specific genre, but this is a common problem in romance novels from beginning writers, where things simply happen to a passive heroine who spends more time agonizing over her problems than acting upon them. Other genres have similar examples – the "chosen one" story trope in fantasy, when mishandled, can lead to a passive protagonist.

Conflict is the first half of a compelling story, but the protagonist taking action to resolve that conflict is the other half.

A passive protagonist who does nothing can be absolute poison to a compelling story. The protagonist must act to attempt to resolve the conflict or problem. Note that he doesn't necessarily have to act effectively (more on that in the next section), but he must take action. In a fantasy novel, the hero must do something to defeat the dark lord or start the quest. In a mystery novel, the protagonist must begin investigating the crime or tracking down the murderer. In a thriller, the hero must battle the terrorists or fight the robbers. In a disaster novel, the protagonists need to deal with the hurricane or the earthquake and its consequences.

If you have a story with a conflict and the protagonists don't take active action to resolve it, that's not a story, that's just an account of bad things happening to people. We can see that every day on the nightly news. While a novel like that would be depressing, it would do something even worse – it would bore the reader.

Don't be boring! Have your protagonists struggle to overcome their difficulties, which leads us to the next iron law.

FOUR: THE PROTAGONIST MUST FACE CHALLENGES AND SETBACKS, AND HIS OR HER EFFORTS TO RESOLVE HIS PROBLEM MAY EVEN BACKFIRE.

WE TOUCHED on this briefly in the chapter on story structure, but one of the chief ways to make a story interesting is to have the protagonists experience setbacks in their efforts to resolve the conflict.

Having the protagonist act to face the conflict makes for a satisfying story, but it can be undone if the hero overcomes the problems without any challenge. This can be a common problem in fantasy and science fiction, especially in the later books of a long series, when a character becomes powerful enough that it's difficult to think up challenges for him or her. For example, how does a writer think up believable foes for Superman, a character who is essentially invincible? In less fantastical settings, this can still be a problem for a character who is a billionaire or who is wealthy enough and powerful enough that it might be difficult to find problems that result in realistic conflicts and challenges.

The key to overcoming these potential problems is to remember two important elements of story plotting. First, every action in life will encounter complications. Second, every action has unanticipated consequences that may result in additional problems.

We have already discussed complications earlier in the book with the example of the trip to the post office encountering car trouble and road construction. Once you know to look for it, you can see this plot technique used in many classic stories. To cite a few examples, in The Lord of the Rings, the Fellowship is forced to divert from their planned route to Mordor into the Mines of Moria, which results in even more challenges. In Pride & Prejudice, Mr. Darcy's first proposal to Elizabeth goes disastrously wrong. In the Sherlock Holmes story The Adventure of the Norwood Builder, Holmes sets out to exonerate his client, only to find absolutely no proof of his innocence and ample evidence of his guilt.

Whenever someone sets out to do something, whether a fictional character or in Real Life, complications and additional troubles are inevitable. Watching a character work through these difficulties makes for compelling fiction.

Unintended consequences are a natural result of unplanned complications that can help with the plot of your novel. In storytelling, unintended consequences occur when a character sets out to do a task or solve a problem, only for something to happen that he did not intend. To return to our previous example of the trip to the post office, let's say you start driving to the post office and hit a deer on the way. The damage to the car is an unintended consequence of the decision to drive to the post office. There could be other unintended consequences resulting from the collison – the insurance company could refuse to pay, or you might have to get a new car, or in all the trouble, you forget to pay the gas bill entirely.

That was a relatively simple example, but you can see its useful application to storytelling. Unintended consequences are a great way to add tension to your plot. For example, you could have a murder mystery where the detective is interrogating a potential suspect for a murder. In a panic, the suspect flees only to be killed by the real murderer to remove a potential witness. This will add further complications to the plot since the detective's investigation suffered a setback, and the detective's superiors might remove her from the case. It also provides the opportunity for additional characterization, as the detective's reaction to the accidental death will reveal a great deal about her.

Of course, any conflicts raised within the story must be resolved, which leads to the final iron law.

FIVE: THE ENDING MUST ABSOLUTELY PROVIDE SATISFACTORY EMOTIONAL RESOLUTION TO THE PROBLEMS RAISED IN THE STORY!

OF ALL FIVE LAWS, this one is the most important. Screw this one up, and readers will be ticked and talk about it on the Internet for years. Whatever crisis comes up in the story, whatever conflict or difficulties, it must be resolved in an emotionally satisfying manner by the end of the story. Note that "emotionally satisfying" doesn't mean that it has to be a happy ending, just that the ending must resolve the story's conflicts in such a way that the reader doesn't feel cheated for having read the book. Your story can have a happy ending, or a sad ending, or a mixture of the two, but the ending must be emotionally satisfying.

What does it mean for the story's conflicts to be resolved in an emotionally satisfying manner? Basically, two different things need to happen at the ending of a story.

First, the conflict has to be resolved.

Second, the characters need to experience change because of resolving the conflict.

Let's look at a few good examples.

The ending of The Lord of the Rings provides an excellent example of this. The object that caused the central conflict of the story – the One Ring – is destroyed, and the Dark Lord is defeated. All the main characters experience change as a result. Frodo is wounded and never really recovers, while Samwise steps up and becomes the leader of the Shire. Merry and Pippin evolve from "young rascals" and become leading figures of the Shire, while Aragorn becomes the King of Gondor and weds Arwen, and Gandalf returns to the Undying Lands, his mission to oppose Sauron complete.

The ending of the movie The King's Speech is another good example of resolving a conflict. (Let's leave out the historical accuracy or lack thereof, which isn't relevant to a discussion about story structure.) At the end of the movie, King George VI addresses the nation over the radio without succumbing to his speech impairment, simultaneously resolving the conflicts over his stammer and his fear of accepting his duties as king. This is an ambivalently happy ending – George VI has overcome his conflicts, but the viewers know that the United Kingdom is about to go through World War II, and George himself will die of lung cancer and heart disease in 1952. Nevertheless, the conflicts within the story have been resolved.

An ending can also be tragic so long as the story's conflicts are resolved. William Shakespeare's play Romeo &

Juliet is a classic example. Romeo and Juliet both commit suicide at the end of the play, but the tragedy of their deaths shocks their families so badly that they end their destructive conflict. All the conflicts in the story have been resolved, albeit at a high price.

STORY STRUCTURE & IRON LAWS

IN THE PREVIOUS CHAPTER, we went through basic story structure, and in this chapter, we showed you some rules to follow while writing your story to keep it as compelling as possible. In the next several chapters, we'll take a closer look at the individual parts of story structure, starting with the introduction.

3

INTRODUCTIONS

"It was a dark and stormy night."

That sentence is perhaps the most cliched opening line in English literature. Of course, the opposite of that is writers who try to make the opening line of their book as shocking and memorable as possible. Like, for example, something like "Today was the day I died for the seventh time." If you read websites and Internet groups where writers frequent, you will often see writers agonizing at length about the opening line of their novel.

Generally, the agonizing is all unnecessary. The introduction to your story has three purposes, and if you keep those functions in mind, it will be much easier to both write the opening line and the rest of the introduction.

First, the introduction should catch the reader's attention.

Second, the introduction should introduce the protagonist and the leading characters.

Finally, it should set the stage for the story's conflict.

We'll go through each of these purposes and then share three methods for getting your story off the ground.

CATCH THE READER'S ATTENTION

AS WE MENTIONED ABOVE, the necessity of seizing the reader's attention and of crafting an interesting opening sentence is the source of much angst in various Internet writers' forums. That said, it's best not to overthink things. The key is to provide just a little mystery, enough to inspire curiosity and encourage the reader to continue further into the book.

The easiest way to be interesting is not to be boring. There are, alas, numerous boring ways to start a book, and you should avoid them. It is best to avoid descriptions of the weather, like the famous "dark and stormy night.". Likewise, it is a good idea to avoid starting your book with lengthy descriptions of the scenery or the setting. Writers who are good at writing lovely prose might pull that off, but I'm not one of those writers, and in my opinion lovely prose is only useful as a vehicle to advance the plot.

Like most advice, "don't be boring" is easy to say and harder to do. How do you provide a little mystery in your novel's introduction? You want to set up a situation where you inspire just enough curiosity in your reader that they keep reading. The first sentence doesn't have to carry the entire load, but it does help.

Let's look at a few examples of opening sentences.

"After dropping my children off at daycare, I drove to the gas station, loaded my pistol, and walked inside." This example might be a bit overdramatic, but it serves to illustrate the point. The narrator is seemingly a responsible parent – dropping his or her children off at daycare before heading to work. Why is the narrator then walking into a gas station with a weapon? For many readers, this will inspire enough curiosity to keep reading.

Here is the opening sentence from my urban fantasy novel CLOAK GAMES: THIEF TRAP (which as of this writing is available for free on all ebook platforms). "One of the earliest things I remember is watching the entire United States Congress commit suicide on national television." Readers have emailed to tell me that this is one of the more effective opening sentences that I have written. It has both a bit of a shock and a mystery hook – why is a small child watching the government commit suicide on TV? If the reader wants to find out why they will have to read on!

INTRODUCE THE CHARACTERS

THE INTRODUCTION of the story must also present the main characters to the reader.

Obviously, you don't need to introduce all the characters to the reader right away, nor all the details about them. The easiest way to introduce any characters in the introduction is to have them engaged in something that reflects their personality and potential conflicts. For example, consider the novel Dracula by Bram Stoker. The book opens with letters written by Jonathan Harker to his fiancée Mina Murray. In the letters, we learn that Harker is a new solicitor on his way to Transylvania to conclude a real estate transaction with an eccentric rural nobleman named Count Dracula. This handily introduces the characters of Harker, Mina, and Dracula, and sets up the stakes. Harker wants to establish himself in his profession so he can marry Mina, and he just needs to conclude his business with Dracula. Unfortunately for Harker, Dracula turns out to be far more dangerous than he initially appears. Soon both Harker and the reader realize that Dracula is an ancient vampire, and the book's conflict begins.

Introducing the characters is a good way to segue into setting the stage for the story's conflict, which we'll discuss next.

INTRODUCING THE CONFLICT

THE FINAL PURPOSE of the introduction is to introduce the reader to the story's conflict or antagonist.

There are lots of fun and exciting ways to introduce the conflict, and I say "fun and exciting" because this is often where the story starts getting quite energetic. In a fantasy novel, it might be when the hero's village is attacked by orcs. In a mystery story, it's when someone stumbles across a dead body. In a thriller, perhaps the hero finds a sinister terror plot that is already well underway.

The conflict can also be introduced more sedately. In an action-themed book, it is easy to introduce the conflict via sudden violence – the attack of orcs or a sudden murder. Other kinds of stories may not involve so much physical danger. The central conflict of most romance novels is whether or not the heroine and the love interest will get together and whether or not they can overcome the assorted obstacles preventing them from having a relationship. A romance novel might introduce the conflict by having the love interest antagonize the heroine in some way. Perhaps he is a lawyer who represents the heroine's business rival, or the heroine is a local law enforcement official, and the love interest is an FBI agent who threatens to take over her case.

Regardless of how the conflict is introduced, the most important part of the conflict is that it must compel the protagonist to take action. If the conflict or the antagonist isn't serious enough to force the protagonist to act, then nothing happens, and you don't have a story. It is possible to have the protagonist refuse to engage with the conflict, only to be forced into it later. For example, take a detective story where the main character (a retired cop) refuses to look into an old case. The retired cop's former partner is murdered, and the grief over his death drives the protagonist into investigating.

Now that you're familiar with the three roles an introduction needs to fulfill, let's take a look at three different methods of writing an introduction – a prologue, bildungsroman (a slow build), or in media res (in the middle of things).

A PROLOGUE

A PROLOGUE IS a short preamble before the main story where you introduce the situation and certain facts about the setting to the reader, facts that your protagonists may not discover until later in the novel. The disadvantage of a prologue is that you will probably need to continue the introduction within the main body of the story since a prologue is usually not enough to introduce the reader to the protagonists and the main conflict in an interesting way. The advantage of a prologue is that you can show the reader vital facts about the story, and obtaining those facts might be a central plot point for the main characters.

I happened to read a good example of an effective prologue before I started writing this chapter – the mystery novel Field of Prey, by John Sandford. The novel revolves around detective Lucas Davenport's efforts to find a pair of serial killers operating in rural Minnesota. The prologue introduces the two serial killers and shows how they stumbled across their preferred method of capturing their victims. In terms of story structure, that means the reader immediately knows who the killers are, even though Davenport and the other detectives do not. The actual plot does not kick off until the first chapter, when a pair of teenagers accidentally discover where the serial killers have been hiding the bodies of their victims. But throughout the book, the reader's advance knowledge from the prologue adds an additional layer of tension to the story, especially when one of the investigators stumbles across the killers without realizing his mortal peril.

Field of Prey had an effective prologue, but I have to admit a prologue is my least favorite technique for an introduction. In the hands of a capable writer, a prologue works, but I've seen a lot of prologues used to dump information on the reader the writer couldn't figure out how to reveal in the story or to introduce a character who doesn't turn up until two-thirds of the way through the book. If you do use a prologue, you will likely have to combine it with one of the other two introductory techniques we will discuss in this chapter.

BILDUNGSROMAN

THE TERM "BILDUNGSROMAN" is a German word that means "education novel" and refers to a genre of fiction that revolves around the education and development of a young protagonist. Nowadays in English we tend to call these kinds of books "coming-of-age" novels. As you might expect, books like this tend to be quite leisurely, following their protagonist from childhood to adulthood.

I have found that this is also a useful shorthand to describe a kind of introduction where the story slowly builds to the conflict. The Lord of the Rings is a good example of a story with a leisurely introduction to the conflict. Frodo doesn't learn that his uncle Bilbo's magic ring is in fact the One Ring until well into the story, and even more time passes before he leaves with the Ring to keep it safe. For that matter, the conflict isn't fully expressed – the Ring must be destroyed, and Frodo is the one to do it – until well into the book.

It can be tricky to hold the reader's interest during a long and leisurely introduction. A good way to keep the reader's interest is to introduce an element of mystery to a long intro-duction. In a fantasy novel, the protagonist might have a secret he has to keep from everyone – perhaps he has magical abilities, and he is hiding them for fear of persecution.

A Study In Scarlet, the first Sherlock Holmes tale, is a good example of a slow introduction, even though the entire book is relatively short. Dr. Watson needs a roommate to help cover his rent, so he moves in with the mysterious Sherlock Holmes. Holmes's many eccentricities lend an air of mystery to him, and finally Watson learns that Holmes is a consulting detective. The actual central conflict - Holmes is brought in to solve a murder - does not take place until well into the story, but the mystery around Holmes himself helps to hold the reader's interest.

IN MEDIA RES

"IN MEDIA RES" is a Latin phrase that translates to "into the middle of things" in English and refers to the kind of introduction where you immediately thrust the reader into the plot without much in the way of buildup.

There are many different methods to do this, and in some ways, it is easier to write than a slower introduction. In a fantasy novel, for example, the protagonist might wake up to find his village under attack by orcs. In a military science fiction novel, the book starts with the protagonist leading his platoon or squadron into battle against the Space Bugs. (This one does seem quite common.) A mystery novel could open with the detective standing over the murder victim and starting the investigation that will be the central conflict of the plot. A legal thriller might open in the middle of a high-stakes trial with the judge issuing a ruling that sets back the protagonist's case and forces her to pursue a different strategy.

The strength of starting a plot in media res is that you can immediately hook the reader with an action scene or some other kind of problem. It's easier to draw the reader's attention with a battle scene or some sort of dramatic sequence than it is with a slower introduction. You can then shift to the next phase of story structure and the conflict once you've gotten through the initial introduction.

The weakness of starting in media res is that you're probably going to skip a lot of important information for the plot that you will need to address later. To return to our previous examples, why are the orcs attacking the protagonist's village? Or why is the protagonist leading his platoon into battle against the Space Bugs? The danger is that you might be tempted to engage in massive "infodumps" later in the book, where characters state obvious things to each other that they already know. Like, for example, "As you know Bob, we're both detectives engaged in a murder investigation." People in real life generally do not talk that way, and using infodumps runs the risk of breaking the story's air of verisimilitude.

The way to avoid infodumps is to use the release of new information as part of driving the plot. As always, the best way to do that is to keep an element of mystery in the story, allowing you to reveal information for maximum dramatic effect. To return to the example of the mystery novel that opens with a detective standing over the dead body, let's say that after the first few chapters, the detective's superior threatens to pull him off the case. There could be any number of reasons – perhaps the detective botched a similar case, or the detective's partner was killed, and the failure haunts him to this day. Or the murder has political implications, and the detective's superior is feeling pressure from his bosses to bury the case. Revealing this information as a complication in the plot rather than an infodump will improve the story.

In our example of a fantasy novel where the protagonist's village is attacked by orcs and the villagers are taken captive, perhaps the human kingdom and the orcs have been at war for centuries. Perhaps the orcs were responding to a human attack, or maybe there is a traitor in the human kingdom who is working with the orcs. Either way, it is better for the protagonist to discover this during the plot rather than explaining it all in the introduction.

Starting the story in media res is a great way to kick off the book, but it can be a challenge not to let things slacken after that. Retaining an element of mystery (and, of course, complications for our protagonist to face) will keep things moving and interesting for the reader.

STARTING THE STORY

IT IS possible to open your book with a combination of a prologue, bildungsroman, and in media res, though you might want to wait until you have more experience writing novels before trying something complicated. The harsh advice "keep it simple, stupid" applies to many areas of life, and keeping things as simple as possible is often useful for writing novels as well.

Of course, the whole point of the introduction is to set up your characters to face the conflict of the story, and in the next chapter, we'll take a look at conflicts.

4

CONFLICTS & ANTAGONISTS

The conflict and the antagonist are the entire reason for the story. To put it another way, if you're building a story structure, then the conflict is the foundation of that structure. If your book's plot boils down to "Bob went to work as an insurance claims adjuster, and nothing happened," that would make for a boring story. But if instead Bob goes to work and gets fired, or Bob goes to work and finds his supervisor murdered in his office, or Bob goes to work and gets kidnapped by alien bounty hunters, you have the basis for a story and a pretty interesting one at that. You would also have the element of mystery to drive the plot forward – who murdered Bob's boss, or why would alien bounty hunters kidnap a human insurance claims adjuster?

In this chapter, we'll take a closer look at the kinds of antagonists and conflicts that make for a compelling story.

THE SEVEN BASIC (OR MAYBE SIX, OR POSSIBLY FOUR) PLOTS

IF YOU'VE SPENT any time researching writing and story-telling, you've probably come across articles stating there are "seven basic plots" or "six basic conflicts." I think the most famous version of this is a book by British author Christopher Booker called "The Seven Basic Plots: Why We Tell Stories," where Booker drew on a combination of Jungian psychology and other academic research to summa-rize seven basic plots. You can find other books and articles that list their versions of the basic plots, though they might use different numbers or organize them differently.

For the purposes of this chapter, I decided to use a list written by Gina Edwards for the ProWritingAid blog on August 2nd, 2020. In that article, she lists seven types of potential story conflict – person vs. person, person vs. nature, person vs. society, person vs. technology, person vs. supernatural, person vs. self, and person vs. destiny. (You can read the article at https://prowritingaid.-com/art/1366/what-are-the-7-types-of-conflict-in-litera-ture.aspx.)

In this chapter, we'll take a closer look at each one of those types of conflict.

Admittedly, the idea that there are only seven basic conflicts might seem limiting, but that is the wrong way to look at it. Think about musical theory – there are only seven basic notes – A through G, and four vocal ranges, soprano, alto, tenor, and bass. Yet from those simple components come the millions and millions of songs throughout human history. The same concept applies to stories and conflicts. Just as the basic components of music can be combined endlessly, so too can the basic conflicts of story structure. Or think about how there are only three primary colors – red, green, and blue, but combined, they create secondary colors and all the countless different variations of colors found in the world.

For that matter, depending on how long your novel is, you will likely have multiple different kinds of conflict within the story.

Let's take a look at each of the seven types of conflict mentioned above.

PERSON VS. PERSON

THIS ONE IS QUITE COMMON, and no doubt you can think of examples off the top of your head – Sherlock Holmes vs. Professor Moriarty, Robin Hood vs. the Sheriff of Nottingham, and others from classic film and literature. In this kind of conflict, the source of the protagonist's conflict is another person.

Why is your protagonist in conflict with this person? The answer to that question will be the source of your story's plot. There are as many different reasons to have conflicts between people as there are people. In a fantasy novel, the conflict could be between a peasant boy and an evil king who destroys his village, or perhaps a knight rebelling against a tyrannical liege lord. In a detective novel, the protagonist might play a game of cat and mouse with a serial killer or a master thief or a corrupt politician. In a legal thriller, the protagonist's nemesis might be a judge or the opposing counsel or perhaps even his own client, or maybe all three, depending on how complicated the book is.

Person vs. person is in some ways the easiest conflict to create because it's not hard to think of reasons for people to fight. Often, conflict begins when people want the same thing – the same house, the same throne, the same romantic partner, the same treasure, and so forth. People can have conflicts for more abstract reasons. Perhaps one man supports the king, and his antagonist supports the rebels. Or one man supports a new housing development to promote economic growth and generate new jobs for the community, while another opposes it because it will damage the environment or push low-income residents out of the neighborhood. Neither person is fully wrong or fully right, and the resolution of their conflict will generate a story – perhaps one will back down, or they will come to some sort of compromise.

Person vs. person is a rich source of story conflict, and nearly every novel has at least some person vs. person conflict, even if the primary conflict of the novel turns out to be something else.

PERSON VS. NATURE

IN THIS STYLE OF CONFLICT, a person struggles against some hostile aspect of nature. Given the implacable power of nature, it is not difficult to think up conflicts that revolve around a character in opposition to the vagaries of the natural world. It could be a natural disaster story, a movie that revolves around a hurricane or an earthquake or a wildfire threatening a community. The conflict would center on the characters' efforts to deal with the natural disaster and save their homes, with no doubt a good deal of person vs. person conflict going on as well.

A survival story would be another good example of person vs. nature conflict. Someone shipwrecked on a deserted island would have to find a way to survive in an unforgiving environment. A character crossing a desert or a frozen tundra would face a similar challenge.

One of the best examples of person vs. nature conflict is the novel Hatchet by Gary Paulsen. In the book, a plane crash leaves a thirteen-year-old boy stranded in the wilderness of a Canadian forest. With nothing but his wits and the titular hatchet, he must find a way to survive until he can be rescued.

Person vs. nature is often combined with other conflicts since natural disasters can bring out both the best and the worst in people. To use the previous example of a natural disaster, the threat of the catastrophe might bring out other conflicts. The mayor and the police chief of a small town might hate one another, and when an earthquake strikes, their conflict erupts. Or the protagonist has a strained relationship with his wife, and surviving a natural disaster gives them an opportunity to resolve their conflicts.

PERSON VS. SOCIETY

IN THIS KIND OF CONFLICT, the protagonist struggles against some aspect of society that he or she finds unjust. Alternatively, the protagonist could find themselves the target of society's injustice and might have to fight or flee.

Both The Hunger Games novels and movies and the

original Star Wars trilogy are examples of people struggling against society, specifically repressive governments. Perhaps one of the oldest examples of this is the Greek myth of Theseus and the Minotaur. In the tale, every year the city of Athens must send seven young men and women to the tyrannical King Minos to be devoured in the Labyrinth of the Minotaur. Desiring to put an end to this, Theseus volunteers to take the place of one of the prisoners and winds up seducing Minos's daughter, killing the Minotaur, and escaping back to Athens.

Basically, conflicts against society tend to take one of two directions. Either the protagonist is struggling to change something about his or her society or is targeted by society for some reason and has to fight to escape or survive. Essentially, one plot is about a reformer, and the second is about the target of repression. Sometimes they are combined when a reformer allies with a target to fight against the aspect of their society they dislike.

Person vs. society conflicts can become quite complicated and lend themselves to longer, more epic stories. If you want to write a shorter book, one of the other forms of conflict might serve better. But if you have an idea for a longer epic story, person vs. society can serve quite well.

PERSON VS. TECHNOLOGY

IN THIS KIND OF CONFLICT, the protagonist struggles against something technological. The most obvious examples are the episodes of Star Trek where Captain Kirk fought an insane computer, but the conflict can be more subtle.

The antagonist can be some kind of new technology that the protagonist finds threatening. No doubt traditional publishing felt and continues to feel that way about indie publishing! In this kind of story, the technology usually has an economic threat to the protagonist.

A classic example of this kind of conflict is the American folk story of John Henry. In most versions of the story, John Henry is a "steel-driving man" whose job it is to pound holes in rock with a sledgehammer to aid in railroad construction. An inventor devises a steam-powered drilling device that would make Henry's job obsolete, so he challenges the machine to a duel. He successfully pounds more holes than the machine but dies of heart failure immediately afterward. John Henry had the moral victory, proving that a human worker could outclass a machine.

This tension between man and machine underlies a lot of science fiction. For as long as humans have used tools, we have feared getting replaced and made obsolete by our tools. The bronze-armored aristocratic warriors of the Bronze Age were made obsolete by iron-wielding soldiers since iron was cheaper and easier to forge. Medieval knights on horseback were made obsolete by professional armies equipped with gunpowder weapons. The process continues in the modern age – expensive fighter jets flown by intensively trained pilots might become obsolete in the face of cheap drone technology. In less violent arenas, there are fears that artificial intelligence will replace audiobook narrators and writers or that artificial intelligence might replace many accountants and lawyers.

One of the modern versions of man vs. technology is the movie Wargames from 1983. In the film, the main character is a teenage hacker. While trying to impress a girl, he hacks into one of the computers controlling the United States's nuclear weapons systems and triggers a wargame simulation. The computer isn't able to distinguish between the simulation and reality, and World War III almost begins as a result. (Apparently, this actually almost happened in 1983 when Soviet computer systems predicted nuclear war with the United States.)

The conflict of person vs. technology can be even more explicit, such as in the Terminator movie franchise, which is about time-traveling robots coming to the 20th and 21st centuries to kill their future enemies before they can become a threat. There is an entire sub-genre of science fiction about people fighting malevolent computers or hostile robots.

Person vs. technology allows for a wide range of different potential conflicts, from the subtle one of someone losing their livelihood to a new kind of technology to a more kinetic battle of a science fiction hero battling evil robots.

PERSON VS. SUPERNATURAL

IN THIS KIND OF CONFLICT, the protagonist battles a supernatural antagonist – a vampire, a werewolf, a malevolent ghost, or some other kind of malign unearthly force. This encompasses most kinds of horror fiction and spills over into fantasy as well.

There are a couple of different ways a writer can approach a person vs. supernatural conflict. You could tell a story where the characters are overwhelmed by the cosmic horror or the evil force, and even if they win, they are badly shaken by having learned Things That Man Was Not Meant

To Know. H.P. Lovecraft's best stories fall into the category. It is tricky to write that kind of story since the ending is depressing. There are readers who enjoy depressing resolutions, but fewer than those who like happy endings.

Another way to address a supernatural conflict is a story where the protagonists suffer and go through trials during the course of the conflict but nonetheless prevail without the sense of cosmic dread, even if they are left scarred by the experience. A good example of this is a story without supernatural elements (though it's still a horror story), the novel Misery by Stephen King. The protagonist escapes from his captor but is left scarred and haunted by the experience.

Alternatively, you could have your protagonists battling supernatural evil fairly often, in a sort of "monster of the week" approach. Stories about vampire hunters or werewolf hunters tend to fall into this category. Bram Stoker's novel Dracula is one of the archetypes of this kind of story. Dracula is a powerful and sinister adversary, but Professor Van Helsing and his allies research and study Dracula's strengths and weaknesses. In the end, Dracula is unable to defeat the combination of Van Helsing's team and modern science.

Person vs. supernatural is a frequent plot in fantasy novels, which overlap on occasion with horror. Numerous fantasy protagonists have battled evil wizards and sorceresses, and vampires, werewolves, zombies, ghouls, and other horror creatures turn up in fantasy novels. In fantasy novels, the battles against the supernatural tend to follow the lines of Van Helsing's battle against Count Dracula. Fantasy readers generally prefer their protagonists to defeat the dark lord or the evil wizard, not to crumble in the face of cosmic horror like a Lovecraft protagonist.

PERSON VS. SELF

IN THIS KIND OF CONFLICT, the protagonist's struggle is against his or her own self. This usually overlaps with another kind of conflict since a protagonist struggling against the self is an internal conflict, and it is common for characters to have both internal and external conflicts simultaneously. To return to our earlier example of the trip to the post office, the external conflict would be the attempt to drop off the mail. An internal conflict would be if the protagonist is a recovering alcoholic and is struggling against the urge to stop by the bar for "just one" drink on the way home, knowing that the one drink would soon turn into nine or ten.

Internal conflicts can take many forms. A frequent example is when a character has mutually exclusive desires or wishes. To use a simple example, a character might need to go to work but really wants to stay home and play in an online gaming tournament. He wants to play in the tournament but needs to go to work to pay his bills. A more serious example could be a character who finds himself in a civil war with most of his family on the other side. He wants to be loyal to his chosen side, but he also wants to remain loyal to his family, which produces an internal conflict since he might not be able to do both.

Addiction is a common internal conflict for a character. In the original Sherlock Holmes stories, it was mentioned in passing a few times that Holmes was a habitual cocaine user until Dr. Watson weaned him off the drug. (Various TV and film adaptations have made this a bigger part of Holmes's character than it was in the original stories.) In the TV medical drama House, one of the long-running conflicts is the titular character gradually losing control of his addiction to painkillers. Addiction issues can make for compelling internal conflict, though it's best to avoid using it as a crutch to create drama.

Generally, internal conflicts are usually combined with external conflicts to maximize the tension within the story. It is possible to write a story that revolves entirely around a character's internal conflict, but frankly, it can be quite challenging.

If you have a character who faces both an internal and an external conflict simultaneously, that can make for an extremely compelling story. The man whose family is on the opposite side of a civil war will face the internal conflict of trying to maintain his family ties and his loyalty to his chosen side while dealing with the dangerous external conflicts of battles. Or a scientist could find himself torn over the ethics of an experiment at his university or of a product that his employer is about to release. A detective might find himself forced to pursue an investigation against a man he believes to be innocent.

In all these examples, the internal and external conflicts play upon each other, making for a more compelling storytelling experience for the reader.

PERSON VS. DESTINY

IN THIS KIND OF CONFLICT, the protagonist battles fate. One of the oldest examples of this sort of conflict is Greek myth and theatre, where protagonists are often fated by the gods to die or fail. Another example can be found in Norse mythology, where the gods know that the world is fated to be destroyed in Ragnarök no matter what they do.

In the modern era, this kind of conflict is not terribly popular and tends to take other forms. People nowadays generally do not believe in fate or destiny, at least not with the intensity that pre-Christian civilizations believed in fate. A good example of a story where the characters really do believe in fate is Poul Anderson's classic fantasy novel The Broken Sword, which is set in a version of Viking-era England where magic is real. Fate binds the main character to his doom, despite all his efforts to escape it.

Another example of this sort of inescapable fate is the character of Turin from J.R.R. Tolkien's The Silmarillion. The dark lord Morgoth curses Turin's father, and so Turin is doomed by the curse regardless of what he does. While Tolkien was a devout Catholic, the story of Turin is nonetheless an excellent example of the pre-Christian sense of inescapable fate.

As you might expect from the previous examples, modern stories about fate or destiny tend to be fantasy novels. Both The Silmarillion and The Broken Sword are classics of the fantasy genre, but in the hands of less-skilled writers, destiny can become a plot crutch. Think about a story where the protagonist must go on his quest or undertake some trial because "destiny says so" and no other explanation beyond that. One would think that destiny would at least show up with a court order!

In stories set in the contemporary world, "destiny" tends to take the form of the character's background or family. These stories have a character who is struggling against their family or social class background – a high school student trying to go to college to escape poverty, for example, or a child of drug addicts or alcoholics attempting to avoid repeating their parents' mistakes. In these stories, family and class background tend to serve as a replacement for the ancient conception of fate or destiny.

RESOLVING CONFLICTS

In this chapter, we've listed seven different kinds of conflicts, but this list is by no means proscriptive. There are other kinds of conflicts we haven't described here. It is important to emphasize that it is rare for a novel to have just one kind of conflict. Usually, the characters will have internal conflicts, and the subplots will often be different kinds of conflicts than the main one.

In the upcoming chapter, we'll take a look at the next important block of story structure: how the characters act to resolve their conflicts.

5

RISING ACTION

We've looked at the first two parts of story structure – the introduction and the conflict. Now it's time to move on to the next portion of story structure, the characters taking action to overcome their conflicts or to defeat their antagonists. In this chapter, we'll explore ways to drive the action once the characters have been introduced and encountered their problem.

GET THINGS MOVING

A QUICK AND easy description of "rising action" is to say that it's the portion of the book when "stuff starts happening." Of course, stuff should already have been happening, but when the protagonists take action to resolve their conflicts, that means the plot will start moving. In The Lord of the Rings, the plot really starts when Frodo decides to leave the Shire to take the One Ring to Rivendell. In a Sherlock Holmes story, usually Dr. Watson spends a few paragraphs setting the stage, a client comes to Holmes with a problem, and then Holmes starts investigating the mystery.

"Stuff starts happening" might be the simple way to describe the rising action portion of story structure, but what kind of stuff? To put it simply, the rising action portion of the story begins when the protagonists start taking action to resolve their conflicts or defeat their antagonists.

AVOID PASSIVITY

ONE OF THE potential problems in any story is a protagonist who is passive instead of active, a protagonist to whom things simply happen.

This is a major problem for two reasons. First, a passive protagonist can inspire dislike or even contempt from the reader. Readers enjoy characters with which they can empathize, and it can be difficult to relate to a character who has problems and does nothing about them. We all like to believe we would take action in the face of difficulties, and so therefore it is often annoying to read about a character who does nothing in the face of challenges.

What do we mean by a "passive" character? Simply put, a passive character is a character who doesn't take action. One way to put it might be a character who has things happen to him rather than taking action, but that might be too simplistic. After all, you could have a character get shot or stabbed – he's at the receiving end of the (unpleasant) action, but obviously that's not an experience most people would passively accept.

Nor does a passive character mean having a character who just reacts to things. Depending upon the kind of plot, your characters might spend a lot of time reacting to events out of necessity. In a fantasy novel, if your main character's village or hometown comes under attack from orcish raiders, the protagonist is going to spend a lot of time reacting to that problem. Or in a thriller novel that involves a terrorist attack or a hostage situation, the protagonist will be forced to react to whatever the bad guys are doing.

A passive character is one who simply lets the events of the story happen to him or her and doesn't react to them or doesn't react in a way that makes sense. A passive protagonist is usually the sign of an inexperienced fiction writer or one who hasn't yet gotten a solid handle on story structure.

For example, consider a protagonist who spends all her time reflecting on her emotions and how she feels about what has happened but doesn't take action in any meaningful way. Such a character will rapidly become tedious. This isn't to say that the protagonist can't have emotions about what is happening, but an emotional response can't be the only action the character displays.

We'll now look at a few ways to make sure that your characters react and that the "rising action" portion of your story is as interesting as possible.

PAIN POINT

SOMETIMES THE CONFLICT of a story is referred to as the "inciting incident." In other words, it is the event that kicks off the plot and pushes the story into motion. In the Sherlock Holmes stories, the inciting incident usually occurs when the client comes to Holmes's flat seeking his help. Of course, the client had his or her own inciting incident that drove them to seek out the advice of London's only consulting detective. (Which is, of course, an excellent example of a character taking action rather than remaining passive – the client took action in the form of seeking out the wise advice of Sherlock Holmes!)

The example of Holmes's client provides a useful way to avoid the trap of a passive protagonist. The key is to make the inciting incident painful enough or serious enough that the character has no choice but to act. Many of Holmes's clients are not the sort of people who get involved in the world of crime and private detectives (and frequently they point this out themselves), but nonetheless, their problem is serious enough that it compelled them to act. It is similar to how in real life not many people enjoy going to see the doctor, but sometimes a medical problem is alarming enough that we are left with no choice but to seek medical advice.

You can also use a sufficiently painful inciting incident to trigger internal conflicts in your characters. For example, let's say you are writing a fantasy novel about a retired soldier who has become an innkeeper. After a lifetime of danger and battles, the former soldier is happy to settle down. But when orcs attack the village and carry off his neighbors, the former soldier has no choice but to take up his sword and pursue the orcs. Indeed, the orcs might have burned his inn and killed some of his friends, creating an inciting incident so painful that the former soldier was compelled to action.

In fact, it can help your story to put the character in a situation where he or she doesn't want to act but is left with no choice but to take action. One of the fundamental rules of physics is that a body at rest tends to stay at rest unless acted upon by an outside force, and this is often true of characters. Your characters could start the story with problems they want to solve, but they might begin the book reasonably content with themselves and their lives. A sufficiently serious problem will compel the characters to take action.

Of course, it is important for the character to act and not just think about his or her problem, which we will discuss in the next section.

THINKING AND FEELING ARE NOT ACTIONS

WHEN SETTING up your conflict and deciding how your characters will respond to the problem, remember that thinking about the problem and having feelings about the problem, from a storytelling perspective, are not the same as taking action.

This is one of the common traps that catch newer writers. We've all read books where the protagonist spends pages and pages thinking about their problems or thinking about how they feel about the problem, but never actually taking action. I suspect this is for much the same reason that people often have difficulty taking action in real life. It is easier to think about problems, talk about problems, and talk about one's feelings about the problems than it is to take action to deal with those problems!

By this, I don't mean that your characters shouldn't have thoughts and feelings. A character without emotions or inner thoughts will come across as an automaton or a lifeless caricature. Your characters will have to think about their situations, and the sort of problems created by the conflict will inspire many emotional reactions.

Rather, it is not a good idea for the character's reaction to the problem to be simply emotional. If the character just rages about the incident, that can work for a little while, but the character will have to take action about the problem. Let's return to our previous example of a man who has to drive to the post office to mail the gas bill only for his car to break down. If you've had car difficulties yourself, you know that situation will obviously inspire emotions, most likely frustration, and probably some anger as well. Yet you cannot just have the character get angry about the situation and do nothing. He might have to call a tow truck or maybe a friend who can repair his car long enough to get home. Or the character might call his friend to pick him up and drive the gas bill to the post office. The character will be annoyed about the situation, maybe even angry, but he will act.

Having a character respond to a broken-down car with emotion and thought rather than action does seem ludicrous, but it is a common problem in fiction written by newer writers. Especially in fiction that doesn't have violent conflicts such as romances or cozy mysteries, but it can turn up in every genre.

A good example of this would be the "Chosen One" story trope that frequently occurs in numerous varieties of fantasy fiction. In this story element, the Chosen One has been selected by destiny or the gods to fight the dark lord or whatever evil force is threatening the world. Obviously, the Chosen One will have an emotional reaction to this revelation, probably a negative one. This will cause a storytelling problem if you let the Chosen One's reactions and actions be entirely emotional. The worst thing to happen will be if the Chosen One becomes an entirely passive character driven by his or her emotions and who only acts when a mentor or the servants of the dark lord compel him. The Chosen One has become a passive main character reacting to the actions of the other characters.

You can use the emotional struggle as part of the plot without making the Chosen One a passive character. Part of the Chosen One's inner struggle could be to deal with his emotions and learning to act effectively. A good way to compel him to do that would be to create more "pain points" like we discussed above, situations that are so unpleasant or dangerous that he has no choice but to act. For example, he decides to ignore the fact that he is the Chosen One, and then the servants of the dark lord attack and kidnap someone close to him. Or his magical powers manifest, and without proper training, he does serious injury to himself.

Another example of a passive protagonist would be the adolescent main character of a young adult novel. One of the challenges of adolescence is learning to manage emotions in an appropriate way since all kinds of bad things can happen to teenagers if they do not. Consequently, becoming paralyzed with emotional reactions while refusing to act is a frequent adolescent problem. Like the Chosen One plot mentioned above, it is possible to have an adolescent protagonist spend the entire book brooding about his or her emotions and not taking action. Of course, like the Chosen One plot, a teenaged character learning to manage emotion and take action would make for a compelling story.

ACTION IS NOT NECESSARILY EFFECTIVE

AFTER READING THE PRECEDING SECTIONS, you might wonder if it is possible to write a protagonist who is too effective at taking action. If your character takes action to resolve the story's crisis, won't that end the story too quickly?

Not necessarily! Just because the character takes action doesn't mean that action will be effective or that it won't have unanticipated consequences or side effects. It may even worsen the story's conflict!

In the next chapter, we'll look at an important part of story structure – complications!

6

COMPLICATIONS

You might have heard of Murphy's Law, which in its most common form states that "Anything that can go wrong, will go wrong, and at the worst possible time." We've all experienced that at some point in our lives, and it's never pleasant when it happens.

But for the writers of fiction, Murphy's Law is a tremendous storytelling tool. Unexpected complications are the difference between short stories and novels, allowing you to extend your story to novel length. Indeed, you can help determine your novel's eventual duration by deciding how many complications your characters will face as they try to resolve their conflicts and defeat their antagonists. Complications are also methods of providing additional narrative tension and plot hooks in your stories since your readers will want to know what happens next.

What do I mean by complications? Specifically, I mean anything unexpected that happens during the characters' attempts to resolve the story conflicts. These complications can either be events that happen out of the blue or unintended things that happen as a result of the characters' efforts.

For example, we have already used the example of a man driving to the post office to put his gas bill into the mail. The problem/conflict is the need to pay the gas bill, and the action the man takes to resolve the conflict is driving to the post office. We've already talked about several potential complications – the man gets into an accident, his car breaks down, the post office is closed or on fire, the character is attacked by alien bounty hunters, he is attacked by orcs, and so forth. (Obviously, the appropriate complication would depend on the story's genre, though it would be pretty funny if rampaging orcs turned up in what was supposed to be a contemplative literary novel.)

Unexpected complications can both make a book interesting and extend its length. Additionally, there are several ways you can use unexpected complications to make a story more compelling, and we'll explore some of those methods now.

AVOID THE IDIOT PLOT

IT's common advice for writers to avoid an "idiot plot," but what does that mean?

An "idiot plot" refers to a character doing something stupid or making a foolish decision specifically to advance the plot. This is especially annoying if a character was previously established as clever or intelligent but suddenly becomes conveniently stupid at a time that allows the plot to continue. Alternatively, this can refer to an entire book whose conflict only works because the characters are idiots who make poor decisions.

The classic example is a character in a horror movie who makes foolish decisions when stalked by a killer or a monster – running alone into the woods, going into the darkened basement with a flickering candle, and so forth. Obviously, people under stress make bad decisions that seem like a good idea at the time, and you can include that in your fiction. The danger to the story comes when the decision is so bad, and so transparently designed to advance the plot, that it breaks the reader's suspension of disbelief.

The examples from horror fiction in the last paragraph are well-known. Every genre has its examples of convenient bad decisions to advance the plot. Romance novels have characters who break up for reasons designed to artificially induce drama and prolong the tension between the lead and the love interest. Thriller novels have the protagonist foolishly leaving the hostage alone in the abandoned building while he goes out to have a look around. Mystery novels have the detective overlook the obvious, which is especially bad if the mystery is obvious to the reader. Fantasy novels have the protagonist ignore good advice from the wizard mentor and almost get killed in the process. Science fiction novels have the characters do things like touch the glowing green space ooze with their bare hands. (It's a good idea in both real life and fiction to never touch glowing ooze with your bare hand.)

But as we mentioned above, people often make bad or irrational decisions while under stress. It would likewise break the suspension of disbelief if your characters always made the right decisions in moments of conflict. Police officers, soldiers, EMTs, and other people with dangerous and stressful jobs undergo lots and lots of training to ensure that they can keep their heads in a fraught situation, training that most people simply don't have, and it is unrealistic to expect characters to act like seasoned veterans in a crisis.

The key to remember is that if the plot requires a character to act like an idiot at a critical moment, then it will probably annoy the reader. People frequently make bad decisions in the heat of the moment, but those decisions almost always seem like a good idea at the time. That alone won't break the reader's suspension of disbelief. But if the entire plot hinges on a character acting like an idiot, indeed, if the plot grinds to a halt if a character doesn't act foolishly (especially in an uncharacteristic way), that will almost certainly annoy the readers and land your story in "idiot plot" territory.

But how to add complications to your story without having to resort to "idiot plot" techniques? One good way is for your characters' decisions to generate unexpected consequences, and we'll explore that more in the next section.

UNINTENDED CONSEQUENCES

THE CENTRAL INTELLIGENCE AGENCY OF the United States is the source of the term "blowback," which began as an informal way among CIA officers to describe a covert operation that had unplanned and unintended consequences, consequences that might even end up undermining the goals of the operation.

You can find many examples of "blowback" or unintended consequences throughout both modern and ancient history, but my favorite example (because it so clearly illustrates the point) is the American experiment in Prohibition from 1920 to 1933. During that time, the Eighteenth Amendment to the Constitution made it illegal to produce or sell alcoholic beverages in the United States. Prohibition was the culmination of decades of work by pro-temperance social reformers dating back to the end of the US Civil War, and in many ways, the passage of Prohibition was their crowning achievement.

However, that achievement backfired. A booming black market for alcohol emerged, fueling the rise of organized crime and more powerful law enforcement to fight the mobsters. When the Great Depression began, public support for Prohibition dropped, and many state and local governments wanted to use liquor taxes as a new source of revenue. Prohibition was repealed in 1933 by the Twenty-First Amendment to the US Constitution, and local restrictions on liquor sales have eroded ever since.

The point of including the story of Prohibition in this book isn't to debate the morality of alcohol consumption but to illustrate the rule of unintended consequences. The goal of the pro-temperance movement was to end alcohol use in the United States, and Prohibition should in theory have accomplished that. Yet the rise of alcohol-related organized crime was an unanticipated consequence, and widespread disregard for the law helped undermine its moral authority. In the end, the net effect of Prohibition was a total opposite of its stated goal. Drinking was even more firmly established in American culture, and cash-strapped state and local governments were unlikely to turn away from a new source of taxes.

(However, in the interests of historical accuracy, it is important to note that the pro-temperance movement did win many smaller and lasting victories, even if it failed on a national level – the establishment of a minimum drinking age was a result of the temperance movement, and state and local laws banning alcohol sales on Sundays or after a certain time of the night can trace their origins back to Prohibition.)

You can use the example of Prohibition to create unintended consequences and backfiring decisions in your stories. These will generate new problems and conflicts for your characters. The complications and unintended consequences will push the story in new directions and create entertaining and attention-grabbing plot twists.

Let's return to our old example of the man who drives to the post office to mail his gas bill. Any number of potential complications could ensue from this simple task. If you're writing a mystery novel, the man might stumble across a crime in progress or find a dead body in the street outside his house. In a romance novel, the man might meet a woman at the post office, starting a potential love affair. On a more prosaic level, any number of complications that we've already mentioned might occur – the character could get into a car accident, suffer engine difficulties, arrive at the post office to find that it is closed for a gas leak, and so forth.

Every genre has ways of introducing unintended consequences to the story. In a fantasy novel, the hero might save his village from orcish raiders only for the victory to draw the attention of a far more powerful orcish warlord. In a mystery novel, a detective could question a witness, and the killer could decide to murder the witness to prevent damaging testimony. In a romance novel, the heroine could go on a date with her love interest, only to enrage her employer, who views her love interest as a business rival. In a science fiction story, a miraculous new technology might have dangerous side effects – a drug to cure an illness could result in unintentional telepathy or other mutations.

Unintended consequences will help make your story more interesting as they present new problems for your characters to solve.

MAKING THE CONFLICT WORSE

A SPECIFIC KIND of unintended consequence can make the story's conflict work even better. Your characters set out to resolve their conflicts, but their actions unintentionally make the conflict worse. In his classic book The Screwtape Letters, C.S. Lewis talked about how opposing evils, instead of canceling each other out, tend to aggravate one another, and you can use this to help drive your story forward.

In real life, we can all think of people who set out to solve problems only to inadvertently make them worse. In fiction, this is an excellent way to add tension to your story. Earlier in this chapter, we discussed the idea of the "idiot plot," where the story only functions because the characters make unrealistically stupid decisions.

The opposite of this is an idea I usually refer to as "the fog of war." The term "fog of war" was originally used by German military writer Carl von Clausewitz to refer to the uncertainty that cloaks any sort of battlefield situation. A commander must make the best decision he can with the best information he can gather, and even when a commander makes the best possible decision based on the available facts, it can still lead to disaster and defeat. Obviously, war is a dangerous and fluid situation that can change quickly, so it is easy to see how a course of action that seems like an excellent idea at the time can nonetheless lead to catastrophe.

In fiction, you can use the "fog of war" to both advance the plot and add tension to the story. This is an excellent way to avoid the "idiot plot" trap because your characters can make intelligent and well-reasoned decisions that nonetheless blow up in their faces because they didn't have all the information or factors beyond their control altered the outcome. It can also have the net effect of worsening the original conflict. Rather than resolving the conflict, the conflict is now even worse than before.

Fantasy is my favorite genre, so we'll use some fantasy-themed examples. We already used the example of a village carried off into captivity by orcish raiders, with the protagonist pursuing them to rescue his neighbors. Let's say the protagonist assembles a plucky band of allies, and together they rescue the villagers from the orcs. That would seem to solve the conflict – but perhaps the orcish raiders are now furious at the slight to their honor and decide to wipe out the village entirely to avenge their defeat. Or the orcs are in service to a powerful evil wizard who decides to take matters into his own hands. Or maybe the fighting accidentally awakens a slumbering dragon, who decides to clear both the human and orcish intruders off his land. In all of these examples, unintended bad consequences spring from the protagonist's decisions and actions.

The same complications could unfold in a mystery plot. A detective must investigate a man killed by multiple gunshot wounds on an abandoned farm. The investigation reveals that the man was killed in a drug deal gone wrong, and the police department decides to set up an ambush to arrest the entire drug ring. Except the ambush goes wrong, and multiple officers are killed as a direct consequence of that investigation. Or the detective realizes that someone within the police department is working for the drug gang and tipped them off about the ambush.

Romance books thrive on the protagonist inadvertently making things worse. The normal plot for most romance novels is that the heroine and the love interest want to get together, but there is some serious obstacle (family divisions, money, she's a public defender and he's a police officer, etc.) standing in their way. In the romance genre, the conflict usually gets worse when the heroine tries to overcome the obstacle and aggravates it. Perhaps she and her love interest find themselves on opposite sides of a contentious legal case. Or the heroine and her love interest's families are business rivals, and her love interest's family wins a victory over her family's business.

Your protagonists can inadvertently intensify the conflict. But if the story's conflict has a villain or antagonist, you can't expect them to take the protagonist's challenge sitting down!

PUSHBACK

WE'VE ALREADY DISCUSSED the dangers of having a passive protagonist in your story. However, if your story's conflict revolves around an antagonist or a villain, it would not be realistic to have the villain ignore the threat posed by the protagonists. Indeed, having the antagonist react to your protagonists is a superb way to enhance the "rising action" portion of your story. Having the villain push back against the protagonists' actions is more realistic, adding to a sense of verisimilitude, and will make both the villain's character and the story more dynamic.

The form this takes varies depending on the genre of story and the specific character of the antagonist. A ruthless antagonist will take more immoral actions than an antagonist who has a strong moral code. For that matter, it's possible to have an antagonist who isn't necessarily a villain. If your protagonist is falsely accused of a crime, he could be pursued by an honest detective. The detective will have scruples that, for example, a drug lord would not, and even if the detective was not completely honest, he would still be bound by the laws governing investigations and would need to at least attempt to follow them so evidence would not get thrown out in court.

There are many ways that an antagonist can react and attempt to shut down the protagonist's efforts to resolve the conflict or to act to resolve the conflict in the antagonist's favor. To return to the previous example of a fantasy novel where orcish raiders carry off the protagonist's neighbors as captives, let's say the protagonist rescues his neighbors. The leader of the orcs is unlikely to accept this. He might chase the rescued villagers, intending to recapture them. He might gather more allies and warriors for another attack on the village. Or, like we mentioned previously, the orcish leader could serve a powerful wizard or a stronger warlord, and the leader appeals to his overlord for help.

Pushback from your antagonist will help add tension and drama to your story. Like any of your protagonist's actions, the antagonist's decisions can have unintended consequences and even set back the villain's cause, which will add an additional element of tension. Indeed, the villain can even be undone by reacting when he might have been better advised to do nothing. In the Sherlock Holmes story "The Adventure of the Norwood Builder," the villain is defeated when he deliberately leaves a bloody thumbprint at the crime scene in hopes of further framing his victim of murder. But Holmes notes the incongruity, which leads to the villain's undoing.

However, to have a compelling story, the conflict must be resolved, and we will discuss how to reach the moment of crisis in the next chapter.

7

THE CLIMAX

In real life, conflicts often drag on for years and years without ever reaching any kind of satisfactory resolution. In fiction, that makes for a very unsatisfying story. To have an enjoyable story, at some point, the central conflict must reach a resolution. In story structure, the moment of crisis that decides the resolution is usually called the climax. At this moment, the conflict is resolved one way or another. The protagonists achieve their goals, the villain is defeated, and the crisis that kicked off the plot is resolved.

While all parts of a story structure are important, the climax and the resolution are especially important. Writing a story without a good ending is a lot like constructing a house with a good foundation, solid walls, and a beautiful interior, but omitting to put a roof on it. No one will appreciate the house's beautiful interior if it floods during the next thunderstorm. Just as the punchline determines whether or not a joke is funny, the climax validates the investment of time the reader has put into the story. No one likes a joke with a bad punchline, and no one enjoys a story with a bad ending.

Everyone reading this can think of examples of stories with bad endings. Indeed, some of these stories might have been wildly successful and critically acclaimed – for example, a cable fantasy show about dragons and ice zombies, another cable show about a New Jersey mob family, a Maine horror writer's fantasy series about a gunslinger questing for a mysterious tower, or the final installment of a popular space opera video game trilogy. It is unfortunate that people mostly remember the disappointing endings because a lot of work went into these TV shows, books, and video games, and they had some amazing installments along the way.

But people mostly remember the bad endings. That is a lesson the writer should never forget.

Let's take a look at what makes a good climax so your story can avoid that fate!

THE BUILDING BLOCKS

THE BEST WAY TO have a good climactic scene in your novel is to do the work before you reach the point of climax.

This sounds like a paradox, but it isn't. The climax is in many ways the pinnacle of the story, but to have a pinnacle, you first need to construct a solid foundation. The climactic scene should pay off the promises made in the introduction, conflict, and rising action sections of the story. We've said before in this book that the ending is in many ways the most important part of the story, but without a solid story before the climax, the best ending in the world won't do any good.

It's a bit like studying for the final exam of a class or preparing to file taxes. If you spent the semester diligently studying and completed the assigned homework, likely the final exam will not be a major problem. But if you spent the semester skipping class and ignoring homework, the final exam becomes a terrifying ordeal. In the same way, if you spend the fiscal year organizing and storing your receipts and paperwork and keeping track of your expenses, filing your taxes will be an annoying but manageable chore. By contrast, if you keep your receipts in a shoebox in the back of your closet and only start on taxes the day before the filing deadline, it will become a major source of stress.

Once you have a solid and compelling story, the climax will be easier to write because the emotional stakes will be so high for the characters. Let's look at some ways to have the strongest climactic scene possible.

EMOTIONAL RESOLUTION

THE MOST IMPORTANT thing to remember about a climax is that it must unfold in such a way that it emotionally resolves the story's primary conflict.

Note that "emotional resolution" doesn't necessarily mean that the story has to have a happy ending. The ending can be happy, sad, bittersweet, or some mixture of those emotions. But it does have to provide emotional closure for the conflict raised in the story.

What do I mean by an emotionally satisfying ending? In his book Poetics, the ancient Greek philosopher Aristotle says that an ending needs to have "catharsis," the purging of the emotions raised during the story. To demonstrate what that means, let's look at one of my favorite examples so far, that of the fantasy novel where the protagonist's village is attacked by orcs.

What emotions are raised by the conflict in that scenario? The protagonist will feel fear, both for himself and for his neighbors. Likely he will also feel anger against the orcs that took his neighbor and maybe anger at the local human nobles who failed to defend the villagers. He may feel determination as he sets out to rescue the captives, and likely new fear once he encounters the orcish raiders again. Ideally, we want the reader to feel these emotions alongside the hero.

The conflict could be resolved in many different ways. The story could have a straightforward happy ending – the protagonist rescues the villagers from the orcish raiders, and they hail him as a hero. Or it could have a bittersweet ending that mixes both happy and sad. The protagonist might rescue the villagers but be killed in the process, becoming a posthumous hero. Or the protagonist's love interest could die, or his closest friends. Either way, the central conflict is actually resolved. The villagers are rescued from the orcs, and the emotions raised during the conflict are purged by the climax.

A bad way of resolving the conflict would be having the protagonist fail, and the orcs slaughter the villagers. In a way, it resolves the conflict since the orcs win. However, the resolution of the conflict must be emotionally satisfying, and as we mentioned above, emotional satisfaction is achieved through the catharsis of the emotions raised during the story. An ending where the orcs kill the hero and slaughter the villagers fails to purge the emotions generated during the plot and the reader is likely left with feelings of dismay, perhaps even annoyance that his or her time has been wasted. This might be the feeling you want to achieve in your reader, but if it is, I am afraid that this may not be the book on writing for you.

This isn't to say that a story can't have a sad ending, but the sad ending must achieve emotional satisfaction. A climax where the hero and his allies die but save the villagers would be sad but nonetheless resolves the conflict in a satisfactory way. This is essentially the ending to the classic film Seven Samurai.

But if you do have a happy ending, how to make it emotionally satisfying? We'll consider that question in the next section.

EARN THE HAPPY ENDING

I SOMETIMES JOKE that before a fictional character can experience happiness, they must first suffer two or three times as much.

That might be a glib remark, but there is a considerable amount of truth to it. Part of having a satisfying story climax is making sure to follow proper story structure before arrival at the climactic moment of the book. Sometimes writers worry that a happy ending will be anodyne or cliché, but that is a mistake. For one thing, a majority of readers generally prefer some level of happy ending. Not entirely happy, but happy enough. There are some readers who enjoy downer endings, but they are a definite minority.

The best way to have a happy ending is to make the

protagonist suffer for it. No one likes a happy ending where the protagonist solves all his or her conflicts and lives happily ever after without first suffering for it, and the reason no one likes this kind of ending is because it fails to offer emotional satisifaction. As we mentioned earlier in the chapter, in story structure one of the functions of the climax is to purge and resolve the emotions raised during the earlier phases of the story. If the characters resolve all their conflicts and receive a happy ending without expending significant effort, no tense emotions are raised in the conflict, and therefore the ending offers no emotional resonance to the reader.

The best way for a story to have a satisfying happy ending is for the protagonist to earn it through tension and suffering. Different genres do this in different ways. In our fantasy novel about a protagonist attempting to rescue his neighbors from orcs, let the protagonist experience setbacks and failures during his quest – his first attempt fails, his allies turn on him, he has to endure cold and hunger – so that way when he does succeed, it feels both earned and satisfying.

Mystery novels provide many good examples of this. In a well-written mystery, the detective has to work hard and sometimes suffer to discover the truth. Along the way, the detective might have friends turn on him, lose the support of his superiors, or even be physically attacked if he gets too close to the murderer. The detective will likely also have to spend a lot of time clearing up false leads and dead-end theories. But in the end, when the truth is revealed and the detective solves the crime, the ending will be all the more satisfying for the amount of work it took the protagonist to get there.

Romance novels can likewise have a happy ending. Typically, the climactic moment of a romance novel is when the protagonist and her love interest declare their love for one another, and this time there are no obstacles standing in the way of their relationship or marriage (depending upon the subgenre of romance). But this happy ending can only be satisfying if the characters first had to suffer. Pride & Prejudice is one of the older examples of this kind of ending. Elizabeth Bennett and Mr. Darcy wind up engaged at the end of the book, but there were a great many obstacles along the way. Elizabeth and Darcy disliked each other at their first meeting, and Elizabeth was offended by Darcy's clumsy first proposal. It was only after Darcy helped Elizabeth's family with a serious problem involving her sister Lydia's poor romantic choices that the two were able to reconcile.

A happy ending is satisfying once the characters have suffered to earn it, but whether happy, sad, or bittersweet, the resolution of the conflict must pay off the emotions raised earlier in the story.

THE CLIMAX MUST MAKE SENSE

IN ADDITION to resolving the emotions and the conflicts raised during the story, the climactic scene must make sense and be logically consistent with what has happened before.

If the ending doesn't make sense, it will grate on readers. We can all think of examples of books, movies, and TV shows where the ending did not make sense at all. Examples include previously unknown characters showing up to save the day or a character suddenly developing stupendous new powers and using them to win the conflict. (This can work, but only if it is sufficiently foreshadowed in the story.)

A good rule of thumb is that the ending should be a surprise to the reader yet nonetheless have been obvious in hindsight. One of the most famous examples of this is the movie The Sixth Sense, starring Bruce Willis. (Skip this section if you haven't seen The Sixth Sense already, because I am about to spoil the ending.) In the movie, Bruce Willis's character is a ghost and doesn't know it, but the movie is structured in such a way that the audience thinks the character is alive for most of the story. In the climactic scene of the movie, the character realizes that he is a ghost, and suddenly various oddities throughout the film make perfect sense. With this revelation, the ending improves everything that came before, and watching the movie a second time is a rewarding experience because the viewer can then see all the subtle clues that indicate that the protagonist died before the movie began.

Obviously, this is easier to say than to do. (Which is true of all good advice.) But if you can write an ending that surprises the reader but nonetheless is obvious in hindsight, you will have a satisfied reader.

DON'T CHEAT THE READER

FINALLY, when writing your story's climactic scene, it's important not to cheat the reader.

Looking back over this chapter, you can see that the

climax of the story is about resolving the conflict and giving catharsis for the emotions raised during the previous phases of that story. The first several parts of story structures offer various promises to the reader. The introduction sets the stage and the characters and telegraphs what kind of story the novel will contain. The conflict and the inciting incident raise the stakes and show the characters working to resolve their conflict despite complications and difficulties.

We've said before that the climax has to pay off the stakes raised by the conflict. In a way, the first few phases of the story are like writing checks to your reader. When the reader gets to the climax, he or she cashes those checks. This means that you do not want your reader to feel cheated by the ending or that his or her time has been wasted by reading your book.

A good example of cheating the reader is the idea of "deus ex machina," where the characters are saved or achieve victory through no effort of their own. This term comes from ancient Greek theatre, where an actor playing one of the gods would be lowered onto the stage with a crane or come up through a trapdoor, and the appearance of the gods would solve the play's conflict and teach a moral lesson to the audience. Greek theatre originally had a religious element, and having the gods appear on stage was part of the story, much in the same way that medieval passion plays would tell the story of the life, death, and resurrection of Christ.

However, modern secular storytelling has a different purpose, to entertain and distract the audience. As we've discussed throughout this book, in story structure, the function of the climax is to resolve the conflict and purge the emotions raised. The more the characters suffer and persevere through their setbacks, the more satisfying the climactic scene will be.

Therefore, you don't want to cheat your reader out of the moment of satisfaction. "Deus ex machina" is one method of cheating. All the characters' efforts don't matter because they're saved by an outside force. Usually, writers employ a "deus ex machina" ending because they've written themselves into a corner and can't find a way out. Even if you don't have an outside force save your characters, you might be tempted to cheat in subtler ways – having an unlikely coincidence save the characters, for example, or one of the characters suddenly revealing a talent or a skill that saves the day.

You can have an unlikely coincidence or a new skill play a part in the plot, but it has to be demonstrated earlier in the story, and it is a good idea to have the protagonist work for it. For example, let's say a knight is on a quest to defeat an evil wizard. The gates to the wizard's castle are secured with locks of unbreakable steel, but the knight knows a dwarven locksmith. That could be a cheat, but let's say the locksmith hates the knight and doesn't want to work with him. The knight would have to find a way to persuade the locksmith to offer help. That would make obtaining the locksmith's help into an unexpected complication, which would fit neatly into the rising action portion of the story's structure. You could even add a few plot twists – the knight gives up on persuading the locksmith and decides instead to scale the wall of the castle and enter that way. The knight soon finds himself trapped by the wizard's soldiers, but the locksmith has a change of heart after seeing the damage the wizard has done to the countryside. The locksmith opens a door that allows the knight to escape from the soldiers, and the story continues.

With a little work, you can keep the reader from feeling cheated.

RESOLUTION

WHAT HAPPENS after the climax and the conflict is resolved? It's time to wrap up the story, and we'll look at how to write a compelling resolution in the next chapter.

RESOLUTION

Your story has come to an end. The knight has slain the evil wizard, the detective has caught the cunning murderer, the action hero has defeated the terrorist cell, and the heroine and her love interest have declared their love for one another or gotten engaged. The ending might be happy, or it might have been bittersweet, with losses and defeats along the way. Either way, your characters have been changed by the experience.

Now what?

We have reached the final phase of story structure – the resolution. This is sometimes called the aftermath, the conclusion, or sometimes the "wrapping-up" phase. In this part of the story, the main conflict has been solved, and the story continues just long enough to see how the characters have been changed by the climax and the resolving of the central conflict.

In this chapter, we'll show you how to write a satisfying resolution and how to set up plot threads for a sequel if you want to write one.

AND THEY LIVED HAPPILY EVER AFTER

THE LINE "and they lived happily ever after" is a cliche from fairy tales, but it is nonetheless a compact and precise resolution all in its own (Cliches become cliches for a reason.) The most long-lasting fairy tales stick closely to the storytelling structure we've described in this book. The knight or prince defeats a dragon or an evil witch, undergoing trials and privations along the way. After defeating the villain, the hero rescues the princess from her imprisonment, and then they live happily ever after. We could delve deeply into Joseph Campbell's "Hero With A Thousand Faces" theories, but "happily ever after" serves the purpose of a resolution. The hero has been changed by his trial, the princess has been rescued, and both of them live happily together after.

Why is "and they lived happily ever after" an effective resolution? Because it fulfills the function of a resolution in story structure – the story continues just long enough to show how the characters have been changed by their experience.

How long the resolution is depends on the needs of the story. Sue Grafton in her Kinsey Millhone series of private investigator mysteries tended to have very short resolutions. Usually, the story lasted only a few pages longer, sometimes only a few paragraphs, after the conflict had been resolved. Since the books were written in the style of Kinsey typing up an investigative report, she usually wrapped up the story in a few pages – mentioning whether or not the murderer had been killed or arrested, a few more comments on the other people involved in the case, and that was that.

By contrast, both the text of The Lord of the Rings and

the film version by Peter Jackson have long resolutions. The climax of the story is when Gollum falls with the Ring into Mount Doom and Sauron is defeated, but both the book and the movie version continue for quite a while after that scene. That is out of necessity – The Lord of the Rings is a long, complicated, and epic tale, and while Tolkien could have stopped immediately after the defeat of Sauron, that would have been unsatisfying. The reader would have missed the various resolving scenes – the coronation of Aragorn, the final downfall of Saruman, the return of the hobbits to the Shire, the voyage into the West, and the resolving scenes with many, many secondary characters.

While you can end the story abruptly after the climactic scene, that is generally unsatisfying. It is a bit trite to say that the resolution should be "as long as it needs to be," but that is the truth. Let the resolution be just long enough to provide a satisfactory look to see how the conflict has changed the characters, but no longer.

SEQUEL HOOK

IF YOU ARE WRITING a book in a series (and if you are self-publishing a series is typically the most effective way to make money), the resolution is also a good place to introduce a sequel hook.

If you want to write in a series, I think it's a bad idea to publish installments as a serial or with a lot of cliffhangers. Writers really like the idea of serials (I've fallen prey to this myself) and get excited about publishing them in hopes of making more money for less work. The problem is that while serials might have been popular in the golden era of pulp fiction, the format was created by the limitations of printing costs and the price of paper. Nowadays, I strongly suspect readers prefer novels, and novels with complete stories at that. Admittedly, this is based on my own experience, but after self-publishing almost 120 novels and nearly as many short stories, that opinion is based on quite a lot of experience.

So every novel you write should have a complete story following the structure we've laid out in this book – an introduction, a conflict, rising action, complications, climax, and then resolution. However, if you want to continue the story with the same characters, there are many excellent ways to do it without leaving the reader feeling cheated, and the resolution is the best place to leave a sequel hook.

A "sequel hook" is something that sets up the next book in the series without leaving the story in the current book incomplete. While you should definitely resolve the main conflict in the story, you can leave a few loose threads to set up the central conflict in the sequel.

For example, let's return to the village raided by orcs. The protagonist has rescued the villagers and defeated the orcish raiders. There are many potential loose threads you can use to set up a conflict in a sequel book. Maybe the protagonists killed the orcish chieftain, and the chieftain has a brother or a son who vows revenge. We already mentioned a potential complication that the orcish raiders are in the service of a dragon or a powerful wizard, and that could be a potential loose thread to set up the next book's conflict.

If you do want to write in a series, there are ways to leave loose threads throughout the story that can set up a new book without writing a cliffhanger. In the next section, we'll look at the dangers of writing a cliffhanger.

AVOID CLIFFHANGERS

WRITERS, especially beginning writers, are often enamored of the idea of a cliffhanger.

The thinking is that the reader will enjoy the story and be so compelled by the cliffhanger and so driven by the need to find out what happens next that they will immediately buy the next book.

In practice, however, it doesn't work that way. A very large percentage of readers, perhaps even a majority, absolutely hate cliffhangers.

Why do they hate cliffhangers? Some of it is the perception that the author or the publisher is "nickel and diming" the readers, breaking up a complete story in hopes of making more money.

A larger part of it is that a cliffhanger is by definition an incomplete story and that incomplete stories are deeply unsatisfying. You have the introductions, the characters, the conflict, a lot of rising action, maybe a few serious setbacks...and whoops! No more book! No catharsis to purge the raised emotions. Break out your credit card if you want to read more. Or, worse, the author got bored with the series and didn't come back to it, leaving the characters hanging from that cliff for a long time, or the series was traditionally published, and the publisher decided to cancel the sequels.

You can see that cliffhangers offer many potential liabilities and few actual advantages for the writer.

That said, I have written cliffhangers a few times. Usually, I write cliffhangers for the second to last book in one of my longer series – for example, GHOST IN THE PACT, the penultimate book in my GHOST EXILE epic fantasy series, or CLOAK GAMES: LAST JUDGE, which I originally planned to be the second to last book in the CLOAK GAMES series, but which actually turned out to be the third to last. All those books sold pretty well and on balance got good reviews, so I don't think the readers were too upset about the cliffhangers.

Why was I able to get away with those cliffhangers? I think it was for two reasons. First, the last few books of my series contained overarching epic stories, even if each of those last few books had individual conflicts and story structures. I suspect this meant that the cliffhanger wasn't completely unsatisfying. Second, GHOST EXILE was nine books long, and I planned for eleven CLOAK GAMES books, but the series turned out to be twelve in the end. By the end of the series, I had established a pretty good track record of turning out books every few months, so the readers knew they would not have to wait very long to find out what happened next.

Nevertheless, I still think that it is best to avoid cliffhangers and to use them judiciously. Previously in this book, we talked about how the conflict and the rising action portion of story structure are checks you are writing to the reader that will be cashed when the climax and the resolution arrive. Writing a story with a cliffhanger ending is like writing a truly enormous check – just make sure you have the money in the bank to pay it!

TIPS & TRICKS

WITH THIS CHAPTER, we've covered all the major parts of story structure. In the next few chapters, I'll show you some tips and tricks to make the writing easier – how to write better descriptions, more interesting characters, and some practical points on the mechanics of writing a novel.

9

DESCRIPTIONS

I f you write any type of fiction, regardless of length or genre, you will wind up spending a lot of time describing stuff. Description is one of the necessary subskills of storytelling. Your readers want to know what your characters and settings look like. If you can make these descriptions come alive in the minds of your readers, that will make your story all the more vivid and will make telling a compelling story easier.

In this chapter, we'll show you some techniques for writing vivid and engaging descriptions.

SOME GENRES ARE HARDER THAN OTHERS

I HAVE WRITTEN books set on created secondary fantasy and science fiction worlds and books set on contemporary Earth (or a near version of it), and I have come to the conclusion that it is easier to write descriptions for stories set in the contemporary world than it is in science fiction and fantasy. Additionally, the farther removed a science fiction and fantasy setting is from the contemporary world, the harder it is to create descriptions.

Why is that? I suspect it is because the average reader is quite familiar with the modern world and what it generally looks like. Therefore, the reader has a sort of mental "shorthand" that a writer can access.

For example, say you're writing a thriller novel, and one of the villains is a corrupt US Senator. (It seems to be one of the rules of thumb that senators are always corrupt in fiction unless the plot revolves around the senator's daughter getting taken hostage.) The description for the Senator would probably be something like this:

"He looked like a typical member of the Senate – red-faced, white-haired, his gut straining against the closed buttons of his expensive suit coat. He moved in a cloud of cologne, applied liberally to mask how much he sweated in the Washington heat. An American flag pin glittered on his lapel, a contrast to the dead, shark-like eyes in the red face."

That passage could be improved, of course, but it immediately paints a mental picture of the character with a minimum of description. When reading that, you probably thought of a politician or some other authority figure that you dislike and juxtaposed his image with that of the fictional Senator.

That is why it is generally easier to create descriptions set in the modern world since you can tap into the reader's own memories to help with the description.

By contrast, this is harder to do in science fiction and fantasy. Instead of a corrupt Senator, let's take his approximate equivalent in a fantasy world – a cruel Baron. The description for the Baron might go like this:

"The Baron stood on the dais, sneering at the guests gathered in his hall. His beard hung to his waist, and his eyes were black wells beneath his craggy brow. His fine black robe had been trimmed with wolf fur on the sleeves and the high collar, and a gold chain hung from his neck, supporting a ruby-studded medallion. His high boots were spattered with mud and crusted blood. The sword on his belt rested in a polished scabbard of cherry wood, but the leather wrapping around the hilt had been stained with sweat and a few flecks of old blood."

Right away, the difference between the two blocks of description is apparent. For one thing, the description of the Baron is quite a bit longer than the description of the corrupt Senator. This is necessary because most readers will have a picture in their head of what a corrupt Senator looks like, and you can tap into it. By contrast, fewer readers will have a mental image of a cruel Baron (unless they happen to be medieval scholars), which means you will have to make a greater effort to create the description.

Both the corrupt Senator and the cruel Baron are humans. It is fairly easy to evoke what humans look like, but what if your novel has something completely alien? One of the creatures from my Silent Order science fiction series is a Final Consciousness infiltrator drone, which (thankfully!) has no equivalent in the contemporary world. Here is the sort of passage I would need to write to describe it:

"The thing was a metal spider the size of a large dog, its carapace sheathed in dark armor. A hairless human head rose from the front of the spider, its eyes blank and lifeless, black veins threading through the gray skin where nanomachines had replaced blood. The sightless eyes rolled back and forth as the spider skittered forward, and the thing reeked of heated metal and rotting meat."

Now, I could have just described it as "cyborg spider with a zombie head," and that would have gotten the point across. Indeed, I have various characters in the Silent Order series describe the creatures that way at various points, usually in moments of stress and danger. But nothing like an infiltrator drone exists in the real world, which means I must create a clearer description so the reader will have a good picture in his or her head.

This can get even more challenging if you are writing a science fiction and fantasy novel with esoteric or abstract concepts. Like, suppose you are writing a science fiction novel where a character encounters a thousand-sided alien prism that simultaneously moves backward and forwards through time? Or a fantasy novel where a character fights a nine-headed dragon goddess, and each one of her nine heads breathes a different kind of fire?

By contrast, describing a scene where two police officers walk into a fast-food restaurant for lunch seems pretty simple.

Fortunately, there are techniques you can use to create vivid descriptions whether you're describing a mundane sight like a fast-food restaurant or a giant alien spaceship, and we'll look at those techniques now.

AVOID LAUNDRY LISTS

ONE OF THE common mistakes of writing descriptions is to employ what is called a "laundry list" description, which is simply a list of what the character is wearing and happens to look like. Here's a typical example:

"She stood about five inches over five feet and weighed one hundred and thirty-one pounds. She had brown eyes and blond hair tied back in a ponytail. She wore a white blouse tucked into a snug black pencil skirt and open-toed high-heeled shoes. She also wore a silver necklace with a pendant, silver earrings, and rings on two fingers of each hand."

The main problems with that kind of description are that it's boring and it doesn't engage the senses. It reads like a description from a police report: "Subject is Caucasian female, five foot five, one hundred thirty-one pounds, blond hair, brown eyes, last seen wearing a white blouse and a black skirt." Granted, if you're writing a mystery novel or a police procedural, such descriptions might be part of the dialogue or the story, but in general, you want more evocative descriptions than that.

You will need a few hard details about the characters' and settings' appearance in your descriptions, but it's best to mix them with metaphors, similes, and sensory details.

METAPHORS AND SIMILES IN DESCRIPTIONS

METAPHORS AND SIMILES are two figures of speech that use comparison to describe something. The quick rule of thumb is to say that a metaphor is an "is" statement, and a simile is a "like" statement. To return to our corrupt Senator above, a metaphor to describe him would be "the Senator is a greedy dinosaur." A simile, on the other hand, would be "the Senator is like a greedy dinosaur."

Metaphors and similes are powerful tools to help you

write vivid descriptions. Like any tools, they can be overused. A common cliché is the purple prose that some writers use during romance scenes. The heroine's emotions inevitably are like "surging tides" or "passionate fire" or "soaring heights" and so forth, or her body and that of her love interest get compared to various architectural features or landscapes.

Sometimes less is more.

We've mentioned that the laundry list technique for descriptions can get tedious, and so can excessive similes and metaphors. One of the ways to avoid that is to combine the techniques since that can result in more compelling descriptions than you would otherwise create. For the corrupt Senator we mentioned earlier, you could have a description like this:

"The Senator lounged in his office chair, thick hands folded on his ample belly, his expensive suit coat undone and his tie loosened. He looked like an overfed tiger contemplating the prospect of another meal."

Like our previous example, this passage brings to mind a corrupt and dangerous politician. We could do the same thing with the cruel Baron:

"The Baron paced down the hall, hand resting on his sword hilt, his black robe swirling behind him. His expression was hard behind his long beard, and he looked like a wolf about to spring upon its prey. The Baron's knights knew that someone was about to come to bloody end."

This is a more evocative description of the cruel Baron than the first example.

ENGAGE THE SENSES

FINALLY, one of the best things that you can do to create powerful descriptions is to engage as many of the senses as is feasible.

Humans have five senses – vision, hearing, touch, smell, and taste. Most of the time, when writing a novel, descriptions revolve around vision and hearing (with the obvious exception of characters with vision or hearing challenges) – characters look at things, and they talk to one another.

Because descriptions based around sight and hearing are the most common, you can both capture the reader's attention and improve your descriptions by integrating the other senses into your descriptive passages whenever possible. This isn't possible in every situation – for example, if the protagonist in a fantasy novel climbs to the top of a hill and sees a wizard's tower in the distance, he will be able to see the tower, but he won't able to touch it, and he probably won't be able to smell it. (Though potentially it could be good foreshadowing if from a distance the tower smells of sulfur.)

Whenever possible, try to integrate at least two of the five senses into any descriptive passages. Some senses are easier to include than others. For example, in our example of a protagonist trying to save his village from orcish raiders, the protagonist is quite unlikely to reach out and feel the orcish warriors' tusks. Unless one of the orcs happens to bite him during a fight, in which case touch and probably smell will be a more significant component of a description.

Smell, in particular, can create very vivid descriptions because smell is strongly linked with memory. Many people find particular smells take them back to powerful memories – the smell of a pizza restaurant associated with a first date, or a particular dinner with a holiday or a relative, or the smell of diesel fuel with a car accident.

Include as many senses as possible when describing something, and your descriptions will be all the more vivid for it.

PERSPECTIVE

A FINAL TIP for descriptions is that different characters will perceive things in different ways, which will be useful for both writing descriptions and creating interesting characters.

Let's use the laptop I'm using to writing this book as an example. I look at it, and in my mind, I see it as a laptop with a 17-inch screen, a 1.8 GHz CPU, and 8 gigabytes of RAM, along with a bunch of other technical details. I think in those terms because I worked in various technical jobs for a long time.

Family and friends who look at this laptop, however, would simply think of it as "Jonathan's laptop" with no additional interest in the technical specs. Someone with more technical knowledge than me might sneer at the laptop since it doesn't have a good graphics processing unit or because it's from a cheaper brand. (Writing a book doesn't take much in terms of computer hardware.) An older person who was already well into adulthood when personal computers became ubiquitous might look at the laptop with resentment, seeing it as yet another computer that has forced its way into his or her life. A person with a criminal history might note the laptop's potential resale value on the Internet.

Everyone views the world through the filter of their own experiences, memories, and opinions, and you can use that to create more vivid descriptive passages and characters. To use another example, imagine that a woman wearing formal business attire walks into the lobby of an office building. How you describe her can depend upon which characters see her. The security guard might note that she's not carrying any weapons or be pleased to see her because she sometimes leaves baked goods for the security staff. A potential romantic interest might note that formal business attire is a flattering look for her. A rival coworker might think that she's wearing too much makeup or has over-dressed for an upcoming meeting. Some there to rob the building might assess her as a potential hindrance to the upcoming heist.

Descriptions filtered through the perceptions of indi-vidual characters will help you create better descriptive passages, and it will also help you create interesting charac-ters, which we will discuss more in the next chapter.

10

CHARACTERIZATION

We've already discussed all the parts of story structure and given you a few tips about writing descriptions. The story is the most important part, but to really hold the reader's attention, a story needs to have interesting characters. We've all read books or watched movies and TV shows that had an interesting story but nonetheless had flat characters.

Characterization is an interesting topic and could be (and has been) a book entirely on its own. In this chapter, we'll give you some tips for making interesting characters that will hold the reader's attention.

THEIR OWN PROTAGONISTS

THE MOST IMPORTANT principle to remember about writing fictional characters is that every character thinks of themselves as the protagonist of their own story, closely followed by the fact that humans are very good at justifying their actions to themselves.

What do I mean by saying that the characters think that they are the protagonists of their own story? It means that each character has his or her own plot arc, challenges, fears, worries, and setbacks. A novel can only focus on so many characters, but it is important to remember that characters will have goals and interests that may not align with those of the protagonists. Indeed, they may view the protagonist's conflict as unimportant or even annoying, or an obstacle to their own goals, which could well make them into one of the antagonists of the story.

This leads to the second principle, that humans are good at justifying their actions to themselves, no matter how badly they have behaved. Most people tend to think that they are one of the "good guys," and if that they have done something immoral, it is because they "did what they had to do." Thieves, for example, will commonly say that they had no choice to act as they did, that they needed the money more than their victim, or that their victim could afford the loss, or that the target had insurance that would reimburse him. This pattern generally repeats all the way from shoplifting up to stock or insurance fraud worth billions of dollars.

You can use this truth of human nature to write interesting and believable characters in several ways. Remember that every character thinks of himself or herself as the protagonist, and the characters will usually be able to justify their actions to themselves. When a character can't justify his or her actions, that can lead to an internal struggle – you could have a character who realizes that he has been acting badly or a character who decides that her lack of action is more harmful than doing something.

One of the best examples I have seen of villainous characters justifying their actions to themselves is in the mystery novels of John Sandford. His books have some seriously nasty villains – murderers and serial killers and worse – and they are believable characters because of how they justify their choices. There is also a hapless human element to them, which makes them more relatable than infallible criminal masterminds. In one book, a murderer hatches a plan to ambush a witness driving a car and then escape into the woods on his snowmobile, only to realize at the moment of crisis he can't actually steer his snowmobile and aim his gun at the same time, and he only barely manages to stop himself from crashing into a bridge while fumbling with his firearm. The killer is a thoroughly evil and unlikeable character, but the human element makes the moment both absurd and darkly funny.

You can use these techniques to make your own characters more realistic, whether they are protagonists or villains.

CONTRADICTORY DESIRES

ANOTHER GOOD METHOD of creating compelling characters is to give them mutually conflicting desires.

What does this mean? Characters usually want something, which helps drive the plot. To return to one of our frequent examples, the man going to the post office wants to pay his bill so his gas remains on, and that is one of the triggers for the plot. But if a character wants two things at the same time and it is impossible to have both of them, that can both make the character more interesting and generate new conflict to help drive the plot forward.

Let's start with a simple example. Right now, I want to do two different things – I would like to finish writing this book, but I would also like to relax by playing computer games with an action movie on the TV in the background. Obviously, I can't choose to do both at the same time, and I probably should choose to work on this book instead of playing computer games. (If you're reading this, then we have proof I chose the book more often than gaming!) But I do have to make a decision between the two activities.

That was a trivial example, but you can use the conflict of wanting two contradictory things to set up both the plot of your book and create more interesting characters. One of the most common examples is the love triangle, where two different men are in love with the same woman, who must then choose between them. (In my Frostborn epic fantasy series, one of the subplots was a love triangle where two women are in love with the same man, and I've probably gotten more email about that than anything else I've written over the last ten years.)

Romance isn't the only area where a character can be caught between two choices. In our earlier example of a protagonist who needs to rescue his neighbors from orcish raiders, the protagonist might have wanted to leave his village and seek his fortune in a nearby city rather than looking after his father's farm. Or, once he is in pursuit of the captives, he might face a hard choice about who to ask for help – a wizard who insists that the protagonist become his apprentice or a paladin who demands that the protagonist become his new squire. The protagonist can't ask both for help and will have to choose between the two.

Having a character torn between two goals can be used

in any genre. In a mystery novel, the detective might want to solve a long-standing cold case, but he could also want a promotion and knows that if he keeps pursuing the cold case, he will irritate his superiors and reduce his chances of advancing in rank. Alternatively, you could have a career criminal who wants to leave his life of crime and go legitimate but knows he will lose a substantial portion of his income since he can't make as much money from an honest job as from crime. In a science fiction novel, a character might want to join the space navy and leave his homeworld but nonetheless feel compelled to remain behind to help with the family business.

VIRTUES & VICES

WHEN WRITING YOUR CHARACTERS, it's important to remember that the good guys have some flaws, and the bad guys will have some positive qualities.

It's possible to take this too far, of course, and give your protagonist so many flaws that he becomes an unsympathetic jerk, and to give the villain so many good qualities that the reader winds up rooting for him instead of the hero. Unless this is your intention, it's best to avoid this.

Nonetheless, it is best to have both sympathetic and unsympathetic traits in all of your characters. A villain needs some virtues, or else he becomes completely ineffective. A villain who spends all day sleeping, overeating, and watching television will not make for a compelling threat simply because he doesn't have the ambition to make much trouble. By contrast, a villain who is self-controlled and disciplined can make a far greater threat to the protagonists simply because he is able to control himself and is therefore more effective.

A good way to explain this idea is with the medieval Christian concept of the seven capital sins and the seven virtues. In the sixth century, Pope Gregory I codified the traditional list of the seven deadly sins – lust, sloth, gluttony, greed, wrath, envy, and pride. These were counterbalanced by the seven virtues, which were chastity, temperance, charity, diligence, patience, gratitude, and humility.

Most characters will be a mix of these fourteen attributes in some proportion or another, and I have found it useful to think in these terms when creating characters. It is easy to use this concept to look at fictional characters. For instance, consider Sherlock Holmes. Holmes in the classic stories displays the virtues of diligence (working determinedly for his client), patience (waiting for the results of his investigation), and charity (taking on cases from impoverished clients if their problems catch his attention). Holmes clearly is not prone to lust or greed. However, he does tend towards pride and a weakness towards gluttony with his cocaine problem. Holmes's chief nemesis, Professor Moriarty, has Holmes's intellect and several of his virtues, but with the addition of overwhelming greed and far more swollen pride.

Ian Fleming's character of James Bond is another who has an interesting mixture of virtues and vices. Bond is physically brave and diligent in the course of his duties (diligence), and he is a good and loyal friend to his allies (gratitude & some humility). Despite that, he does have numerous negative qualities – excessive consumption of alcohol and rich food (gluttony), frequent womanizing (lust), and a tendency to take brutal revenge on his enemies (wrath).

Sherlock Holmes, Professor Moriarty, and James Bond are all somewhat extreme examples of this. Most people in real life have a mixture of positive and negative qualities – we've all had an experience like learning a hated coworker turns out to be a good and diligent parent to their children, or a disliked boss is nonetheless scrupulously honest in all business dealings. You can use this truth of human nature to make more realistic characters.

For example, the protagonist of our fantasy novel about orcs could be humble and hardworking yet suffer from wrath and fly into a fury whenever someone insults him. One of the protagonist's allies could be a lazy and gluttonous knight who nonetheless takes care of the widows and orphans on his lands with generous charity.

You can also have the characters be aware of their flaws and work to overcome them, adding a layer of internal conflict to the story even as the characters struggle against the central conflict.

11

PRACTICAL POINTS

In the previous chapters, we've looked at all the components of story structure and provided a few tips on characterization and descriptions. Now we'll look at a few practical aspects of novel writing – how long your book should be, chapter length, and so on.

HOW LONG SHOULD YOUR NOVEL BE?

THIS IS A COMMON QUESTION, and it has less of a definitive answer than you might think. The customary answer for "how long should your novel be?" usually is "as long as it needs to be." This is rather less than helpful – I once had an accountant tell me that the definitive answer for many areas of tax law was "yes or no, but maybe," which we both agreed was not terribly illuminating.

That said, "as long as it needs to be" is a good metric. We've all read novels where the writer clearly got bored or needed to finish to meet a deadline and so rushed the ending. We've also all read novels that went on way too long, where the writer should have wrapped things up five chapters ago, but either had a contractual obligation to hit a certain number of words, or in more modern books, was padding the length of the novel so the audiobook version would be a more attractive purchase.

In the end, the proper length for your novel is long enough to resolve the conflict in a satisfying manner.

How long does a story have to be to qualify as a novel? Again, this is an area of some disagreement, but generally speaking, most people consider 50,000 words to be the minimum length for a novel. I've written a few novels that were in the 40,000 to 50,000 words range, but any shorter than that, and it's a long novella. After writing almost one hundred and twenty novels, I've found that the sweet spot is around 80,000 to 100,000 words. People generally like longer books, and 80k to 100k is a good length.

Any longer than 100,000 words, in my experience, gets difficult. The longest book I've written was about 145,000 words, and every ten thousand words after 100k seems harder and harder. Too much longer than that, and it might be a good idea to split up the book into two pieces, which can aggravate readers. Between 80,000 and 100,000 words seems to be the best length for both reader enjoyment and the sanity of the author.

HOW LONG SHOULD THE CHAPTERS BE?

CHAPTER LENGTH IS another common question. I once had a very annoyed reader email me that my chapters tended to vary in length, and I have seen beginning writers worry about how long chapters should be, or whether they should write in chapters at all. The late Sir Terry Pratchett famously did not use chapters in most of his books, pointing out that real life did not occur in neatly numbered chapters. By contrast, Stephen King often has written books that have tiny chapters, sometimes no more than a page or two.

Like novel length, the real answer to the question of chapter length is "as long as it needs to be," which is once again somewhat less than helpful. In practice, when I'm outlining my books, I usually assume that I will end up at about three thousand to four thousand words per chapter. Most of the time, it averages out to that. While I was working on this book, I also wrote a new novel called GHOST IN THE TALISMAN, which came to 90,000 words and 22 chapters, which is an average of about 4,090 words per chapter. That said, the longest chapter in the book was about 6,900 words, and the shortest a little over 2,000.

Why such a wide variation? I find that it is best that a chapter contain a complete scene and some scenes are longer than others. Basically, a complete conversation or character action – a detective interrogates a suspect, the protagonist in a fantasy novel leaves a city or finds an object on his quest, and so forth. During action-heavy chapters, a scene can be spread out among multiple chapters. If I'm writing a chase scene, my characters might have gotten away from one group of enemies, only to turn a corner and find a rival group of foes waiting for them. The longest chapter in GHOST IN THE TALISMAN was a heist scene, and I wanted to fit it entirely in the single chapter since the heist was a precursor to the main plot.

There's nothing wrong with "cliffhanger" chapters since the next chapter will follow. In fact, that is a common technique when writing books with multiple protagonists or point-of-view characters. Protagonist A's chapter will end with a cliffhanger, and then we'll switch to Protagonist B for the next chapter and then return to Protagonist A. This helps build suspense and tension within the plot, pulling the reader along through the story.

If you do that, bear in mind that the readers will be unsatisfied if you don't resolve the conflicts of all the protagonists by the end of the book, and that the more point of view characters you have, the longer the book will be. I have found that I can typically assume that every point of view character will add an additional ten to fifteen thousand words on top of the book's base length.

CHARACTER NAMES

THIS IS A SMALL POINT, but a practical one. Try to avoid having characters whose names start with the same letter or sound the same, since this will confuse some readers.

This can be a particularly challenging point for fantasy and science fiction writers since we make up many names. In my books, I have had characters named Agrimnalazur, Gothalinzur, Tamurvalrax, and Azurvaltoria (among others), and readers have told me that sometimes they don't bother to learn the names and just think of the characters as "that woman with the A-something name." Indeed, that is one of the reasons that people who prefer mysteries, thrillers, and romances will not read fantasy or science fiction since they do not want to learn the rules of a new world.

But trying to give your characters distinct names is a good idea no matter what genre, since it will help avoid reader confusion. Having two characters named Nancy and Nanette, for instance, or Carol and Caroline, or Joshua or John, can cause readers to get the two mixed up. This is especially true if you're writing science fiction and fantasy and you've invented the names. (I should note that Azurval-toria and Agrimnalazur were characters in separate series and were never in the same book together.)

I have made that mistake myself, and recently. As I mentioned, I also wrote the novel GHOST IN THE TALISMAN while I wrote this book. The main character is a woman named Caina, and during the book, she works with her half-sister Calvia. GHOST IN THE TALISMAN is the eighth book in the series, and I wrote the first book in the series back in 2017. In that book, Caina learned that she had a half-sister named Calvia that she had never known about, but Caina didn't meet Calvia for the first time until the seventh book in the series, which I wrote in 2020.

I had originally named the character Calvia because her personality would be similar to Caina's, but I didn't realize the similarity of the names would be a problem until I started writing the seventh book and kept transposing the two names in dialogue. Of course, by the seventh book, it was too late to do anything about it, and I just had to roll with it.

Learn from my mistake! Don't have two characters with similar names if at all possible. This will both reduce reader confusion and the amount of mistakes you make while writing your book.

ANNOTATIONS

I've spent the last eleven chapters talking about story structure, so it's time to provide you with a concrete example!

What follows is a complete copy of my science fiction novel SILENT ORDER: IRON HAND. I chose this book because it is relatively short, only ten chapters long, but it is a complete example of story structure and has examples of everything I have talked about in this book. Before every chapter, I will write an annotation describing which parts of story structure I used in the upcoming scenes. Then you can read the chapter yourself and see how I applied the ideas about story structure.

Everyone learns in different ways, and sometimes the best way to learn something is to watch someone else do it. By reading the annotations and SILENT ORDER: IRON HAND, I hope you will see a good example of story structure and realize how to apply it to your own books.

Let's get started!

ANNOTATIONS ON SILENT ORDER: IRON HAND CHAPTER 1

C hapter 1 introduces us to the setting, the main character, and the conflict of the story.

SILENT ORDER: IRON HAND is a science fiction novel set one hundred thousand years in the future when mankind has used hyperspace travel to spread across the galaxy. Humanity used to be ruled by a single Terran Empire, but that fractured two thousand years before the start of the book, and now there are many different human interstellar nations, some allied with each other, some hostile.

The book takes place on the fringes of the Kingdom of Calaskar, one of the major interstellar nations. Calaskar is a constitutional monarchy locked in a cold war with the Final Consciousness, a nation of human cyborgs joined in a hive mind and bent on brutal conquest. Calaskar's foreign intelligence and black ops agency, called the Silent Order, frequently conducts operations against Final Consciousness agents within Calaskar and in neutral powers. Both the Final Consciousness itself and its sympathizers are often called "Machinists," since the ideology of the Final Consciousness seeks to perfect mankind with a perfect fusion of human and machine, though the brutal and tyrannical reality of the Machinists is a far cry from their utopian vision.

Our protagonist, Jack March, is an Alpha Operative of the Silent Order, which makes him one of the agency's chief field operatives. He was formerly an Iron Hand, an elite special ops soldier of the Final Consciousness. After witnessing the brutal atrocities carried out by the Final Consciousness, March rebelled against the hive mind and wound up joining the Kingdom of Calaskar and the Silent Order. He has since fought against the Final Consciousness in many different covert operations.

Chapter 1 introduces us to the setting of the Kingdom of Calaskar and to March, and hints at some of his internal conflicts and motivations. We also meet Censor, the head of the Silent Order and March's handler, who gives him a new assignment. Two Calaskaran nobles, Roanna and Thomas Vindex, were dabbling in a political group associated with the Final Consciousness and are taking a starliner flight to Rustbelt Station, a lawless asteroid base on the fringes of Calaskaran space. March's assignment is to fly to Rustbelt Station, pick them up, and bring them back to Calaskar before they can get into any more trouble.

Of course, as a veteran operative, March knows this assignment will likely be more complicated than it appears. And as a reader of this book who now understands story structure, you know that the protagonist will face unexpected troubles and complications before much longer!

The first of these complications appears in this chapter when March is attacked by a Final Consciousness covert agent named Simon Lorre. March eludes the trap, but Lorre escapes.

With the setting and protagonist introduced in Chapter 1, we can continue to Chapter 2, where the action begins.

14

SILENT ORDER IRON HAND CHAPTER 1: ORDERS

J ack March had traveled to a hundred different worlds and spoken to a dozen different alien races, had fought on two different sides in a vast war, but no matter what he did, the pain in his shoulder never quite went away.

Another man might have considered that an omen or maybe a sign from God, but he ignored the pain. The shoulder always hurt, and it wasn't supposed to hurt. Allegedly, the software interface ought to filter out any pain from the cybernetic arm grafted to his left shoulder, but nonetheless, the shoulder always had at least a mild ache.

Sometimes he thought it was his punishment for leaving the cybernetic hell of the Final Consciousness for the Silent Order.

But as punishments went, it was a mild one, so he endured it.

The chiming of his ship's pseudointelligence woke him from a restless sleep.

"Captain March," said the female voice with a crisp, cool Calaskaran accent. "We are approaching the terminus point of our hyperspace tunnel. Advise that you proceed to the flight cabin at once."

"Right," said March, grimacing at the ceiling of his cabin above his narrow bunk. He had just about given up attempting to sleep anyway. "Time?"

"Ten minutes," said the cool female voice.

"Thank you," said March, getting to his feet. He rubbed his face with his right hand, the stubble rasping against his palm. Time for a shave? No, better head to the flight cabin. Never knew when something would go wrong coming out of hyperspace. "Start the procedure for bringing the dark matter reactor to standby, along with the primary and the backup resonator coils. I'll take manual control for the approach to Antioch Station."

"Acknowledged."

"Thank you, Vigil," said March. Some pilots named their computer's pseudointelligences, some did not. March did, partly because it felt odd to converse with something without a name, and partly because the Final Consciousness did not give names to any of their artificial intelligences, only numerical designations. It was a minor act of rebellion, considering that he had abandoned the Machinists for the Silent Order and Calaskar, but he enjoyed it nonetheless.

"You are welcome, Captain," said Vigil.

March pulled on his coat over his flight suit, slinging his gun belt around his hips. Then he pulled on a black glove over his left hand, concealing the gleaming metal fingers and stepped out of his cramped cabin and into the dorsal corridor of his ship.

The air smelled a bit dusty. Once March arrived at Antioch Station, he would have to do a maintenance check on the life support systems. March walked past the galley, the gym, the armory, the passenger cabins, and into flight cabin. The *Tiger* was a Mercator Foundry Yards Class 9 light freighter, which was a polite way of saying "blockade runner," and a class of starship favored by independent traders, privateers, and pirates across the starfaring nations of civilized space. March might have been an operative of the Silent Order of Calaskar, but the Silent Order, like all intelligence organizations, was stingy, so March actually was a licensed privateer. The Class 9 light freighter had been designed for a crew of six, but March flew the ship alone, aided only by Vigil.

It worked, but sometimes maintenance tasks fell through the cracks. Hence the dusty smell in the corridor.

The flight cabin was a small, narrow room with four stations, each with their own acceleration chairs. March dropped into the pilot's chair, the smart foam of the padding closing around the shape of his body, and powered on the piloting console. Holographic displays flared to life, blue text and images upon a black background, and he flicked through the checklist, preparing the *Tiger* for the transition from the perils of hyperspace to normal space.

Not that normal space didn't have its own dangers, of course.

"Captain," said Vigil in her precise Calaskaran accent. "We are approaching the terminus point."

"Very well," said March, gripping the appropriate levers. Many of the *Tiger's* controls were holographic or on touch-screens, but the vital controls were hardwired, and the hyperspace controls were one of them. "Give me a countdown."

"Five, four, three, two, one...now."

March pulled the levers, and the *Tiger* exited its hyper-space tunnel and returned to normal space.

Dozens of minor things happened in the flight cabin. The sight of hyperspace could induce insanity in a normal human mind (and that was one of the better possible outcomes), so the exterior views had been blanked. The viewscreens now lit up with views of the Antioch system and the surrounding star field, the planets and the moons brighter dots against the blackness. The dark matter reactor and the resonator shut down, and the *Tiger's* kinetic shields came online to block micrometeors and other debris. The fusion drive kicked on, and the ion thrusters powered up.

The sensor displays flickered with readings of Antioch Station, and March switched one of the viewscreens to target the station.

He had seen a lot of space stations in his travels, but he had to admit Antioch Station was an impressive sight. The Antioch system was the outer edge of the core worlds claimed by the Kingdom of Calaskar, and the station looked like the kind of giant installation found in orbit around worlds with populations in the billions. The station was five thick, concentric rings of gleaming metal, the largest nearly five kilometers in diameter. Racks of solar panels rose from the rings, and the *Tiger's* sensors detected hundreds of ships of varying size docked with the station. The sensors also picked up powerful weapon systems, and two Royal Calaskaran Navy destroyers patrolling the station's defense perimeter.

To his amusement, he felt a flicker of patriotic pride. He had not been born Calaskaran but had joined the Kingdom after his escape from the Final Consciousness. Such feelings should not have been possible in his machine-scarred soul, but there it was. He had to admit the station looked impressive, even beautiful.

Certainly, nothing the cybernetic slaves of the Final Consciousness built looked anywhere near as graceful.

One of his displays lit up as a traffic control officer from Antioch Station hailed him. March responded and fed his credentials and ship registration into the computer. Because of the nature of his work, he had several dozen different sets of forged ship registrations and credentials, but at a Calaskaran station, he could use the *Tiger*'s legitimate registration.

As he expected, the registration generated a response, and after a moment the traffic control officer appeared on the screen.

"Your name?" he said. He was a young Calaskaran, clean-cut and sober looking.

"Jack March," March answered.

"Occupation?" said the officer.

"Independent freighter captain," said March. "Licensed privateer holding letters of marque."

"And the reason for your visit to Antioch Station?" said the officer.

"Stopover for supplies," said March, which he supposed was true enough. "I plan to head to the outer colonies and the asteroid mines. They are always looking for freighter space. I can pay for my supplies with hard currency, no credit."

"Any cargo to declare?" said the officer.

"None," said March.

"Very good, Captain March," said the officer. He worked on something off-screen for a moment. "You are hereby assigned to dock at Airlock Thirty-Seven on Ring Three. That will be tight for a Class 9 Mercator Yards runner, but you should be able to manage it. Standard docking fees. Any questions?"

"None," said March.

"Welcome to Antioch Station, Captain March," said the officer. "Remember that Antioch Station is sovereign territory of the Kingdom of Calaskar, and the law of the Kingdom applies here. Have a pleasant stay."

The screen went dark. Antioch Station loomed larger on the central display, with Airlock Thirty-Seven flashing on Ring Three.

"Manual control, Vigil," said March, flipping a series of switches and gripping the flight yoke.

"Are you certain, Captain?" said Vigil. "It will be a precise docking maneuver."

"I know," said March, using the ion thrusters to ease the *Tiger* towards Ring Three, one of the Calaskaran destroyers passing overhead. "That's why I'm doing it. Best to stay sharp."

"Is that why you spend all that time in the gym with the gravity dialed up?" said Vigil.

"Precisely," said March. "I'm in a dangerous business. Skills can't be left to rust. Stay quiet so I can concentrate."

He set the *Tiger* on a vector towards Ring Three. A kilometer from the station, he cut the fusion drive, taking the ship in with just the ion thrusters. He spun the ship around, using the dorsal thruster to glide the *Tiger* towards the ring, and then eased the ship's cargo airlock against the side of the ring.

A moment later he felt the vibration as the station's airlock clamps locked on, and the displays flashed confirmation of a successful docking.

"We are docked, Captain," said Vigil. "Nicely done."

"Thanks," said March, setting the *Tiger*'s systems back to standby.

"Would you like to arrange for standard maintenance?" said Vigil.

"Just for the life support systems," said March. "Run the standard diagnostics, and have our repair drones go over the ship. If you find anything wrong, give me a call. Else I don't want to spend the money."

"Very well, Captain," said Vigil. "Enjoy your stay at Antioch Station."

"I doubt it," said March.

He unstrapped from the acceleration seat, got to his feet, and made his way from the flight cabin, down to the cargo bay and to the stern airlock. The outer door cycled, and March stepped over, checking his gun belt and the weapons hidden up his right sleeve.

Then the inner door cycled, and Jack March walked onto Antioch Station.

He had been here before, and he knew that the public concourses and market areas of the station were built of gleaming white metal, with plenty of hydroponic plants and solar lamps to simulate sunlight. Alas, Airlock Thirty-Seven on Ring Three did not share such luxuries. The chamber beyond the airlock was built of dull gray metal. Instead of a welcome officer or robot, a computer screen on the wall cycled through a slideshow displaying a listing of the station's businesses and advertisements for ship repair and supplies.

March walked past it without looking and stepped into the corridor beyond. The long corridor ran the length of Ring Three, with regular archways leading to the other airlock chambers and cargo bays.

He expected the corridor to be deserted.

He did not expect three men to be waiting for him.

All three looked tough and dangerous and stood as if

they knew how to handle themselves in a fight. The three men wore the jumpsuits of cargo handlers, an unfamiliar logo on their arms, likely the corporation the Kingdom of Calaskar had hired to manage the freighter traffic through the station.

The man in the center did not look like a cargo handler.

He had the lean, tight build of a competent fighter, and a thick scar went down the left side of his face, turning his lip into a permanent sneer. Unlike the others, he wore a brown coat over his cargo handler's jumpsuit, one hand resting in his hip pocket. All three men moved to block the corridor, and the man in the center offered a friendly smile, though the scar ruined the effect.

"Welcome, Captain," said the man in the brown coat.

A mugging? No, that wasn't it. An isolated part of the station was perfect for a mugging, but frankly, anyone coming through this corridor wouldn't have anything worth stealing.

Which meant they were waiting for him, specifically.

"Hi," said March, coming to a stop a meter away from them. "Suppose you're the welcoming committee, right?"

The scarred man grinned. "That's right, I am. Why don't you come with us? We'll take you to the hospitality kiosk."

"Nah," said March. "Think I'll find my own way if you don't mind. Stretch my legs after all that flying."

The scarred man kept grinning. "I think you'll want to come with us." He produced a small black plasma pistol from inside his pocket, leveling the emitter at March's chest. "I think you'll want to come with us right now."

The other two men laughed.

They stopped laughing when March moved.

His left hand shot out and seized the end of the pistol. The servos in his cybernetic arm made no sound, but he felt their vibration as they engaged. March closed his fist and crushed the pistol before the scarred man could pull the trigger. The scarred man yelped and jerked his hand back, and March punched him in the stomach with his right hand.

The other two men attacked as their leader fell back, and March exploded into motion. The other two men were good, but they did not have March's cybernetic arm. They did not have the nanotech swimming through his blood. And most importantly, they did not have the brutal lessons that the trainers of the Final Consciousness had beat into him, the lessons that he now used against his former masters.

The lessons that he now turned against the other two men, men he suspected of being paid hirelings of the Final Consciousness. Even on Calaskar, the Machinists had friends and sympathizers, useful idiots for the cause of the Final Consciousness

And if there were useful idiots on Calaskar itself, why not on Antioch Station?

One of the men produced a knife, and March caught it in his left hand, his fingers crushing both the weapon and the man's hand. The man screamed as his fingers snapped, and March kicked him in the knee and sent him sprawling. The third man punched, and March parried with his right hand, ducked under a second blow, and kicked the man from his feet.

For a moment his enemies were stunned, and March considered his options.

The logical solution was to kill all three, and March drew his gun from its holster. Yet killing them was more risk than it was worth. He had spotted a security camera in the ceiling a few yards down the corridor, and Antioch Station was a law-abiding place. March couldn't trust that his attackers had been smart enough to disable the cameras. If he shot them all, he would be arrested, and he would have to invoke the authority of the Silent Order to deal with the matter.

That would annoy his superiors to no end. The only thing Censor hated more than a mess was official attention from the other authorities of the Kingdom. The whole point of the Silent Order was to remain silent and unseen.

March considered interrogating his attackers to learn more but discarded that idea. There wasn't time to do it properly, and he doubted he could find a location free of security cameras on short notice.

All three men stared at the emitter of his pistol.

"Wallets," said March. "On the deck, now. If you're professionals, I'm sure you know the routine."

They reached into their pockets and dropped their wallets on the deck. Two of the men looked sheepish. The man with the scarred face was cold and calm and collected, his eyes boring into March as if marking him for future vengeance.

Maybe it would be better to just shoot him now.

"On your feet," said March, gesturing with his gun. The men got to their feet. "Turn around and run as fast as you can while counting to a thousand. When you get to a thousand, you're done. Go!"

The men ran down the corridor, boots thumping against the deck. March stooped and picked up their wallets. He supposed they could call the station authorities and claimed that he had mugged them, but then he would have the authorities pull the video from the camera, proving that they had attacked first.

No, if they came after him again, they would choose a different avenue of attack.

He tapped the collar of his jacket, where he had clipped a microphone paired to his phone. "Vigil?"

"Captain," said the pseudointelligence.

"Maximum security on the ship," said March. "Some Machinist goons just tried to mug me. Not sure if they're true believers or hired help."

"Any identification?" said Vigil.

"Yeah," said March. He flipped open the wallets. Some credit notes, which he claimed for himself. There were ID cards, which he was sure were fake. Nonetheless, he pulled out his phone and ran the camera lens over them, sending the images to Vigil and the *Tiger's* computer system. "Run these through our database and see if you find anything."

"Acknowledged," said Vigil.

With that, March pocketed the wallets and decided to use their money to buy himself lunch while he waited for his call.

March strode down the corridor until he found a lift heading from Ring Three to Ring One. He stood with a crowd of bored-looking cargo handlers and various starship crewers until the lift came to a halt. His gloved left hand drew a few stares, but no one commented. Cybernetic replacements were common, since even the best medical science sometimes could not keep the immune system from rejecting cloned limbs. But given how many wars Calaskar had fought against the Final Consciousness, those with cybernetics tended not to flaunt them while within the systems of the Kingdom.

Especially those who, like March, had once been part of that Final Consciousness.

Sometimes if he closed his eyes, he could still imagine

the thunderous chorus of the Final Consciousness filling his thoughts, bestowing him with certainty and purpose and direction...

March hated lifts. They gave him too much time to think.

Finally, the lift deposited him on Ring One. The outer three rings of the station were for docking and cargo. The second ring housed industrial workshops, power plants, weaponry, shields, and other station utilities.

The inner ring housed lots and lots of shops.

March emerged from the lift and entered one of the commercial concourses of Ring One. It looked like a massive three-story mall with balconies running along the walls. Most of the businesses catered to the crews of the ships that came and went from Antioch Station – repairs, supplies, upgrades, weapons, and restaurants. Screens mounted here and there displayed films from the Ministry of Information, showing a pretty woman in a dark jacket discussing the history of Calaskar while arguing that a parliamentary monarchy like the Kingdom was the best system to prevent both anarchy and tyranny. A church of the Royal Calaskaran Church occupied part of the second level, and despite the time of the day, there were already many worshippers. March had no doubt there was a well-regulated and licensed brothel tucked away in a discreet part of the station, but he had no wish to visit one.

He made for one of the cheaper restaurants. Calaskaran nobles and naval officers preferred to dine at more formal restaurants that followed the rigid manners of the Kingdom's upper classes. The restaurant that March chose was a bar that happened to serve food. The air was heavy with cigarette smoke, the filters in the ceiling giving off a loud whine as they struggled to keep up. Crewers and enlisted men sat at the tables, eating and drinking and laughing. Over the bar hung a picture of King Alexander XVI of Calaskar, and if anyone offered the King an insult in a place like this the offender would be lucky to escape with nothing worse than broken bones.

"What'll it be?" said the bartender, a middle-aged man in an apron.

"Bacon, eggs, coffee," said March. "A private booth, if you've got it." He tapped the phone at his belt. "Expecting a call."

The bartender nodded and pointed to a booth in the corner as March handed him some bills adorned with the portrait of a long-dead King of Calaskar. March seated himself, checking the booth over. No one could overhear him here, and he did a quick search for listening devices. Nothing stood out to him, and the noise of the crowd would drown out any microphones.

Still, best to be careful. Those men had been waiting for him at the airlock.

A moment later a pretty waitress arrived with his food. Sometimes places like this relied on androids to cut costs, but it was hard for a robot to compete with the charm of a pretty girl. Out here, the bacon and the eggs had been grown from Rustari algae protein in a hydroponics lab's vat, and the coffee had been vacuum sealed and shipped from one of the farms on Calaskar, but it was still better than the food aboard the *Tiger*. March thanked the waitress and picked up the fork.

Naturally, that was the moment that Censor chose to call.

March sighed, put down the fork, and drew his phone from his belt. The call was coming from the *Tiger*, and the Vigil reported that the call had arrived from the entangledtachyon communications relay on Antioch itself. Quantum entanglement tachyon technology was the basis for any faster-than-light telecommunications. It was also hideously expensive. March wondered how much these calls cost Censor and decided he didn't want to know.

He waited until the confirmation flashed on the screen, and then accepted the call and lifted the phone to his ear.

"Hello," he said.

"Captain Jack March," said a familiar male voice, dry and cool with the accents of the Calaskaran nobility. "I trust you are well?"

"Well enough, sir," said March.

"Good," said the man known as Censor, the head of the Silent Order, the leader of the Calaskaran intelligence services, and possibly the most dangerous man in the Kingdom of Calaskar. "We have a great deal of work to do, Captain."

Censor had recruited March into the Silent Order, and ever since then, Censor had been his handler and had given him assignments. March had never met the man, had never even seen his face. For all that March knew, Censor might not even be a man – software voice masking had been available for thousands of years. Given that the head of the Silent Order was a prime target for Machinist cells, it made sense for Censor to hide his identity.

"I'm ready, sir," said March.

"Excellent," said Censor. "Are you familiar with a place called Rustbelt Station?"

"I am, sir," said March. "It's in an unnamed system – NB8876X, I think. The Kingdom claims it, but there are no habitable planets and no colonies. The station used to be an asteroid mine, but the mine played out. Now it's a place off the beaten track that caters to people who do not want to be found – smugglers, pirates, criminals, exiles."

"And privateers," said Censor.

"And privateers, sir," said March. "I have been there three times. Twice since I joined the service, and once from my time...before."

His right hand held his phone, but his left arm of metal ached a little at the memory.

"Very good," said Censor. "You're familiar with the station, which is why we have chosen you for this task. Another question. Are you familiar with the names Roanna Vindex and Thomas Vindex?"

"No," said March. He thought for a moment, staring at his food. His stomach rumbled, but there was no way he would eat while on a call with Censor. "The name sounds familiar, though. A noble house of Calaskar?"

"Correct, Captain," said Censor. "One of the oldest and most powerful of the Kingdom. In the aftermath of the collapse of the Fifth Terran Empire two thousand years ago, the Vindex family was one of the first families to settle upon Calaskar, and they have played critical roles in the history of our Kingdom ever since."

"Yes, sir," said March, connecting the dots. "I assume there is a reason that two members of a noble family would find themselves in a place like Rustbelt Station?"

"Yes," said Censor. "Nor is it a good one. I fear they have been dabbling with a cell of Machinists sympathizers."

March felt something in him grow cold. "Then this is a termination assignment, sir?"

"Not necessarily," said Censor.

That wasn't the same as saying no.

"Roanna and Thomas are twins, and are close as often

happens with twins," said Censor. "It seems that Thomas fell in with the Machinist sympathizers, as sometimes happens with bored young men possessed of more money and time than wit. Lady Roanna possesses better sense and went to retrieve her brother. Apparently, she succeeded in convincing her brother to break away from the Machinists, and they both fled from the cell's meeting place somewhere in uncharted space. Unfortunately, they have run out of funds. They were able to secure passage on a smuggling ship heading for Rust-belt Station, but will be unable to go no further. Roanna contacted her father for help, but we intercepted the request."

"Then you want me to fly them home," said March. "With respect, sir, it seems that an Alpha Operative would be better employed elsewhere."

"An Alpha Operative is deployed where the Silent Order sees fit," said Censor with mild reproof. "As it happens, this situation requires an Alpha Operative. The cell took Thomas's defection badly, and they have decided to kill him. He knows too much. Enough to get them all imprisoned or hanged. To save themselves, they have to kill both of the Vindex twins."

"Is this cell competent?" said March. "To be honest, sometimes these Machinist cells are the bored children of rich men playing at being rebels."

"That is true," said Censor. "And sometimes the cells are the sort who can plan a terrorist attack like the Orbital Ship-yard Bombing or the incident at the Outer System Dock. I'm afraid that the Vindexes' friends fall into that category."

"I see, sir," said March.

"Alpha Operative March," said Censor, and March felt himself sit up a little straighter out of habit. "This is your official assignment. You will proceed at once to Rustbelt Station and await the docking of the *Fisher*, the smuggling craft holding the Vindexes. There you will intercept the Vindexes, and convince them to come with you. To persuade them, you will say that their father Lord Vindex hired you to take them from Rustbelt Station. Once they are aboard your vessel, you will take them to Antioch Station and deliver them to the offices of the Royal Calaskaran Navy. Do you accept this assignment?"

"Yes, sir."

"Good." Censor's voice was satisfied. "Relevant data is being sent to your ship's pseudointelligence. Do you have any questions?"

"Yes, sir," said March. "I think this mission might have already been compromised."

"How so?" said Censor.

"When I arrived at Antioch Station to await orders," said March. "I was attacked at the airlock. Three men."

"Did you kill them?" said Censor.

"No, sir," said March. "Didn't want trouble with station security. I took pictures of their IDs. They're in my ship's computer system. The pseudointelligence will share the images."

He lowered his phone and hit a few commands on the display, telling Vigil to send the images, and then put the phone back to his ear.

"Ah," said Censor a moment later. "Yes, these men are known to the Silent Order. The two followers are unimportant. Local hired muscle. They will get arrested by station security sooner rather than later. The leader, though, the fellow with the scar. He's an extremely dangerous high-level operative for the Machinists."

"Why hasn't he been killed yet?" said March.

"He's too slippery," said Censor. "He goes by a dozen different names, but his most common alias is Simon Lorre.

Most likely he intended to assassinate you but underestimated you instead." A dry note entered his voice. "It has happened before."

"Thank you, sir," said March.

"And at the moment the Final Consciousness and the Kingdom are technically in a state of peace," said Censor, "but you know as well as I do that they assassinate our operatives whenever possible."

"And a new war is only a matter of time," said March. "Sir, it's also possible that the Machinist cell realizes that the Vindex twins are backing out, and are trying to capture them."

"Your conjecture is entirely accurate, Captain," said Censor. "You asked why we sent an Alpha-level Operative on this mission? You have your answer."

"Thank you, sir," said March. "I will depart at once."

"Very good, Captain," said Censor. Again, that dry note entered his voice. "Be sure to finish your eggs first."

March grunted. "How did you know I am having eggs, sir? I paid in cash."

Censor laughed. "You are a man of simple tastes, Captain."

"There are worse things, sir," said March, looking at his gloved left hand. He had eaten no eggs when he had been part of the Final Consciousness, only meal packets of flavorless paste. There had been no coffee, only water. And there had been the colossal voice of the Final Consciousness in his skull, filling him with its implacable purpose and its desire to enslave all humanity. "There are far worse things."

"Indeed," said Censor. "And our work is to keep those worse things from happening. God go with you, Captain. Do not make contact until you have mission results."

"Yes, sir," said March, and Censor ended the call.

March returned his phone to his pocket and contemplated his mission. He had joined the Kingdom of Calaskar, but he had never much cared for the nobles, at least for those not in the military.

Still, he had his mission, and he would execute that mission.

First, though, he would eat his meal. Censor might say March had simple tastes, but he did like the taste of vat-grown eggs.

15

ANNOTATIONS ON SILENT ORDER: IRON HAND CHAPTER 2

With his new assignment, March travels to Rustbelt Station aboard his ship, a blockade runner named the Tiger. During the journey to Rustbelt Station, March reviews the information Censor sent him about the Vindex twins, adding uncertainty to the plot. Were the twins innocent victims who blundered into things over their head or active allies of the Machinists?

During the journey, March is attacked by a pirate ship. He drives off the attack, but this adds to the element of uncertainty. Was it just a random attack, or were the pirates working for the Final Consciousness?

March also begins to encounter the first unexpected complications when his ship arrives at Rustbelt Station. Administrator Heitz, who manages the station, and Ronstadt Corporation, who provide the security, are both corrupt. Additionally, Simon Lorre has arrived at the station ahead of March and is probably there to kidnap or kill the Vindex twins. Fortunately, March has an ally in his old friend Constantine Bishop, who heads the local branch of the Silent Order. March and Bishop start to prepare for the Vindex twins' arrival, knowing that they might have to stop Lorre from assassinating or kidnapping them.

This chapter features both rising action and unexpected complications.

16

SILENT ORDER IRON HAND CHAPTER 2: RUSTBELT

A fter his meal, March left the bar and took the lift back to Ring Three.

Censor had told him to leave as soon as possible, and March always followed orders to the best of his ability.

That said, he had to make some preparations first.

He might have been an Alpha Operative of the Silent Order of the Kingdom of Calaskar, but his cover was a privateer, the captain of a small, well-armed trading vessel. A cover had to be maintained. March looked for a cargo heading towards Rustbelt Station.

Fortunately, after he logged into the station's network, it did not take him long to locate a cargo. March found a load of prepackaged meals, the kind of sealed and nano-prepared food that kept for centuries, scheduled for transfer to Rustbelt Station. The job paid just enough to meet the costs of traveling to Rustbelt Station and turn a small profit, and it was exactly the kind of cargo an independent freighter captain would take. Even better, the meals were to be delivered to a man named Constantine Bishop who owned a restaurant and bar on Rustbelt Station called the Emperor's Rest.

March knew Bishop well, and he also knew that Bishop was the local head of the Silent Order's branch on Rustbelt Station.

He accepted the job, and the station's cargo office scheduled a time to load the meals on the *Tiger* later in the afternoon.

After that, March busied himself preparing for his trip to Rustbelt Station. His housekeeping was often lackadaisical, so he hired a set of cleaning drones and set them loose on the ship. He restocked the ship's stores with food and drink, and made sure the oxygen and water supplies were topped off and the life support ready. No doubt the Vindexes were used to more luxurious accommodations, but if they had wanted luxury, they shouldn't have gotten involved with a Machinist cell.

Their comfort wasn't March's mission. Their survival was his mission, and March cared about the mission most of all. The Final Consciousness had made him that way, and the trait persisted, even if he had broken free and transferred his allegiance to the Kingdom of Calaskar.

While he made the preparations, March kept a careful eye out for any trouble. If this Simon Lorre had been sent to assassinate him, the Machinist agent might try again, or he might attempt to sabotage the *Tiger*. After the failure of his first attempt, he might hang back and watch to gather more information. That was what March would have done in his position.

Yet he saw no sign of Lorre, nor of anyone else watching. Despite its excellence as a cover story, it was regrettable he had to take that cargo to Rustbelt Station. It advertised that

March was going there. On the other hand, security on Rustbelt Station was much lighter.

If Lorre showed up again or attempted to interfere with the mission, March would simply kill him and dump his body into empty space. He knew what crimes the Machinists had committed on the worlds they had enslaved. March had no qualms about killing Machinist agents whenever they crossed his path.

And if the Vindexes were Machinist agents...

March dismissed that thought. That was for Censor and the others in the Silent Order to decide.

By late afternoon, the preparations were complete. March returned to the *Tiger*'s flight cabin and started the preflight checks.

"Welcome back, Captain March," said Vigil. "We are departing for system NB8876X?"

"That's right," said March.

"I have begun calculating the entry point for our first hyperspace tunnel," said Vigil. "I estimate it will take approximately three and a half days to reach NB8876X and Rustbelt Station, depending on local conditions, and a total of fifteen hyperspace jumps."

"Acknowledged," said March, running through the checklists. All the maintenance had been completed successfully, and he started warming up the fusion drive and the ion thrusters.

"Additionally, your employer left a collection of files for your perusal during his call," said Vigil.

"I'll read them while we're in hyperspace," said March.

He finished the preflight preliminaries while Vigil used most of the ship's computing power to calculate the hyperspace tunnel. Once he received clearance to leave, he undocked from Antioch Station, spun the *Tiger* around, and headed for the vector that Vigil's calculations indicated. The fusion drive, the gravitics, and the inertial absorbers all showed green, so March turned his attention to the hyperdrive. He fired up the dark matter reactor and the dark energy resonator. Hyperspace was filled with macrobes, energy creatures that could possess living human minds, and without a resonator to keep the macrobes away, the crew and passengers of a starship in hyperspace would suffer macrobe possession, followed immediately by homicidal insanity and dark energy-based mutations.

Of course, because of alterations the Final Consciousness had made to his physiology during his time as an Iron Hand, March was immune to those dangers, but if he was taking on passengers, best to make sure they did not become homicidal mutants.

Vigil finished the first of the hyperspace computations, and March activated the hyperdrive. The hyperspace tunnel opened before the *Tiger*, invisible to the naked eye, but a vortex of writhing energy on the dark energy sensor display. The *Tiger* shot into the tunnel and into hyperspace, and then the computer blanked all the external displays to prevent any crew and passengers from looking into hyperspace and going insane.

March set the computer to alert him if anything went wrong, and left the flight cabin. Interstellar travel was a bit like stepping from stone to stone to cross a creek, albeit a creek of unimaginable distance. To aid in navigation, the easiest method of interstellar travel was to jump from system to system, one at a time, using the star's gravity well to collapse the hyperspace tunnel at the appropriate instant. March's first jump was to an unnamed system with the chart number of NB4633J, and it was nothing but gas giants and uninhabitable rocky inner planets. From there, he had another jump to calculate, but he had three hours before they reached NB4633J.

So he headed to the *Tiger's* gym.

He had converted one of the cabins and half the galley into a gym equipped with free weights, a treadmill, and a few other exercise devices. The early training given to all Iron Hands remained with him, and he felt restless if he did not maintain his exercise routine. The nanotech in his blood could do many things, but it could do far more with a healthy, fit body than it could with a weak one. For that matter, the rigors of interstellar travel were hard on the body, and the stronger he was, the better off he would be.

And given how often he found himself in combat, he needed physical strength.

Exercising with his cybernetic arm was a challenge, but he had long ago mastered it. His left arm could easily lift four or five times the weight of his right arm, so he refused to rely on his left arm in training. The cybernetic limb had inhuman strength, but the rest of him had to be strong as well.

He exercised while the ship made its way through the hyperspace tunnel. He did squats, overhead lifts, and dead lifts, interspersed with stretches and forms he had learned as part of his unarmed combat training. March worked through each form until he reached muscle exhaustion, and then moved onto the next set.

As he recovered between sets, he used a tablet computer to read the files that Censor had sent him on the Vindex twins.

The Silent Order kept records on powerful and wealthy Calaskaran citizens, and the House of Vindex was no exception. The current head of the House, Lord Sebastian Vindex, was the Earl of Sundrex on Calaskar, held a seat in the

Congress of Lords, had served in various government ministries, was friends with the King, and fantastically wealthy. He had nine children, and Roanna Vindex and Thomas Vindex were his youngest. It seemed they had not been disciplined as his elder children had been, all of whom either served in the Royal Calaskaran Navy or had posts in the ministries of Calaskar's various colonies. No one in the family had shown any Machinist sympathizes until Thomas.

March did another set of military presses, and then read the file on Thomas as he caught his breath.

The file included a picture. Thomas Vindex looked like a charismatic young man, with thick black hair, bright blue eyes, and commanding features. The file noted that he had been on the typical career path of a young Calaskaran noble until he had befriended some dissidents who had been later arrested as a part of a terrorist plot. Thomas had joined a Machinist cell, changed his mind, and wanted out.

His sister had gone to rescue him.

Thomas had been charismatic, but Roanna Vindex, if the picture was any indication, was beautiful. The features that made her twin brother look commanding became forceful beauty on her. The Silent Order's report noted that her character included a strong selfish streak combined with an altruistic impulse, along with a tendency to make decisions on an emotional basis and rationalize them later.

Such women, March knew, were trouble. It explained why she had taken off after her brother to get him back from the Machinists. An emotional decision rationalized later. March wasn't sure if she would become a Machinist or not. It seemed unlikely. Most probably she was arrogant enough to reject the ideology of the Machinists out of hand.

He looked at her picture a moment later, and then shut off the tablet.

"Captain," came Vigil's voice. "We are ten minutes from the terminus of our hyperspace tunnel."

"Acknowledged," said March.

He toweled off and walked back to the flight cabin.

The *Tiger* returned to normal space without incident. The dark matter sensors detected a few active ship reactors scattered around the NB4633J system, likely gas miners prospecting the gas giants, but no threats. Vigil calculated the next jump, and the *Tiger* entered the hyperspace tunnel without any difficulty.

The trip fell into a familiar pattern. March exercised during the hyperspace jumps or practiced his marksmanship in the cargo hold with a low-power hand laser. He also attended to various maintenance tasks. The *Tiger's* maintenance drones could do a lot of things, but some repairs had to be done manually.

The first thirteen jumps passed without incident.

As the *Tiger* exited its fourteenth hyperspace tunnel, things got interesting.

The system was called Wyatt's Folly, evidently due to a doomed colonization effort a few centuries ago. The colonists had slaughtered each other in a political dispute, and the system had remained empty ever since.

The *Tiger's* sensors lit up as it locked onto a starship about three million kilometers away, its reactor hot and its defensive systems activated. March keyed for a sensor focus, and information about the ship scrolled across his screens. It was a Mercator Foundry Yards Class 5 patrol craft, sold to planetary navies for use as a customs enforcer and long-distance patrol ship. The *Tiger's* database had the official specifications of that class of ship, and it was generating way more power than it should have. The visual scan picked up additional weapons emplacements and missile racks on the patrol ship, and its hull armor had been replaced and thickened.

"They are on an intercept course," said Vigil.

"Send a standard greeting," said March, running through the checklists for the weapons systems.

"Greeting sent, no answer," said Vigil. "There are no standardized identifying markings on the hull, and the ship is not broadcasting an ID signal."

A visual came up. The Class 5 patrol craft was sleek and narrow, with back-swept wings for both aesthetic appeal and to present a smaller targeting profile. The lines were marred by the addition of missile pylons to the wings, and the clunky shape of extra armor plating. On the wings, March saw a crudely painted symbol – a gray wolf's head, fangs bared in a snarl.

"Missile lock detected, Captain," said Vigil. "Recommend immediate switch to battle configuration."

"Do it," said March, flipping switches as his combat reflexes came to the fore, his heart speeding up, his mind slowing down. This was the kind of battle fought while sitting in a chair and pressing buttons, but it was a fight nonetheless, and his body responded as if he was about to go into combat with his fists.

The *Tiger* switched to battle configuration. All external communications shut down, to reduce the risk of a successful hacking attempt. The shields powered up, both the kinetic deflector to block missiles and projectiles, and the radiation deflector to absorb the damage from beams and plasma bursts. The *Tiger*'s own weapons came online, four forward-facing plasma cannons, a keel-mounted railgun that flung tungsten rods at dangerous velocities, and a dorsal laser turret and a ventral laser turret for point defense. It would take time for the plasma cannons to build up enough active particles to fire, but the railgun and the defense turrets were ready.

Which is just as well, because a shrill alarm filled the flight cabin.

"Missile launch detected," said Vigil, red text scrolling across the display.

"Give me manual flight control," said March, gripping the flight yoke and spinning the *Tiger* around with a burst from the ion thrusters. "Calculate a firing solution for the turrets."

March fed power to the drive, and a faint shudder went through the ship as the drive pushed them forward, the gravitics and the inertial absorbers unable to quite keep up. The sensors identified the missile as a standard fragmentation warhead. It would hit the *Tiger*'s kinetic shield and shatter, and the resultant explosion would hurl thousands of small fragments at the ship. That many contacts might overwhelm the kinetic shield and send the fragments hammering into the hull.

The *Tiger* hurtled towards the patrol ship, the missile burning close. March turned the *Tiger* so that the ship's nose pointed towards the oncoming missile, which also meant the dorsal and ventral turrets could target the missile.

"Firing solution calculated," said Vigil.

March glanced at the displays, noting the targeting information and the remaining charge time on the plasma cannons, and hit the firing switches for the lasers. The turrets rotated, locked, and let out invisible beams of light. The missile was not shielded, and the beams sliced into the missile's side, breaching the reaction chambers of its ion thrusters. March jerked the *Tiger* to starboard, and the missile tried to follow, but with its thrusters damaged it could not change course.

The patrol ship kept flying towards him, and March adjusted his vector, locked on with the plasma cannons, and squeezed the firing triggers. Bolts of superheated plasma burst from the cannons, hammering into the patrol ship's radiation deflectors, and both of his laser turrets added their power to the barrage. If the patrol ship's radiation deflector collapsed, the plasma bolts would rip through the armor and into the hull.

The next volley of plasma bolts missed as the patrol ship banked, and the battle turned into a dogfight, with March trying to keep the *Tiger* on his enemy's tail. The patrol ship was more maneuverable, but the *Tiger* had heavier armor, and the two ships circled and spun around each other, their relative velocities moving closer and closer. March only managed to hit the enemy with the plasma cannons a few more times, but the laser turrets kept their invisible beams fixed on the patrol ship, and March watched his enemy's radiation deflector weaken. If it collapsed, the laser turrets could slice apart the hull, or a volley from the plasma cannons could rip open the patrol ship.

As abruptly as it began, the fight ended.

The patrol ship turned, and an alarm blared as March's sensors picked up a surge of radiation from a dark matter reactor. He spun the *Tiger* and fed power to the drive, blazing away from the patrol ship as it opened a hyperspace tunnel. An instant later the patrol ship vanished from real space, leaving behind only a fading signature of dark energy and conventional radiation.

"Calculate their vector," said March.

"Calculating," said Vigil. A moment later the pseudointelligence spoke again. "Deep space, vector leading to no nearby systems. Probability indicates that was an emergency jump to escape."

"Check the sensor logs and calculate their original position," said March. "Did that ship come from NB8876X?"

He waited as Vigil crunched the numbers. They were far from the core systems of the Kingdom of Calaskar, far from the solar systems of any major power, and this system was exactly the sort of place a pirate ship might decide to prowl. Nevertheless, it seemed an unlikely coincidence. This solar system was vast, with hundreds of potential terminus points for hyperspace tunnels from the neighboring systems. Combined with the fact that Lorre and his thugs had been waiting for March at Antioch Station, stumbling on a pirate ship waiting at exactly the route from the Antioch system to Rustbelt Station was an improbable coincidence.

"Calculation complete, captain," said Vigil. "I estimate a fifty-two percent chance that ship originated in the NB8876X system. However, based on its original position and vector, there are at least nineteen surrounding systems the ship could have used as a starting point before jumping here."

"So a pirate," said March, "or someone waiting specifically for us."

"Most likely," agreed Vigil. "Either conclusion fits the available facts. Without further data, it is impossible to reach a definitive conclusion."

"I suspect," said March, "we're about to get further data. Calculate a jump to NB8876X, with our terminus near Rustbelt Station. Once we're in hyperspace, I'm going to do as much of a maintenance check on the weapons as I can without doing a spacewalk. I expect we might need them before we get to Rustbelt Station."

"Acknowledged," said Vigil. While the computer calculated the jump, March did the usual pre-jump check on the hyperdrive, the dark matter reactor, and the resonator coil. Sometimes he wished for additional crew on board. He could fly, operate, and repair the *Tiger* himself, though he did have to hire some things out. Still, it wasn't as if he had the funds to hire additional crew, and any crewers would have to be members of the Silent Order to satisfy the need for operational security.

Once they were in hyperspace, March went to the cargo bay, threaded his way past the pallets of prepackaged meals, and opened the weapons access panels. He would have to do some of the weapons' maintenance outside of the ship, but from here he could clear some of the crystallization from the plasma cannons' capacitors and make sure the reaction chambers hadn't developed any flaws. Once that was done, he went to the laser turrets and made sure the servos and gears in the turrets were operational, and that the railgun's coils were ready.

By then there were only a few moments until the *Tiger* reached the terminus of its hyperspace tunnel, so March returned to the flight cabin, made sure the shields and weapons were ready to power up, and waited.

The ship exited hyperspace, and the *Tiger* returned to normal space in the NB8876X system.

March looked at the sensor displays.

NB8876X was a binary star system, with a smaller blue star and a red supergiant. The first nine planets were rocky but too close to the suns to hold an atmosphere or too far away to support life. The remaining twelve planets were gas giants, and each one held a constellation of moons, some of them the size of a planet, some of them no more than captured asteroids. The system had two asteroid belts, one between sixth and seventh planets, and another beyond the ninth planet, at just about four and a half AU from the stars

The system was deserted of any life save for Rustbelt Station.

The station occupied an asteroid in the outer belt about forty million kilometers from the *Tiger's* exit point. As the *Tiger* drew closer, March watched the sensor data scroll across his displays. The asteroid was shaped like a lumpy potato and was about fifty kilometers in diameter at its thickest point. The radar and ladar picked up dozens of metallic domes clustered near the asteroid's southern pole, and the radiation sensors detected several active fusion reactors. The sensors also registered enormous empty spaces within the asteroid, places where the mining equipment had cut into the rock. Once the asteroid had been home to some rare ores, and a mining company had tried to exploit them. The market prices had changed, driving the company out of business, and the mine had shut down.

But Rustbelt Station remained, catering to those who wished to conduct their business far from official eyes. Smugglers and pirates and drug runners turned up here, along with people involved in far more serious crimes, such as slaving and kidnapping. Naturally, spies from the various starfaring nations and races visited Rustbelt Station as well.

"Vigil," said March. "How many ships are docked here?"

"Ninety-seven," said Vigil. "Mostly light freighter craft the size of the *Tiger*, but several larger vessels. It is possible that additional starships are docked inside the caverns of the asteroid where our sensors could not penetrate." One of the displays started flashing red. "Also, several missile turrets have locked onto our ship, and we are being hailed."

"Acknowledged," said March, and he reached for the communication controls. "This is Captain Jack March of the *Tiger* calling Rustbelt Station control. Requesting docking permission."

"*Tiger*," came a dry male voice, "this is Administrator Heitz of Rustbelt Station. Identify your purpose for visiting the station."

"I am carrying a load of prepackaged meals," said March, "to be delivered to one Constantine Bishop and his restaurant the Emperor's Rest."

An amused snort came from the speakers. "More swill for Bishop's dive? Fine. The docking fee is seven hundred and fifty credits. Hard currency, nothing electronic. We're a long way from any communications out here."

March scowled. "A bit high for a docking fee, isn't it?"

Some smugness entered Heitz's voice. "We're also a long way from civilization out here, Captain March. There are additional expenses. Everything has its price at Rustbelt Station. Consider it a good faith gesture, proof you're not a pirate or a troublemaker." The sensors reported another missile turret locking onto the *Tiger*. "And if you're not willing to make that good faith gesture, well...no one will miss another pirate. You understand me?"

March understood extortion when he saw it, but he didn't see any way around it. "Fine. I'll pay."

"Excellent," said Heitz. "You are cleared for Bay 93." The coordinates flashed on a display. "I will meet you there to collect the docking fee in person."

"Fine," said March again. "Will I have room to unload my cargo? I don't want to pay a shuttle to ferry it to a different dome."

"Yeah, yeah," said Heitz. "You can get to Bishop's restaurant without any trouble. You're cleared for landing. Don't try anything clever, or else you and your ship will be on the scrap market."

The call ended.

"A good faith gesture," muttered March with disgust.

He shut down the main drive and used the ion thrusters to guide the *Tiger* towards the asteroid. There were dozens of landing pits scattered around the metal domes of the station, and one of them flashed on his screen. March rotated the *Tiger*, extended the landing struts, and put the ship down.

"Landing successful, Captain," said Vigil.

"Thanks," said March, watching the displays. A static atmosphere barrier appeared over the entrance to the bay, sputtering a few times before it caught. He made a mental note to take a breath mask in case the barrier failed. "Do the usual maintenance routines, but keep the ship on standby in case we have to leave in a hurry. Also, maximum security, and keep the laser turrets charged if someone tries to break into the ship. Inform me if anything unusual happens."

"Acknowledged, Captain," said Vigil.

March unstrapped and stopped by his cabin long enough to retrieve his coat, his knives, his gun belt, and a few other useful tools. From a safe in the wall, he took fifteen hundred Calaskaran credits in 50-credit denominations, tucking the money into a pocket. He picked up his phone and connected it to Rustbelt Station's local network, downloading the public directory and map.

"Captain," said Vigil as March stepped back into the dorsal corridor, "four men have just entered the landing bay. All of them are armed, and based on voiceprint analysis one of them is Administrator Heitz."

"He's here for his bribe," said March, checking his gun. "If it comes to a fight, use the laser turrets."

He descended to the cargo bay, opened the loading ramp, and walked into the landing bay. The *Tiger* fit snugly, the brilliant star field visible overhead beyond the static barrier. The air smelled of laser-cut rock.

Four men stood near the airlock leading into Rustbelt Station proper. Three of them had the look of private security contractors, hands resting on their gun belts. They wore black jumpsuits with the logo of crossed laser pistols on the right arm. The fourth was obese and sweating a little, and wore a suit that he should not have been able to afford on a civil servant's salary.

"Captain March?" said the fat man, and March recognized Heitz's voice.

"I am," said March. "You're Heitz?"

"Administrator Heitz," he said. "Alas, our governor died seven months past, and the Crown has not seen fit to dispatch a new one. Until the King appoints a new governor, I'm afraid I must manage all the affairs of Rustbelt Station." He offered an oily smile. "Your docking fee?"

March withdrew fifteen 50-credit notes from his pocket. He resisted the urge to shove them into Heitz's mouth. "Here."

"Thank you," said Heitz. He pocketed the money. The royal government and the Silent Order took a dim view of corruption, and sometimes the Order dispatched operatives to arrange "accidents" for officials who indulged in too much corruption. March had carried out a few of those assignments. Perhaps he would pay an official visit to Heitz one day. "Welcome to Rustbelt Station. Security arrangements and public order are overseen by members of Ronstadt Private Security Corporation." He nodded to his goons, who were no doubt also on the take. March had dealt with Ronstadt a few times, and the Corporation ignored the law whenever it could get away with it. "They are authorized to carry out all law enforcement functions within the station. But so long as you behave yourself, you should be fine. If you have any questions, there are public directories available on the local network."

"A question," said March as they turned to go.

Heitz stopped with a sigh. "What?"

"I was attacked on the way here," said March.

"Rustbelt Station is not liable for any damages your ship or your property might have incurred on the way..."

"I fought them off without damage," said March. "But they had a logo painted on their hull, a wolf's head. I wondered if you've had trouble with pirates or renegades."

"The Graywolves," said one of the Ronstadt men.

"A mercenary company," said Heitz with a scowl. "Damned troublemakers, the lot of them. When they can't find proper jobs, they work for crime lords and the sort of petty warlords you find out in the unclaimed systems. And when that doesn't pan out, they turn pirate." A flicker of disgust went over his face, and he spat upon the rough-cut rock of the floor. "They'll even work for the Machinists."

"You don't approve?" said March.

"Damned Machinists," said Heitz, anger flaring in his tone. "I was at Martel's World when they bombed it at the end of the last war. Machinist sympathizers are not welcome on Rustbelt Station. If I find a Machinist sympathizer, out the airlock he goes." He leveled a thick finger at March. "If you're a sympathizer, you'll disappear, and that will be that."

"I'm not a Machinist sympathizer," said March, "and I've never been one." He supposed that was entirely true. He had been an Iron Hand, part of the Final Consciousness, and never a sympathizer. "God save the King."

Heitz grunted and walked away. The Ronstadt men gave March a hard look, and he kept a bland expression on his face, training and experience mapping out how he could kill all three of them.

But the security men walked away. March stared after them for a moment, rolled his aching left shoulder, and strode into Rustbelt Station.

It was indeed a rough place, especially compared to his previous stop. Antioch Station was the height of Calaskaran engineering. Rustbelt Station was an asteroid mine that had gone bankrupt. March strode down a wide cargo corridor with a metal grill floor, rough walls of laser-cut rock on either side. The walls gave off a distinct chill, which did not speak highly of the station's life support systems. From time to time he passed a worker in the coveralls of a cargo handler, or a drone truck rattling past with a load of crates and barrels in its bed, but the corridor was otherwise deserted.

The cargo corridor was a perfect place for an ambush from somebody like Simon Lorre and his helpers, but no attackers presented themselves. March consulted the map for a moment, then turned right, walked through an airlock, and stepped into a wide concourse cut from the rock of the asteroid. Shops lined the walls, and unlike at Antioch Station, the shops catered to men accustomed to violence. One shop sold hand weapons, everything from plasma guns to portable missile launchers. Another specialized in ship repairs and upgrades. March saw three bars and two brothels, one specializing in human women, and another in androids of various models designed to cater to every perversion. On Antioch Station, such a place would have been shut down and its owner arrested within an hour. Here, it was the busiest shop on the concourse. Armed guards stood at every establishment, watching the crowds with cold eyes.

March ignored them and walked to a restaurant at the end of the concourse. A sign labeled EMPEROR'S REST hung over the restaurant, and March stepped through the front door. Like most of the other rooms in Rustbelt Station, it had been carved from the rock of the asteroid. Metal tables and chairs dotted the room, about half of them occupied with crewers and cargo handlers eating lunch. A long bar ran the length of the wall, and waitresses in tight skirts and T-shirts carried out trays of food from the kitchen. March had been in a hundred restaurants like this in a hundred systems, and he was familiar with the guards at the door, the cold eyes of the waitresses, and the fact at least some of the men at the tables and the women in tight skirts would be informants for the intelligence services of the various starfaring nations.

March leaned against the bar.

"What will it be, traveler?" said the woman at the bar, giving him a wide smile that did not touch her brown eyes. She had shaggy blond hair and sharp features, her mouth red with lipstick and her eyes encircled with dark lines of makeup.

His eyes flicked to the inflated prices on the menu boards, and then looked back at her. "I need to speak with Constantine Bishop."

"Oh, you do, do you?" said the bartender. "What are you, a debt collector?"

"That's exactly right," said March without smiling. "I'm a debt collector. So I'd like to talk to Constantine Bishop, and I'd also like you to get me a beer first."

The bartender laughed, and this time the smile did touch her eyes. "Fine." She named a price, twice as much as the beer would have cost on Antioch Station, and March handed over the credit notes. The bartender grinned at him and produced a beer. March took a sip. It tasted better than he expected. The bartender turned and vanished into a door behind a neon sign for a Calaskaran brewery. She was wearing high heels, and March couldn't help but notice that the short skirt fit her excellently.

He pushed aside the thought with annoyance. He was working, and that was not a time to allow distractions. Another sip of beer, and he glanced around the restaurant, but no one seemed to be paying him any attention.

"Well, well," said a familiar voice, deep with the accent of a Calaskaran commoner. "Look who wandered in with the trash."

March turned his head as Constantine Bishop strolled out of the back room, the bartender walking behind him. Bishop was a huge man, nearly seven feet tall, though he was developing a bit of a stoop from spending so much time in cramped quarters. He had ragged blond hair and a bushy blond beard and wore an odd mixture of clothes – steel-toed work boots, cargo pants, a red silk shirt, and a formal black coat. He owned the restaurant, and he was also in charge of the Rustbelt Station branch of the Silent Order.

"Jack March," said Bishop, grinning. He extended his left hand, and March shook it with his left. It was a gesture of trust. Bishop knew perfectly well that March could have crushed his left hand into hamburger. "You still flying that barge?"

"The *Tiger* is a good ship," said March, smiling.

"He said he was a debt collector," said the bartender.

"Captain March is a privateer," said Bishop. "I suppose he would do debt collection if we paid him enough. Thank you, Anne. Bring us a pair of beers on the house. Captain March and I need to catch up."

Anne produced two more bottles of beer, and March took one and added it to his half-finished bottle. He followed Bishop through the door behind the bar and into a storeroom stacked with cases of beer and prepackaged meals. Bishop opened the door and stepped into a small office with a plastic desk, the walls lined with photographs of Bishop posing with various dignitaries.

"Have a seat," said Bishop, dropping into his desk chair with a sigh.

March seated himself. "I have a delivery for you. Prepackaged meals."

"And thank God for that," said Bishop. "My inventory was running low, and Rustbelt Station is the only place I can sell those wretched things at a three hundred percent markup." He grinned and drained a third of his bottle with a single swig. "And having you deliver my inventory is an excellent cover story for getting an Alpha-level Operative out here in the wilderness."

"Censor's talked to you, then?" said March.

"Message only got here four hours ago," said Bishop. "Takes a while for anything to make its way out here. It didn't have many details. Some trouble with a noble-woman?" He leaned forward, his chair creaking under his bulk. "She went over to the Machinists?"

"Not quite," said March. "At least, I don't think so. Seems like young Lord Thomas Vindex was flirting with a cell of Machinist sympathizers and realized it was a bad idea. His twin sister Lady Roanna came to rescue him, and they're on a smuggler ship called the *Fisher* heading for here. Ought to arrive tomorrow. Censor sent me out here to pick them up and bring them back to Antioch Station."

Bishop grunted and swirled his beer in the bottle. "Think their story's on the level?"

"Damned if I know," said March. "Maybe Lady Roanna is telling the truth. She did ask us for help. Or maybe they both went over to the Machinists and are planning on starting a new cell on Calaskar. Or the Machinists scooped out half their brains and replaced them with cybernetics, and they're part of the Final Consciousness now."

"Which one do you think it is?" said Bishop.

"I don't know," said March. "I've seen all three before. I suppose I'll know when I talk to them." He shrugged. "Anyway, I'll take the two of them back to Antioch Station, and Censor can figure out whether they're traitors or if they're just stupid."

"It's never that simple, Jack," said Bishop. "There are going to be complications."

"There already have been," said March. "You ever heard of a mercenary gang called the Graywolves?"

Bishop scowled. "That I have. Though calling the Graywolves mercenaries is giving them too much credit. They're more of a pirate gang that hires out from time to time. They'll work for anyone who pays them, even the Machinists. Heitz won't let them dock openly at the station, though they've got men here on their payroll."

"Heitz," said March. "Is he trustworthy?"

"Of course not," said Bishop with a smile. "The man's a greedy slug. He's a predictable slug, though, and he hates the Machinists and the Final Consciousness something fierce. Guess he lost some friends on Martel's World when the Machinists bombed the place, and he won't let them on the station." Bishop took another swig of his beer. "If he finds any Machinist sympathizers, his goons from Ronstadt have them killed."

"Is that why you haven't had Heitz removed?" said March.

"He's corrupt, but he's not a traitor," said Bishop. "Rustbelt Station is in the middle of nowhere, so no one cares what happens here. If I have him killed, the King will appoint a proper governor for Rustbelt Station, and that would be inconvenient. Right now, this place is a honey trap, and we can use it to learn all kinds of secrets about Calaskar's enemies. Why did you ask about the Graywolves?"

"On my way here," said March, "a Graywolf ship attacked me without warning. Drove them off after a few shots."

Bishop grunted. "They could have been going pirate."

"To steal your load of overpriced prepackaged meals?" said March.

"Out here, food is sometimes worth more than anything else," said Bishop. "It could have been a coincidence."

"Maybe not," said March. "You ever hear of a man named Simon Lorre?"

Bishop's expression hardened. "I have. He's a Machinist agent. The Final Consciousness gives him dirty jobs inside the boundaries of the Kingdom from time to time. He's been here twice, and both times I tried to kill him, but he got out of the trap both times. Lorre has the devil's own cunning."

"He tried to kill me on Antioch Station," said March.

"Must have wanted to stop you from rescuing the Vindex twins," said Bishop.

"He tried to kill me," said March, "an hour before I got this assignment from Censor."

They sat in silence for a moment. March finished his first beer and opened the second one.

"Aw, hell," said Bishop at last.

"Yeah," said March.

"I hope you killed him," said Bishop.

"Didn't," said March. "If I had known who he was, I would have shot him. As it was, there were too many cameras, and if I had shot him, I'd have gotten arrested by

Antioch Station security." He sighed and took a drink of his second beer. "I think I'd have saved myself a lot of trouble if I had."

"He would have had a way out," said Bishop. "He always does. Have to admire him for it, really. It's good to see a man think things out in a professional manner. Pity he's working for the Final Consciousness."

"Well, let's follow his example and think things out," said March. "The Vindex twins' ship. You know when it's coming in?"

Bishop set down his beer, opened up a laptop on his desk, and started typing. "The *Fisher*, right? Let's see...ah, here it is in the flight schedule."

March snorted. "A restaurant owner has access to the station's flight schedule?"

"It's amazing what bribes can accomplish when a man like Heitz is in charge," said Bishop. "Anyway, the *Fisher* should be docking at Bay 156 tomorrow at noon, station time." He leaned back, his chair creaking. "How do you want to play this?"

March thought for a moment. "The Machinists have already tried to kill me. First at Antioch Station, and then in empty space with that Graywolf patrol ship."

"That could have just been a pirate," said Bishop.

"True," said March. "But the ship was waiting for me when the *Tiger* came out of hyperspace. That's a hell of a coincidence, and we're in the wrong business for coincidences. Right now, I figure that that Lady Roanna got her brother away from the Machinists, and they're running here. Either she or her brother, or maybe both, learned something the Machinists don't want us to know. So, they sent Lorre to make sure I wouldn't be there to give the Vindex twins a ride home, and they'll probably try to kill the twins here."

"Makes sense to me," said Bishop. "Unless there's something we don't know."

"Isn't there always?" said March. "Let's pretend we're Machinist agents." His left shoulder throbbed as dark memories flickered through his skull, and he pushed them aside. "Simplest way to kill them is to blow up their ship. An Iron Hand wouldn't care about collateral damage, and the hirelings of the Machinists wouldn't care either, so long as they get away clean. Think the Graywolves will shoot down the *Fisher*?"

Bishop glanced at his laptop screen. "No. They won't be able to pull it off. The *Fisher* will exit a hyperspace tunnel too close to the station. This place is a hole, but it does have a lot of firepower. If the Graywolves try anything, Heitz will shoot them down. The *Fisher* will probably make the station in one piece."

"Then the Machinists are going to kill the Vindex twins on the station," said March.

"Probably," said Bishop.

March gave an irritated shake of his head and finished his second beer. "There are a million ways to kill someone on a space station, even by accident."

"Yes," said Bishop, "though some of them are more practical than others. And given your previous professional experience, my friend, you would have a better chance of sorting out the practical methods from the impractical."

"True," said March, thinking it over. "I want to have a look at Bay 156." He pulled out his phone and looked at the map of the station. "The *Tiger*'s at Bay 93, and it's only a walk of about two kilometers from there. Maybe I can meet the

Vindex twins when they land, walk them to the *Tiger*, and get out of here as soon as possible."

"Efficient," said Bishop. "But you'll have a hell of a job convincing the nobles to follow you."

"I can be very persuasive," said March.

Bishop raised an eyebrow.

March sighed. "I'll tie them up if I have to. Censor said to get them to Antioch Station alive and in one piece. He didn't say that they had to like me when I'm done."

"As ever, your optimism cheers me, my friend," said Bishop, lifting his bottle in a mock salute.

"I'm not an optimist."

"Your optimism is matched only by your sense of humor," said Bishop.

March shrugged and dropped both his bottles into the bin next to Bishop's desk. It was already three-quarters of the way full. Bishop seemed to enjoy his own inventory quite a bit. "I can't argue with that. Want to show me Bay 156? Better to do it now before they start prepping it for the *Fisher's* arrival."

"A good idea," said Bishop. He unlocked a drawer in his desk, produced a small pistol, and tucked it into the interior pocket of his jacket. "Always good to have a stroll after a drink or two, isn't it?"

March nodded and followed Bishop out of the office, through the storeroom, and back to the restaurant floor. Anne looked up as they passed and flashed a wicked smile in March's direction.

"Captain March has delivered our inventory for the next three months," said Bishop. "You're in charge until I get back."

Anne laughed. "Well, don't I feel special." She looked

back at March again. "You're dressed funny for a debt collector."

"Whatever gets the job done," said March.

It wasn't a joke, but she laughed anyway.

They left the restaurant and entered the concourse.

"I think she likes you," said Bishop.

March snorted. "Running a brothel now, are you?"

"Certainly not," said Bishop. "One must have some standards, you know. I do not hire prostitutes, and throw out any customers who attempt to harass my workers."

"And that gains you a trustworthy workforce?" said March.

"Rustbelt Station is something of a harsh place for women with no money," said Bishop, "and the brothels are always hiring. None of my employees know my true business, of course, but within certain bounds they are trustworthy. And I do think Anne likes you."

"Doesn't matter," said March. Bishop led them towards a waiting cab drone, which looked like a plastic cart with four seats and no roof. March dropped into the back, the plastic cushion creaking beneath him. "I don't like distractions while I am working."

"A night with Anne," said Bishop, "and you would be much less distracted. And if that seems like too much work, you could visit one of the brothels and hire an android for an hour." He tapped the drone's panel. "Bay 156."

"A waste of good money," said March. The drone's electric motor whirred, and it pulled into the flow of pedestrians, the computer display showing ads for various local businesses.

"You need a woman, March," said Bishop.

"You say that every time we work together."

"That is because your need clearly has not lessened."

March rolled his eyes and let Bishop talk as the drone headed towards Bay 156, grunting from time to time and nodding when appropriate. Constantine Bishop did like to talk, but March tolerated it. They had been on numerous missions together, and Bishop had saved his life several times.

The cab drone reached the cargo corridor, and after a drive of a few moments came to a stop in front of a massive airlock labeled Bay 156. March got out as Bishop paid the cab, and the vehicle rolled away on another call. Bishop went to the airlock's control panel, tapped in a code, and the double steel doors slid open with a metallic groan.

Bay 156 was a big pit dug from the side of the asteroid, large enough to accommodate a mid-sized passenger liner. The *Tiger* was only seventy-five meters long, and a dozen of March's ship could have landed in the pit. Right now, the bay was mostly empty. He looked overhead and saw the stars beyond the flickering of the atmosphere barrier. There was a heavy repair gantry bolted to the rock wall, currently retracted, and a pile of metal crates and barrels against one wall. There were fuel lines across the floor, and a set of four stalls held repair drones.

"Bay 156," said Bishop. "What a pit."

"Literally," said March, looking around. There were possibilities here.

"So," said Bishop, "if you were going to kill someone in here and you didn't care about casualties, how would you do it?"

"Bomb would be the easiest," said March. "I'd hide it in those access points on the floor. Blowing out the atmosphere barrier would be another way to do it, but I'd have to sabotage the airlocks as well, make sure they couldn't get away. Setting fire to the fuel lines would kill a lot

of people if I timed it right." March looked towards the
stacked creates. "I suppose there is likely a service corridor
there, isn't there?"

"There is," said Bishop. "It runs through all the landing
bays, hooking up to the atmosphere barrier generators and
the other equipment."

March nodded. "That's how I would do it. Those
damned crates shouldn't be stacked there. What kind of
ship is the *Fisher*? An Olympic-class passenger liner?"

"That's what the flight record said, yeah," said Bishop.
"Old model the Mercator yards churned out a few decades
back. The *Fisher* is independently owned, still ferries people
around the outer reaches of the Kingdom. Not a lot of
money in that, so I bet the operators pad their profit margin
with a little smuggling here and there."

March took three steps to the left. "They would disembark from the main passenger ramp, and it would be right
about here." He glanced at Bishop, and then back at the
crates. "If I hid behind the crates, I would have a perfect line
of fire at the passenger ramp. I would just sit there, wait
until I saw the Vindex twins, and shoot them. There aren't
any security cameras in here, and I doubt there are any in
those service corridors. I could get away clean. So long as I
disposed of the gun properly afterward, no one would ever
catch me." He saw it all like a map in his head, the training
of both the Final Consciousness and the Silent Order
showing him the possibilities. "I would..."

He froze, a burst of intuition cutting into his thoughts.

If he wanted to set an ambush for someone, those crates
would be the perfect place to do it. And if he had been a
hired thug of the Machinists, sent to kill a pair of nobles,
then the sensible thing to do would be to remove any
obstacles.

Such as killing any operatives of the Silent Order that might interfere.

There was a glint of light behind the crates.

"Down!" snapped March, throwing himself to the left. Bishop might have been a restaurant owner, but he was still an operative of the Silent Order, and he moved with alacrity, hitting the ground and rolling as he snatched his gun from within his jacket.

Two plasma bolts hit the ground where they had been standing, blasting chunks of hot stone from the floor, and March heard the ricochet of a bullet. He sprinted forward, yanking his gun from his holster and leveling the weapon, spraying shots at the stack of crates. He glimpsed three men crouched behind the crates, guns in hand. March's reckless charge had forced them onto the defensive, but in a moment, they would recover and shoot him dead.

March's left arm drew back and then shot forward with all its cybernetic strength driving the metal limb forward. His palm slammed into one of the crates. It had to weigh at least a hundred pounds, but the power of the blow hurled the crate as if it had been made of paper.

The stack of crates collapsed backward with a series of deafening clangs, followed by a furious barrage of curses from the men. March seized one of the remaining crates with his left hand and heaved, pulling himself up with a single fluid motion as he leveled his pistol at the stunned men.

"Drop them!" he snarled.

Two of the men had the look of starship crewers, both wearing blue coveralls, shocked expressions on their faces. The third man was wearing nondescript clothes beneath a leather overcoat, his face twisted with fury beneath a prominent scar.

It was Simon Lorre.

March took aim at Lorre's head and squeezed the trigger.

Lorre, however, was already moving. March's plasma bolt missed his head by half an inch, blasting splinters of hot rock from the wall. Lorre darted into the entrance of the service corridor behind the crates. March fired again, but door clanged down behind Lorre, and the plasma bolt carved a molten groove into the metal.

He almost pursued, but the two men on the floor started to raise their weapons, and March swung his gun down to point at them.

"I said to drop them," said March. "Now."

His tone left no room for argument. Both men dropped their weapons and raised their hands over their heads.

"Gentlemen," said Bishop with a wide smile, strolling towards the downed gunmen, his own weapon pointed in their direction. "You did just try to kill us, but there is no reason to hold a grudge. Business is business, right? Let's all be reasonable. You tell my friend and me what we want to know, and there is no reason at all you can't simply walk out of here." He sighed and shook his head. "Of course, if you don't want to be reasonable, my friend and I shall take the sensible course and shoot you both in your head and feed your bodies into the hydroponics recyclers."

As it turned out, both men were reasonable.

The first one was named Marco Clarkson, and the second Damian Thompson. Their names matched the ID cards in the wallets March dug out of their pockets, and their other cards identified them as crewers aboard a freighter called the *Nominson*. Both Clarkson and Thompson said they had been hired by a man who called himself Torres, which was no doubt the alias Simon Lorre had used. He had promised them five thousand credits each in exchange for helping to kill two men in Bay 156. Neither Clarkson nor Thompson seemed all that bright, and they had believed the promises of "Torres" that he would dispose of the bodies and take care of destroying the evidence. March had no doubt Lorre would have killed his hired help alongside the two agents of the Silent Order.

Unfortunately, Lorre's reputation proved justified. He had told nothing useful to either men, and all their meetings had taken place in a bar several kilometers away in one of the station's habitat domes. Bishop checked a few pieces of information on his phone, nodded, and then handed their wallets back.

"Very well, gentlemen," said Bishop, kicking their guns towards March. "I am glad you have chosen to be reasonable. Always good to be polite, eh?" He offered them a sunny smile. "Run along, now. The *Nominson* is leaving later today, and you won't want to miss it. I trust you've learned your lesson?"

"Yes, sir," said Clarkson, rubbing his legs where the crate had landed on them.

"This really isn't your line of work," said Bishop. "You got lucky. And if you have any ideas of trying again..." He looked at March.

March stooped, picked up one of the pistols in his left fist, and squeezed.

Metal squealed, and plastic cracked, and the shattered remnants of the gun clattered against the rock floor.

Clarkson and Thompson gaped at him.

"Best to head out, gentlemen," said Bishop. "You don't want to be late for the *Nominson's* departure. Have a good flight."

The two crewers needed no further prompting. They all

but ran from Bay 156, and March watched as they vanished into the cargo corridor.

"They got lucky?" snorted Bishop. "I got lucky. I'm a damned idiot. I walked right into that ambush. If you hadn't been here, I would be dead. How did you know?"

"I got lucky, too," said March, flexing the fingers of his gloved left hand. His left shoulder always ached after he used his cybernetic arm in a fight. "That was how I would kill someone in here. And if I could figure out the best way to kill someone, then so could Lorre. Any chance we can track him down?"

"Doubtful," said Bishop. "There aren't any cameras in there, and the only sensors are for equipment failure. No, our good friend Mr. Lorre planned this well."

"The reason he did this," said March, "is because he's going after Roanna and Thomas Vindex tomorrow. Whatever he's got planned, he didn't want us in the way."

"Then what does he have planned?" said Bishop.

"I don't know," said March. "But whatever it is, we're going to stop it."

ANNOTATIONS ON SILENT ORDER: IRON HAND CHAPTER 3

In Chapter 3, we see more rising action and unexpected complications for March.

March and Bishop prepare to meet the Vindex twins when they arrive and protect them from any ambushes and assassination attempts. Except only Roanna Vindex arrives, with no sign of her brother Thomas. To make things more complicated, Roanna is traveling in the company of Sam Heath, a naval officer who went AWOL to help her. As March tries to figure out what is happening, the Machinists attempt to use a bomb to kill Roanna and Heath. March manages to disarm the bomb and takes Roanna and Heath to speak with Bishop so they can get to the bottom of things.

The rising action continues in this chapter, along with additional unexpected complications with the absence of Thomas Vindex and the arrival of Heath. Additionally, there is an element of new mystery to act as a plot hook – why is Heath traveling with Roanna? And why is a wealthy noblewoman traveling with an AWOL naval officer to a place as dangerous as Rustbelt Station?

SILENT ORDER IRON HAND: CHAPTER 3:
THE NOBLEWOMAN

March spent the rest of the day preparing.

Bishop called in favors and applied bribe money liberally. March rigged a surveillance system and placed the cameras on the service gantry in Bay 156, setting them to transmit to the *Tiger*. Vigil took control of the feeds and sent the images to March's phone and Bishop's office computer. Bishop also set up a tap for Vigil, connecting the *Tiger*'s computer to the computer monitoring Bay 156. That way, hopefully, they could keep Lorre from venting the atmosphere or inserting toxins into the local environmental system.

Bishop's bribes arranged for extra Ronstadt Security personnel to guard the cargo corridor and the bay. March hoped that Lorre and the Machinists did not have any agents among the Ronstadt men, but Bishop thought they were clean. One of Bishop's bribes also got Vigil a tap into Rustbelt Station's weapon systems. That would let Vigil take control of the station's weapons for one shot. The station's pseudointelligence would lock her out after that, but if necessary, it would let March shoot down any ships attempting to fire on the *Fisher*. For that matter, if Lorre had hacked into the station's systems (and knowing the Machinists' expertise with AIs and cybernetics, that was a possibility), Vigil could shut down any attempt of the station's weapons to shoot down the *Fisher*.

"This is getting expensive," said Bishop after he finished tallying up the bribe money in his office.

March grunted. "No one got rich in the Silent Order."

"Yes, I'm beginning to see why," said Bishop, rubbing his face. "I can't think of anything else. Can you?"

"No," said March. They had taken every precaution he could think of, given the resources they available. "All that's left to do is to wait for the *Fisher* to arrive."

"Yeah," said Bishop. "The ship's scheduled to land at 12:00 hours tomorrow." He squinted at his computer. "04:00 now. You might as well get some sleep. Your ship is monitoring the video feeds, and will send an alert if anyone sets foot in the bay."

"Suppose so," said March, setting the alarm on his phone for 10:00 hours.

"There's a cot in the storeroom," said Bishop.

"Height of luxury," said March.

Bishop grinned. "You're the one who said we don't join the Silent Order to get rich. Besides, this is a restaurant, not a hotel."

The cot was fine. March had slept in far more uncomfortable places, and he fell asleep at once.

He had bad dreams most of the time, but the night before a Silent Order operation, the dreams became especially vivid. Most of the time he dreamed about the week the surgeons of the Final Consciousness had taken him and transformed him into an Iron Hand. There had been no anesthetic. It was a final test. The Iron Hands were the elite force of the Machinists, the best of the best, and surviving the surgeries without dying or going insane was the last trial. March had survived, but he remembered the lasers slicing into his flesh, the metal grafting against his muscles, the waves of blinding pain – and through it all the thundering chorus of the Final Consciousness filling his thoughts through the hive implant in his skull. The Machinists believed that the Final Consciousness, all humanity joined together in a single cybernetic hive mind, would allow mankind to become God and rule the universe, and listening to the voices in his head, March had believed it.

Other times he dreamed about the missions he had undertaken as an Iron Hand, all the death he had inflicted until that final mission on Martel's World had broken the Final Consciousness's hold upon him.

The alarm went off at 10:00 hours, and March awoke rested and in a calm, tranquil rage for what had been done to him. Ever since he had left the Machinists and joined the Kingdom of Calaskar and the Silent Order, he had vowed to make the Final Consciousness pay in whatever way he could, and today he would have another opportunity.

The thought put him in a good mood.

Then he put aside all emotion because emotion was a hindrance in his line of work. He used the bathroom in Bishop's office, washed his face, and walked into the main floor of the restaurant. It was crowded with crewers and cargo handlers having breakfast, and Bishop leaned against the bar, chatting with some of his customers. March looked around for Anne and then realized that she would have the morning shift off, and then rebuked himself for allowing his attention to wander.

"Captain March, good morning," said Bishop, pushing away from the bar. The only sign of the late night was a bloodshot tinge to his eyes. Other than that, he wore a crisp suit, his beard trimmed and his blond hair styled. He did not look out of place as the owner of a overpriced restaurant, but the businesses on Rustbelt Station tended towards showmanship if their garish ads were any indication. "Thank you for delivering my inventory."

"Pleasure," said March. Bishop held out his right hand, and March shook it.

The cool plastic of an earpiece pressed against his palm.

March left the restaurant and stepped into the morning crowds upon the concourse, slipping the bit of plastic into his left ear. He heard a crackling noise, and then a chime from his phone as it synced to the little device.

"March?" came Bishop's voice as March joined the flow of pedestrians heading for the docking bays or their jobs at the station's hydroponic facilities. "Can you hear me?"

"Clear as a bell," said March.

"Captain March," came Vigil's voice next. "I have successfully synced to this communications channel. Quantum encryption is at the maximum level allowed by the available processing power. We should be able to communicate securely."

"Why, March," said Bishop. "You didn't tell me your ship's computer had such a charming voice. No wonder you had no need to seek out female companionship."

March would have rolled his eyes, but he wanted to keep an eye on the crowds around him. "For God's sake, Bishop. You can't flirt with a pseudointelligence."

"I take that as a challenge."

"That's been the downfall of a hundred spacefaring human civilizations since the discovery of hyperspace," said March. "Some lonely fellow programs an artificial intelligence to flirt with him, and it goes berserk and wipes out all the organic life it can find."

"Fortunately, I am a restaurant owner, not a software developer," said Bishop.

"Well, thank God for that."

The crowds remained heavy as March approached the cargo corridor outside of Bay 156. Several freighters had come in, and cargo handlers unloaded and loaded crates and barrels and pallets of goods, assisted by drones. March wove his way through the crowds and came to Bay 156's airlock. Four men in the jumpsuits of Ronstadt Private Security Corporation stood there, sidearms holstered at their belts, their faces locked in a scowl as they glared at everyone in sight.

"What's your business here, friend?" said one of the security men.

March reached into his jacket, a flicker of amusement going through him as the Ronstadt men reached for their weapons. He produced one of the documents that he and Bishop had forged last night and handed it over. "Courier. Got a bonded and sealed thumb drive for one of the passengers on the *Fisher*."

The security man looked at the paper identifying March as an official courier of the Royal Message Corporation, grunted, and handed it back. "Fine. You can wait in the bay. You got a breath mask?" March nodded and tapped the mask and goggles that hung from his belt. "You might need that. The atmosphere field sometimes cuts out during landings."

March shrugged. "I've got my instructions. I'll wait."

"Suit yourself," said the security man, jerking his head towards the airlock. "It's your funeral."

March walked through the airlock and into the

cavernous bay without another word. Save for a few additional scorch marks on the stone from plasma bolts, there
was no sign of yesterday's fight with Lorre's thugs. March
and Bishop had restacked the crates before leaving the bay,
and March checked them over. There was no one hiding
within them or behind them, and the door to the service
corridor was locked, the metal still scarred from a plasma
bolt.

He did a complete circuit of the bay, checking everything, and climbed onto the service gantry, examining the
integrity of the fuel lines and the other equipment. Everything seemed to be in working order, and he found no
bombs or waiting traps. He then checked the atmosphere
field generator and found it in better condition than he
expected. Whatever Lorre had planned, it didn't involve
sabotaging Bay 156, or it was so subtle that March had
missed it entirely.

No. March couldn't second-guess himself. Too much of
that and he would leave himself unable to act when the
moment of crisis came. His brutal trainers among the
Machinists had emphasized that no plan of battle survived
contact with the enemy, and the ability to think flexibly and
adapt was the hallmark of the successful warrior. His
trainers had done their job well. Perhaps too well – March
had been able to think so flexibly that he had left the Final
Consciousness behind and defected to the Kingdom of
Calaskar.

So he would simply have to keep his eyes open and react
to stop whatever Lorre intended. March disliked the
thought. In his experience, whoever took the lead and
forced his enemy to react tended to win the fight.

Still, he had his own advantages. Vigil was monitoring
from the *Tiger*, and all March needed to do was to get the

Vindex twins, get them to his ship, and head for hyperspace. Bishop's bribes had ensured that Ronstadt security personnel patrolled the cargo corridors from Bay 156 to the *Tiger*'s bay. March supposed it was possible that Lorre had bribed some of the security men, but March could take a number of them in a fight.

For now, though, he could do nothing but wait, so wait he did.

March positioned himself in the corner, not far from the sealed door to the access corridor, and waited. He had spent a large amount of his life waiting, both in his years as an Iron Hand and since he had joined the Silent Order, and he was good at it. His mind sorted through his plans in an orderly fashion, while he stressed and relaxed the muscles of his leg and his arm of flesh in a systematic way, not enough to induce muscle fatigue but enough to keep the muscles from getting stiff.

About an hour later, an alarm began blaring, the red warning light flashing over the airlock door. March looked up towards the roof of the landing pit and saw the blaze of ten thousand stars overhead.

Then something blocked out the stars, something big and metallic with running lights along the side.

"Here we go, Jack," came Bishop's voice in his ear. "The *Fisher* is beginning its final approach to the station. ETA for docking in three minutes."

"Any sign of attackers?" said March, reaching for his belt and drawing his breath mask and goggles over his face.

"Negative, Captain," said Vigil.

"There are only five other ships outside the station," said Bishop. "Three ore freighters, a privateer departing with what is probably a falsified flight plan, and an ice miner heading to harvest some water from the rings of one of the gas giants in the outer system."

"What about that privateer?" said March, watching the bulk of the *Fisher* maneuver overhead. Sometimes passenger liners looked sleek and streamlined. The *Fisher*, alas, looked like a stack of cargo containers welded together in a vaguely rectangular shape. No wonder the owners had to supplement their incomes by smuggling. "If I was going to blow up the *Fisher*, I would use a privateer."

"I would, too, and it's a heavily armed craft," said Bishop, "but your computer says the privateer's vector is all wrong."

"It is, Captain March," said Vigil. "The other craft are not well-armed enough to attack the *Fisher* before it reaches Rustbelt Station."

"What about the station's weapon systems?" said March.

"Everything looks green," said Bishop. "All of the systems are on standby, and none of the warheads or beam emitters are even armed yet."

"All right," said March. "So we can assume that Lorre isn't going to shoot down the *Fisher* before it docks. He's going to let it land. Whatever he's got planned, it's going to happen between here and the *Tiger*."

"There are no signs of anomalous or suspicious activity in the *Tiger*'s landing bay," said Vigil.

"Hell," said March. He wanted to scratch his jaw, but the mask made that impossible. "Suppose it would be too much to hope for something obvious. But knowing Lorre, anything obvious would be a distraction. Constantine, keep an eye on the security cameras from here to Bay 93."

"There aren't many," said Bishop, "and some of them are off-line."

"Better than nothing," said March, and then a gale of wind drowned out his words.

The *Fisher* was coming in for a landing, disrupting the atmosphere barrier as it descended. March stepped to the side, gripped the doorframe of the service corridor door with his metal arm, and anchored himself there, the wind tugging at his jacket as the decrepit liner maneuvered into the bay. The *Fisher* extended its landing struts and landed with a thump that made the stone floor vibrate.

March waited as the *Fisher*'s pilot finished the landing procedures, no doubt preparing a bribe for Heitz in the process. Two ramps opened on the bottom of the craft, a ventral one for passengers, and a wider one at the stern for cargo. The airlock door to the cargo corridor hissed open, and both cargo handlers and drones came into the bay, heading for the ramp at the stern of the ship.

Passengers began to disembark from the dorsal ramp, and March waited, drifting closer to ramp as he did. In the increasing chaos of the crowd, no one paid any attention to him, but the flood of cargo handlers and drones provided ample cover for any assassins. He grimaced, pulled off his breath mask and goggles, and waited, scanning the passengers. Most of the passengers were young and middle-aged men, either young men coming to the outer reaches to find their fortunes or middle-aged men to rebuild their lives after some disaster. Very few women and children, which ought to make it all the easier to spot Roanna Vindex and her brother. March took another look around the crowd, trying to find any assassins or attackers in their midst, but nothing caught his eye.

He turned his head again and saw Lady Roanna Vindex descend from the ramp.

March had thought her picture beautiful, but the picture had not done her justice. Her hair was thick and black, her eyes bright and blue, her features strong and sharp. She wore a loose travel jumpsuit of dark blue, the sort that could be sealed against a vacuum in the event of a hull breach, but even the baggy garment could not completely hide the curves of the body beneath it. To his great annoyance, March found her attractive, almost compellingly so. He disliked the feeling since it could interfere with his mission.

Because he was so focused upon Roanna, it took March's brain a second to notice the obvious.

There was no sign of Thomas Vindex.

Censor had said that the twins were traveling together after Roanna had gone to get her brother away from the Machinist cell. A man walked alongside Roanna, speaking to her in a low voice, but March didn't recognize him, and there had been no mention of him in Censor's report. The man was older than Roanna but younger than March, fit and strong with close-cropped brown hair and brown eyes in a shaven face. Everything about him – his stance, his posture, the way he gestured as he spoke with Roanna - screamed that he was an officer of the Royal Calaskaran Navy. Probably a junior officer.

So what was Lady Roanna doing traveling with a junior officer instead of her brother?

"Constantine," said March. "You see Lady Roanna?"

"That I do," said Bishop. "Fine looking woman, isn't she?"

"You see Lord Thomas?" said March.

"No, I don't," said Bishop. "I don't recognize the man with her, either."

"Vigil?" said March.

"I ran facial recognition algorithms based on available data," said Vigil. "Based on camera footage, I calculate a ninety-eight percent chance Lord Thomas Vindex is not visible on our camera feeds."

"Complications," said Bishop, voice grim.

"Hell," said March. "All right. I'm going to make contact. Keep an eye out."

He walked through the crowd, heading straight for Roanna and her companion. Roanna did not notice him approaching. The young man did, and he straightened up, putting himself between March and Roanna. The noble-woman blinked in surprise, and her blue eyes fell on March with an intensity that he did not like.

"Whatever you're selling, we're not interested," said the man. He even sounded like a crewer of the Royal Calaskaran Navy, with the same crisp, precise voice the drill sergeants beat into their charges.

"Not selling anything," said March. "I need to talk to you about something urgent."

"No," said the man.

"Sam," said Roanna, touching his arm. Sam subsided at once. "Who are you, sir, and what do you want?"

March glanced around the crowds. "Not here. I bet you don't want anyone to hear what I have to say."

"This is a risk, my lady," said Sam.

"Obviously," said Roanna with a hint of asperity. "When I have done anything else for the last two months? But there is no harm in talking. We might learn something useful."

"Very well," said Sam. Like March, he wore a dark jacket over his jumpsuit, and he opened it just enough to let March see the shoulder holster under his arm. "But we don't want any trouble."

March could have killed them both before Sam's hand had gotten anywhere near the gun.

"I'm not fond of trouble myself," said March. "Over here, please."

He jerked his head towards the base of the service

gantry, and Roanna and Sam followed him. March noticed how confidently Roanna walked, just as he noticed the pleasing sway of her hips beneath the jumpsuit. He also observed how Sam hovered over her like a protective shadow, his scowl never wavering as he watched March. Clearly, he had concluded that March was dangerous – which was a point in his favor, come to think of it.

"I'll level with you," said March once they were out of earshot of the other passengers. "My name's Jack March. I'm a privateer with a light freighter, and Lord Sebastian Vindex hired me to pick up his two youngest kids and get them off this rock and to Antioch Station."

"Lord Sebastian hired you to kidnap Lady Roanna, then?" said Sam, his hand twitching towards the gun beneath his jacket.

"No," said March. "He hired me to take Lord Thomas and Lady Roanna to Antioch Station aboard my ship. He didn't tell me the whole story. Said there was trouble and he wanted it kept quiet, and he pays well enough, so I didn't argue. Anyway, my ship is a short distance from here. Once Lord Thomas disembarks, we can all head there and leave at once." He decided to play a hunch. "Your boyfriend can come, too."

Roanna only blinked, but Sam flinched as if March had slapped him, his face reddening a little.

"Lieutenant Samuel Heath is my bodyguard, Captain March," said Roanna with perfect calm. "I fear you have misinterpreted the nature of our relationship."

To judge from Heath's expression, March didn't think he was the only one.

"I don't spend much time around nobles," said March. "But I know you're in danger, and I know that the sooner you leave Rustbelt Station, the better. As soon as Lord

Thomas joins us, I can take all of you to Antioch Station immediately."

Roanna drew herself up, her cool expression turning imperious. "Captain March, you overstep yourself. I am at Rustbelt Station entirely by my own decision, and I will remain here for at least three days, probably more. Once I have completed my business, you can then take me to Antioch Station at my leisure, but do not presume to give me orders."

March stared at her. The cool mask remained in place, but he saw the tightness around her eyes, the pulsing vein in her throat.

"You're in trouble," he said.

"Sir, you presume..." she started.

"You're in trouble," he said, his suspicion hardening into certainty. "And you don't know where your brother is."

Roanna said nothing. For a moment the mask cracked, and beneath the hauteur of a Calaskaran noble, he saw a terrified young woman.

Or she was an excellent actress.

"Not...presently," said Roanna.

"My lady," said Heath.

"I know where he is going to be in three days," said Roanna. "Which is the essence of the problem."

"We cannot trust this man, my lady," said Heath, glaring at March. "He could be working for...our enemies."

"The Machinists, you mean?" said March, and a little twitch went through Roanna, while Heath's scowl hardened. "I know your brother got himself involved with some bad people. I know you went to get him out once he came to his senses. And I know the Machinists want you dead for it."

"You're very well informed, Captain March," said Heath.

"Yup," said March. "So you're in trouble."

"Why would you bother yourself with my troubles?" said Roanna.

"Because I don't get paid unless you and your brother get to Antioch Station," said March.

Roanna laughed a little. "Clarity of purpose is a fine thing."

"What can you do to help us?" said Heath. His eyes were still narrow, but he hadn't pulled Roanna away.

"For one, I have a ship," said March. "For another, if your brother is in trouble, I have a lot of experience with trouble. Might be able to get him out of it."

"I don't trust you, Captain March," said Heath.

"Of course you shouldn't," said March. "Trust isn't necessary. Let's go to a neutral location and talk." He would have preferred to have gotten Roanna onto his ship, but he could see there was no way he could talk Roanna and her bodyguard into that. "Then we'll see if I can help with your trouble."

"Very well," said Roanna. "We…"

"My lady," said Heath. "This is a mistake."

"Maybe," said Roanna, "but we have to take some risks, Sam. Captain March is not incorrect. We have indeed found trouble, and we will need help dealing with it. You have a location in mind, Captain March?"

"Friend of mine owns a restaurant," said March. "He won't mind some visitors."

"A friend?" said Heath. "Yes, and I'm sure this friend of yours isn't a slaver or a pirate or some other lowlife."

Bishop laughed in March's earpiece. "Charming young man."

"If he was a lowlife, he wouldn't own a restaurant," said March.

Heath's scowl did not waver. "If…"

"Enough," said Roanna, her voice quiet. "Very well, Captain March. We shall put ourselves in your hands. Please lead the way."

"Right," said March. "Follow me. Keep your eyes open."

"You're expecting trouble?" said Heath.

"Always," said March. "This way, please."

He walked across the bay, joining the last of the crowds leaving the *Fisher*. Fortunately, most of the passengers had disembarked, and the flood of people had drained away, leaving only a few stragglers. March stepped into the cargo corridor and looked around. A steady stream of cargo drones rolled away from the *Fisher*, carrying the ship's cargo to its destinations on the station. The Ronstadt men stood the entrance to the bay, scowling at everything in sight. Nothing seemed amiss, so March turned, intending to lead Roanna and Heath to the Emperor's Rest.

He took one step and then stopped.

"What is it?" said Heath.

"Something's wrong," said March.

"What?" said Heath. "I don't see anything."

March said nothing for a moment, watching the line of loaded cargo drones rolling away down the corridor. A steady stream of them left the *Fisher*, but there was one cargo drone heading towards the bay. His first thought was that it was another one sent to help with the unloading of the *Fisher*, but the drone was carrying a half-dozen metal barrels in its bed. Undoubtedly the *Fisher* would take on more cargo before departing Rustbelt Station, and for a second March's alarm eased.

Yet why would a loaded drone come while the *Fisher* was still unloading? It would just get in the way and slow the entire process. Spaceport cargo controllers always unloaded first and then loaded freighters. Trying to do both at once invariably caused problems.

March took three quick steps to the right.

The cargo drone shifted direction. It was subtle, and March wouldn't have seen it unless he had been paying attention, but the drone changed direction to follow him. As March moved, he also saw the labels on the barrels in the drone's bed. All kinds of red warning labels covered the barrels, warning about the toxic engine coolant within. The stuff did an excellent job of cooling down fusion engines, but it also was supremely toxic, and a deep breath of the gas would turn a pair of human lungs to sludge.

A bomb in the cart would shatter the barrels and kill everyone in the cargo corridor. There were still dozens of people in the corridor, and perhaps the gas would spread far enough to kill hundreds.

The Machinists did not care about collateral damage.

All this flashed through his head in a second.

"What's wrong?" said Heath again.

"There's a bomb on that cargo drone," said March, his voice calm. Heath said something, but March ignored him. "Bishop, Vigil. Cargo drone CR-8897. There's a bomb on the thing. Can you disable it remotely?"

"Negative, Captain March," said Vigil.

"It's not showing up on the system," said Bishop. Likely Lorre had disabled its antenna and programmed it for autonomous action.

"We should inform the guards," said Roanna. "We..."

"No!" said Heath. "My lady, those barrels hold engine coolant. If even one of them is breached, the gas might kill everyone in this corridor."

Roanna flinched, the color draining from her face as the cart continued rolling towards them.

March looked to the side. "Bishop, we're outside Bay 173. What's the nearest unoccupied bay?"

"207," said Bishop.

"Is there access to the service corridors there?" said March.

The drone began to roll faster, the whine of its electric motor reaching March's ears.

"Hang on...yes," said Bishop.

"Good," said March. "Run, both of you. Bay 207. Run!"

Both Roanna and Heath started running, and March followed them. He shot a glance over his shoulder and saw the cargo drone break free of the line, shooting towards them. The Ronstadt security men shot it a bemused look, but the useless idiots took no action to stop it. Well, at least they weren't on Lorre's side. The men could have drawn their weapons and shot them all down while pursued by the cargo drone.

Roanna reached the airlock door to Bay 207 first, followed a half-second later by Heath. March joined them, the whine of the cargo drone's engine getting louder, its tires squealing against the rock floor as it accelerated. The bay door was unlocked, and March triggered it, the wide doors sliding open with a hiss and a clang. The bay beyond was about the size of the one that held the *Tiger*, a large oval pit carved into the rock of the asteroid, a service gantry mounted to the wall.

There was also a door leading to the service corridors.

"This way," said March. "Hurry!"

He ran across the bay and reached the service door first, sliding it open. Beyond stretched a narrow corridor with a metal grill floor, pipes and bundles of wires lining the walls in racks. The air within stank of machine oil and insulation foam and emergency lights hung in small metal cages from the ceiling. Heath urged Roanna into the corridor, and March followed them, drawing his pistol from its holster and thumbing its selector to maximum power.

"Bishop!" said March. "When I give the word, close the airlock door to Bay 207 and lock it down."

"All right," said Bishop, and March heard a keyboard clattering in the background. "We...yes, here we go. Say the word, and I can close the airlock."

"Good," said March, sliding the access door almost closed, leaving only an inch-wide crack open. With his right hand he gripped his pistol, and with his left hand, he grasped the door handle. He would have exactly one chance to get this right.

"What are you doing?" said Heath.

March didn't say anything, his whole attention on the airlock.

"What are..."

"Quiet!" said March. He heard Heath start to move forward, then Roanna said something that March didn't catch, and Heath subsided.

The cargo drone rolled into the bay, the barrels of coolant clanking in the bed.

"Bishop!" said March. "Now!"

He aimed and squeezed the trigger, sending the plasma bolt streaking towards the nearest barrel, and as he did he slammed the door the rest of the way shut.

A lot of things happened at once.

There was a roaring noise, and a jolt went through the floor. The door bulged out from sudden pressure, and the impact sent March stumbling back. He caught his balance, but not before he stumbled into Roanna, and he felt the warmth of her hands against his right arm she helped him to stand up. A klaxon wailed in the distance, and he heard frantic voices, both from his earpiece and from Roanna and Heath.

March ignored it all, his eyes focused on the damaged door. If it decided to fail and flood the corridor with the released gas, they were all about to die.

But the door held. Despite the slipshod maintenance standards aboard Rustbelt Station, this door at least was airtight. At least for now. Given how badly the door had been stressed, it might fail at any moment.

"What happened?" said Roanna and Heath.

"What happened?" said Bishop.

"I shot one of the barrels, and that set the bomb off," said March. "Bishop, did you get the airlock sealed?"

"Yeah," said Bishop. He let out a low whistle. "Like two seconds before the cargo drone exploded."

"It was actually 0.67 seconds, Mr. Bishop," announced Vigil.

"Are you insane?" said Heath. "That was reckless! You could have killed Lady Roanna!"

"A lot of people would have died when that bomb went off," said March. "There wasn't time to play it safe. Bishop, what's our status?"

"The cargo corridor is locked down," said Bishop. "Maintenance teams and security are rushing to the landing bays. Looks like you've kicked over the beehive, Jack. Are you in the service corridors?"

"Yeah," said March. "We can't get back to the Emperor's Rest or the *Tiger*. And if Lorre knows about us, we've already been compromised. I need another location to take Lady Vindex while we figure out what to do next."

"There's a bar in Dome 7," said Bishop. "I don't own it, but the owner's a friend, and he owes me some favors. I'm sending directions to your phone. Head there and I will meet you there as soon as I can. Hopefully, we can make some sense of this mess."

"Thanks," said March. "I'll meet you there. Good work."

Bishop snorted. "Me? You're the one who just saved a noblewoman and a few hundred other people. Keep your eyes open, Jack. I'll call if anything comes up."

He ended the connection, and March turned back to Roanna and Heath. The naval officer glared at him, while the noblewoman only looked pensive.

"Captain March," said Roanna. "I would appreciate an explanation."

"There's a Machinist agent named Simon Lorre on your trail," said March. "He sent that bomb to kill you, and he's been trying to kill me, which means he knows about you. The bomb's given us a moment of chaos, and we had better exploit it. Follow me. A friend of mine is going to meet us there, and we can figure out what to do."

Roanna gazed at him for a moment and then nodded.

"Lady..." started Heath, but she spoke over him.

"So be it, Captain March," said Roanna. "You've dealt honestly with us so far. It seems we must place our lives in your hands." She smiled a little. "Please endeavor not to drop them."

"I have very steady hands," said March, which was truer than she knew. He fished out his phone and glanced at the map Bishop had sent him. "This way, please."

ANNOTATIONS ON SILENT ORDER:
IRON HAND CHAPTER 4

In the confusion after the failed bombing, March slips away with Roanna and Heath, taking them to a bar where they can confer with Bishop. Roanna lays out the problem for March – her brother Thomas has been taken captive by Machinist sympathizers, and they are demanding a ransom for his return. March realizes that Heath is infatuated with Roanna and has come along to help her and hopes of winning her affections. Neither Roanna nor Heath fully trust March, but they have no choice but to work with him.

This chapter acts as more rising action and complications, showing how March's mission has changed and how he must adapt to the new circumstances.

SILENT ORDER IRON HAND CHAPTER 4:
OUT OF PLACE

For the moment, confusion ruled in Rustbelt Station, but despite that, the area around Dome 7 seemed quiet.

March led the way through the service corridors, his gun in his right hand and his phone in his left. Roanna followed him, and then Sam Heath. March had been concerned that Heath might get excited and accidentally shoot him in the back, but Heath handled his gun properly and even went around corners with smooth skill, his pistol sweeping to track for any potential enemies. His steady competence seemed an odd contrast to his infatuation with Lady Roanna, and March wondered how Heath had gotten involved with the Vindex twins and their troubles.

Another complication. March wasn't surprised. When things went wrong, they tended to go wrong in unexpected ways.

"Here," said March, stopping before an access hatch. He slipped his phone back into his jacket and gripped the handle, the hatch swinging open on creaking metal hinges. Beyond was a corridor hewn from the rock of the asteroid, lit by dim red lights, and March heard a distant bass thumping.

"What is that noise?" said Roanna.

"Music," said Heath. His scowl deepened. "Of a sort."

"Watch your step," said March, testing his balance on the corridor floor. "The gravitics here feel like they need maintenance." The noblewoman and the naval officer followed him into the corridor, and March led the way into Dome 7.

It looked as if it had once been a hydroponics bay. The metal dome arched overhead, its central third made of a clear alloy that offered a view of the stars. Where hydroponics pods had once grown food now stood a variety of seedy-looking businesses – pawn shops, questionable druggists, shops offering "escorts," and various gambling establishments. The largest business was a bar lit with flickering green lights, and the pulsing music came from within its doors. Two guards stood before the doors to the bar, stun batons in their hands.

"That does not seem like a reputable establishment," said Roanna.

"It does not," said March, and he led the way forward. The two guards looked them over, their eyes settling on Roanna with gleeful interest. That made Heath bristle, and March hoped the damned hothead would not start a firefight.

"Here to audition as a dancer, miss?" said one of the guards, grinning. Tattoos covered his thick, muscled arms. "You can get started here. Take off your clothes and give us a twirl or two, and if we like what we see, you can dance for the boss."

Heath started to snarl an answer, but Roanna spoke first.

"I'm afraid your establishment couldn't afford me, sir," she said with a chilly smile.

"Bishop sent us," said March, meeting the guard's eyes with an unblinking stare.

The guard grunted, glanced at March's gloved left hand, and then tapped an earpiece. He listened for a moment, then nodded.

"Go on in," said the guard, stepping to the side. "Booth in the corner, the opposite wall of the stage. Don't make trouble."

"I've never made trouble in my life," said March.

The guard snorted but waved them through.

March walked into the bar.

He had been in a lot of places like this during his duties, but to judge from the way that Roanna's eyes went wide, Calaskaran noblewomen did not often come to establishments of this nature.

The bass rumble of the music filled the air, and the patrons sat at the tables and drank, eerie in the green light. Waitresses in translucent halter tops and short skirts tottered past on stiletto heels, carrying trays of drinks. On the stage, three women wearing string, glitter, high heels, and nothing else twisted and danced in time to the beat of the music. A large crowd of men had gathered at the base of the stage, many of them holding credit notes.

March's eyes swept the room, looking for threats. Despite the alarm klaxon, most of the crowd was indifferent, either focused on their drinks or on the dancers. No one was paying any attention to them. He glanced at his companions. Roanna's face had settled into a cool, aloof mask. No doubt that had been drilled into her since childhood. Heath's face had turned red, and he looked like he didn't know where to put his eyes.

"Here," said March, gesturing to the booth in the corner. Roanna sat down, a bit gingerly, while Heath followed her. March sat across from them, making sure he had a view of the crowd and the door.

"This is not a suitable establishment for a Calaskaran noblewoman," said Heath, indignant.

"Probably not," said March. "It's also the last place anyone would look for her. Which is why we are here. My friend should arrive soon, and we can make a proper plan."

Heath scowled but didn't argue further.

"I suppose it is nothing I have not seen before," said Roanna, trying to keep her voice light.

Heath gave her an astonished look.

"There were communal showers after gym class at the Queen's Academy on Calaskar," said Roanna.

"Ah," said March. He jerked his head at the stage. "Can't imagine that went on in the showers, though."

Roanna gave him a shocked look and then laughed. Even Heath smiled a little. "No, sir, it did not. Captain March." She took a deep breath. March tried not to notice how her jumpsuit pressed against her chest as she did. Heath might have become besotted with her, but he had come by it honestly. "Thank you for saving our lives."

March inclined his head.

"Unless it was a ruse to gain our trust," said Heath.

Roanna frowned at him, but March spoke first. "If it was, that was a crap way to do it. Death by engine coolant gas is a bad way to go. No, if I wanted to gain your trust, I would have hired a couple of these idlers," he jerked his head towards the crowd at the stage, "to attack you in the corridor. Then I would have swooped to the rescue." He shook his head. "No, that was a bad business. If it had gone wrong, a lot of people would have died."

"That coolant gas," said Roanna. "Would it really have killed everyone in the corridor?"

"Yes, my lady," said Heath. "The stuff is toxic. It's not even supposed to be transported through pressurized corridors. It's safer to have a tug carry it through the vacuum. That must have been what tipped Captain March off."

"It was," said March, ignoring the suspicion in the younger man's voice.

"All this just to kill me?" said Roanna. "Why?"

"Think you know more about that than I do," said March, and Roanna swallowed. "Here comes my friend. Might be time to put all our cards on the table."

Heath started to protest, and then Bishop approached the booth. He had changed to a dark business suit, though it was shabby enough to match the other patrons of the bar. It made him fit in, which was no small feat for a man of his height.

"I do apologize for my lateness," said Bishop, dropping into the booth next to March. The seat creaked a bit beneath their combined weight. "Your little adventures have caused quite the tangle in the station's transit systems."

"This is your friend?" said Heath, eyeing Bishop.

"Oh, of course," said Bishop, sticking out a callused hand. "Constantine Bishop." Heath gave the hand a cautious shake. "And you..."

"This is Lieutenant Samuel Heath the Royal Calaskaran Navy," said March, "and Lady Roanna Vindex, daughter of Lord Sebastian Vindex, the Earl of Sundrex on Calaskar."

"A pleasure, Lieutenant, my lady," said Bishop. "Do forgive the lack of a proper bow. I don't wish to draw attention to us."

Roanna raised one eyebrow. "As if I have not already drawn attention by being the only clothed woman in here."

Bishop laughed. "The waitresses are clothed, at least according to the minimal legal standard of the word. But we ought to be unobserved for the moment." He waved a hand at the room. "You will see that none of the patrons or the employees have abandoned this establishment, despite the alarms. No one here wishes to be noticed."

"What happened after the bomb went off?" said March. "Was anyone killed?"

"No," said Bishop. "Luring it into the empty bay, that was clever. The gas was vented into space and didn't spread to anywhere else within the station. Ronstadt still has the cargo corridor sealed off, and the rest of the station is on temporary alert. Heitz is fit to be tied, but the official story is that there was an accident with coolant gas. This is an inconvenience, but it will hinder our friend Mr. Lorre as well."

"Who is this Lorre person?" said Heath. "You mentioned him before."

"He's a Machinist agent," said March. "Think he was sent here to kill Lady Roanna. He tried to kill me on Antioch Station when I was hired to fly her and Lord Thomas off this rock, and he tried to kill me again when I arrived here. He likes to work through hired thugs and sabotage. A bunch of gas barrels on a hacked cargo drone is exactly his style."

"Why would he try to kill you at Antioch Station?" said Heath. "You're just a privateer. Does he have a grudge against you or something?"

"He probably does now," said March.

"Why are you helping us?" said Roanna. "You said my father hired you to get me off the station...but why?"

"What happened to your brother?" said March.

"Before I answer that question," said Roanna, "you need to answer a question of mine, Captain March. You and Mr. Bishop both."

"What question is that?" said March.

"Why have you invested so much effort into helping me?" said Roanna.

"Because I was hired to do it," said March.

"No," said Roanna. "There is more to it than that. You're a privateer, and Mr. Bishop is a..."

"I like to think of myself as an entrepreneur," said Bishop with a wide smile. "I own a restaurant and bar near the station's spaceport complex, and have several other interests, both on Rustbelt Station and out-system."

"My point," said Roanna, "is that both privateers and entrepreneurs are motivated by money. My father might have hired you to get me to Antioch Station, but he certainly did not hire you to deal with my other problems or to handle assassination attempts. No. Something more is motivating you, I think." She folded her hands on the metal table. "Is it money? Favors?"

"Neither," said March.

"My lady," said Heath. "I think...they might be Silent Order."

Roanna flinched as if he had jabbed her in the side. "Is this true?"

March and Bishop shared a look, and finally, Bishop inclined his head.

"If we take you into our confidence," said Bishop, "then we will be burdening you with secrets that you will have to take to your graves."

"Then you are Silent Order," said Heath.

Roanna closed her eyes for a moment. "I had hoped the

account of my brother's...foolishness would not become general knowledge."

"We're not in the business of sharing knowledge," said March.

Heath snorted. "No, just collecting it."

March considered them for a moment. Roanna only seemed resigned, while Heath remained distrustful. Perhaps it was time to extend a little trust.

"Mr. Bishop looks after the Silent Order's interests on Rustbelt Station," said March. "My job is more of a troubleshooter. On Antioch Station, I received instructions to head out here, pick up Roanna Vindex and Thomas Vindex, and fly you both back to Antioch Station."

Roanna sighed. "What did your instructions say about us?"

"That Thomas had fallen in with a Machinist cell," said March. "You found him, convinced him to repent of his folly, and then escaped aboard the *Fisher*, heading for Rustbelt Station. My superiors thought your funds had run out, so I was sent to bring you back to a Calaskaran outpost."

"Then you aren't to take...direction action against Thomas?" said Roanna. "You aren't going to execute him?"

"My orders are to take him back with me to Antioch Station," said March. "If he has gotten into trouble, he'll have to deal with it then. Otherwise, no, I won't do anything to him. Unless he has actually betrayed the Kingdom to the Machinists, or if he has become a Machinist agent. Then I will shoot him on the spot..."

"No!" said Roanna, color flaring in her cheeks. "No, he has not!"

"Sure of that?" said March.

"I am entirely certain of that, Captain March," said

Roanna, biting off every word. "I have known my brother my entire life. There is not a malicious bone in his body. He would never hurt anyone. He was just...excessively enthusiastic. And bored. He got caught up in something he did not understand."

"All right," said March. "Where is he, then?"

Roanna hesitated. "It...seems that we come to the point where I must trust you, sir."

March waited, letting her sort through her thoughts. Heath scowled at March and at Bishop. For his part, Bishop set the pleasant, bland expression of a charming businessman upon his bearded face.

"I don't recommend that," said Heath. "The things I've heard about the Silent Order..."

"What have you heard about us, Lieutenant?" said Bishop with genial calm.

Heath grimaced and met his eyes. "That you execute anyone even suspected of associating with the Machinists without trial. That you kill corrupt officials without warning..."

"Well, corrupt officials do need killing from time to time," said Bishop.

"And I suspect that you are here to kill Lady Roanna and her brother," said Heath.

"You're not wrong," said March.

All three of the others gaped at him.

March looked at Roanna. "If you've joined the Machinists, my lady, I will shoot you in the head and drop you out the nearest airlock. And I'll do it without losing a wink of sleep." He looked at the wary Heath. "Same goes for you, lieutenant. No threats, just promises. That's just what I'll do. And if you knew the Machinists the way I do, you would understand. But if you haven't gone over to the Machinists, then I'll do my best to take you and Lord Thomas back to Antioch Station."

No one spoke for a while.

"As ever, Jack," said Bishop with a snort, "your eloquence never ceases to amaze."

"No," said Roanna. "I believe you." She took a deep breath. "Very well. It seems I must once again place myself in your hands, Captain March."

Heath looked ready to protest. March supposed Heath would rather put his hands on Roanna Vindex, but he pushed the thought of his mind. He would deal with that complication later, and only if it threatened the mission.

"So," said March. "Lady Roanna. Tell me what happened."

"Well," she said, "my brother and I are twins, as you undoubtedly know, and we have always been close. Thomas has always been...restless. Yes, that is the word. Restless. Myself, I have been content with the role of a noblewoman of the Kingdom of Calaskar, even happy with it. Thomas has never been content. By now he should be a junior officer in the Royal Calaskaran Navy or have a post in one of the colonial administrations, but he...rather sabotaged his chances. Father used to let him explore his passions, do whatever he wanted, but Thomas was drummed out of the Naval Academy over some misunderstanding, and the Ministry of Colonies took a dislike to him."

March nodded, saying nothing. He could fill in the details well enough. Undoubtedly Thomas Vindex had been the spoiled youngest son of an old man. No doubt Thomas had found the discipline of life in the Navy or the Colonial Service unpalatable and had offended his potential superiors and any social connections from his father's friends.

And if Roanna had found the life of a Calaskaran noble-woman congenial, what was she doing here? March didn't care, but her motives might jeopardize his mission.

"Because he was discontented, he found friends who were also discontented," said March.

"You guess correctly," said Roanna. "Not everyone among the nobility is happy how Calaskar is dominated by the Royal Church, the Royal Navy, and the King. Others are less content how the Congress of Commons, the Congress of Lords, and the Congress of Admirals determine legislation and policy."

"They ought to be content," said Heath with some heat. "Calaskar is the oldest and most stable of mankind's star-faring nations. Others have collapsed into chaos and anarchy, or have been enslaved by AIs and alien races, or devoured by the Final Consciousness. Other worlds and nations have collapsed, but not Calaskar."

"No," said March. He had traveled farther than Heath, and he knew that Calaskaran society tended towards puritanical social stratification. Yet the system mostly worked. Calaskar had stood defiant against the Final Consciousness for two centuries, and the Kingdom had not been conquered by an alien race, nor had it fallen into the social chaos that often engulfed human worlds.

"Your patriotism is commendable," said Bishop, "but we wander afield from the point. Lady Roanna, if you could continue your narrative?"

"Thomas fell in with some dissidents," said Roanna. "They were all afire with enthusiasm and plans for reform. He was invited to a meeting on Tamlin's World. Do you know it?"

"I do," said March. It was an unclaimed planet with a harsh desert climate. Various races and powers had attempted to found colonies there, and all had failed. Consequently, those with shady business often conducted it in the ruins upon Tamlin's World.

"Thomas was invited to a meeting there," said Roanna. "In retrospect, it seems naïve, of course. He left, convinced he had found his purpose in life. I tried to talk him out of it, but his mind was made up. For six weeks, we heard nothing from him. Then I received a message from him. He realized that the dissidents were a front group for the Machinists, and he wanted out. But he had no money left, and he needed someone to come get him quietly, without risk of scandal..."

"Hence, you," said March.

Roanna kept talking as if he had not spoken. "You see why we had to keep this quiet, yes? If there is even the slightest word that Thomas was involved with the Machinists, he'll be ruined. Recovering from youthful follies is one thing. But if word gets out that he was involved with Machinist sympathizers, even unintentionally, he'll be ruined."

"Then you came out here to give him a ride home," said March.

"Yes," said Roanna. "We hired a ship to Tamlin's World."

"Must have been expensive," said March. "It's something like a hundred and fifty jumps from Calaskar to Tamlin's World."

"One hundred and fifty-six," said Heath with a grimace.

"We arrived at Tamlin's World...but found that Thomas had been taken captive," said Roanna, sighing. "It had all been a trick. The entire thing had been a false front to capture a Calaskaran nobleman, and Thomas had fallen for it."

"How did you know it was a ransom?" said Bishop.

"A letter was left for me with detailed instructions," said Roanna. "Thomas had left his coordinates on Tamlin's World in his message to me, in one of the ruined human colonies there. The ransom letter was waiting for me. The instructions said I was to proceed to Rustbelt Station and meet Thomas's captors. We would then make the exchange. I could cover the cost of the ransom myself, but it would take everything I had, and there would be no funds left to arrange transit home. I had no choice but to send a message to my father, and hoped he could send someone to help us."

"I see," said March. "How did you send the message?"

"Courier," said Roanna.

March shared a glance with Bishop. That explained how the Silent Order had learned of the situation. March was sure there were honest couriers somewhere among the civilized systems, but he had yet to meet one. It also explained how the Machinists had learned of Lady Roanna's problems, and how they had known March would be the one sent to her assistance.

"We will, of course, need to review the ransom letter and its instructions," said Bishop. "If you will forgive my bluntness, the Machinists are quite capable of killing both you and Lord Thomas and taking the ransom money."

"Yes," said Roanna. "Yes, that was one of my fears."

"When is the exchange to take place?" said March.

"In three days' time, in one of the old ore processing facilities," said Roanna.

"Good," said March. "That will give us time to prepare. Perhaps we can yet turn the tables on the Machinists."

"There is one point that I am curious about," said Bishop, "and I'm sure that Captain March is as well."

"Which point is that, Mr. Bishop?" said Roanna.

"Lieutenant Heath," said March. "How did you get

mixed up in this? Junior naval officers generally aren't given leave for this kind of thing."

Roanna flushed, and opened her mouth and closed it. For once, Heath looked at a loss for words.

"Ah," said March. "You're AWOL."

"It is not like that at all," said Heath. "I would never betray Calaskar and the King."

"Then you received leave from your commanding officer to escort Lady Roanna to her destination," said March.

"Not...precisely," said Heath. "I was stationed on the RCS *Raymond*, a destroyer. Lady Roanna came aboard to inspect the vessel before we set out. I saw her weeping in the corridors, and I was moved to help her. No true Calaskaran man could refuse a lady in her hour of need."

That was a polite way of saying he had fallen for her and decide to abandon his post to run after her on this fool's errand. March's gaze turned towards Roanna, and he caught the flicker of shame before she controlled herself. She knew full what she had done, and she had encouraged Heath to do it, letting the chivalrous fool destroy his career and expose himself to a military court to help save her brother.

"How gallant," said Bishop, the sarcasm carefully hidden.

"But before we accept your help," said Heath, "there is something we need to know about you."

"What's that?" said Bishop.

Heath pointed at March. "What is under the glove?"

March glanced at his left hand. He was wearing his jumpsuit and his coat, but over his left wrist and arm he wore a leather bracer and a black glove. Sometimes the leather creaked when he made a fist.

"Sam, that's rude," said Roanna.

"No," said March. "I demanded the truth of you, so it's only fair that you ask it in return."

Bishop sighed, rolled his eyes, and settled back into his booth, though March saw him shift his weight to move his hand closer to his gun.

March unlocked the bracer on his left arm and pulled away the glove, revealing his left hand. It almost looked as if he wore a glove of overlapping and interlocking metal plates. The metal was dull gray, almost like pewter, though it was infinitely stronger and far more resilient than any natural metal.

Heath's eyes widened, and March saw his hand twitch towards his gun.

"Don't do that please, Lieutenant," said Bishop. "If you shoot someone in here, we'll be thrown out, and the drinks are passable."

"It's a cybernetic prosthesis, obviously," said Roanna with exasperation. "There's occasionally social stigma attached to them, so of course he wears a glove..."

"That's not just a cybernetic arm," said Heath. "It's a Machinist cybernetic implant."

Roanna's eyes widened, and she sucked in a startled breath.

"And it's only his left arm," Heath said.

Roanna's eyes widened further. "That means..."

"He's an Iron Hand," said Heath. "All this time we've been sitting here talking to a damned Iron Hand."

"An Iron Hand," said Roanna, staring at March.

"The Machinists' elite death commandos," said Heath. "Fighters and assassins without peer."

"I know what an Iron Hand is," said Roanna, her fear obvious.

"They never leave the Final Consciousness," said Heath. "They are fanatically loyal. They fight to the death."

"Not always," said March. He retrieved his glove. Both Heath and Roanna flinched, but March donned the glove and his bracer without hurry. "If you like, you could cut my right arm and test the blood. If you cut an Iron Hand, he bleeds black, because his blood has been replaced with nanobots. Though I suppose that would be obvious on my face." He reached with his right hand and opened the collar of his jumpsuit, showing the top of his chest and the hints of the scars there. "No armor plating, either. Or hive implant, if you want to scan my brain and spinal column."

"Then you were an Iron Hand," said Roanna.

"Yes," said March. "Now I'm not."

"Why?" said Roanna. "Why did you leave the Final Consciousness?"

March shrugged. "Which reason would you like? Revenge? I'm from the Calixtus system, and they ruined the planet. Revulsion? I saw what they did on Martel's World, and I left the Final Consciousness and Silent Order soon after that. Survival? You know how the Machinists deal with traitors. You can pick any one of those reasons you like. I suppose they're all true. But I want to hurt the Final Consciousness and the Machinists however I can, and saving you and your brother will do that."

No one spoke for a while.

"Good speech," said Bishop at last.

"Thanks," said March.

"I believe you, Captain March," said Roanna. "How should we proceed?"

"Very well," said March. "This is what I have in mind..."

ANNOTATIONS ON SILENT ORDER: IRON HAND CHAPTER 5

March and Bishop decide to keep Roanna and Heath secure on March's ship until the hostage exchange can take place. Meanwhile, March and Bishop plan to scout the location where the exchange will take place in preparation for any treachery. Roanna tries to seduce March, partly to have greater influence over him and partly because she is frightened, but March rebuffs her advances.

Heath overhears the conversation and confronts March, much to March's exasperation. Heath explains that he came on this trip partly because he is in love with Roanna but partly out of a debt of loyalty to Roanna's father. March accepts this explanation and allows Heath to accompany him on the scouting trip.

This chapter continues the rising action of the story structure and allows Heath some character development as he accepts that he made a bad decision following Roanna but plans to make the best of it.

SILENT ORDER IRON HAND CHAPTER 5: PLANNING

They slipped away from the bar and headed towards Bishop's restaurant.

The alert from the explosion in Bay 207 had died down, and the main corridors and lifts were open again, but at March's insistence, they headed back into the service corridors, walking single file through the maintenance areas of the station. By now, March knew, Lorre would have realized that his attempt in the cargo corridor had failed and would be making plans for another attack.

Except that didn't make sense.

If the Machinists were planning to ransom Thomas back to Roanna, why would they send Lorre and his goons to kill her? It was hard to obtain a ransom from a dead woman. March supposed that different factions within the Machinists' agents might be working to different purposes, but that was unlikely. Though it was possible that Lorre might have his own agenda, or that the Machinist agents holding Thomas Vindex captive might be planning to turn a personal profit before liquidating the Vindex twins. The

Final Consciousness cared less about methods and more about results.

March would worry about it later. Right now, he needed to make sure both Roanna and Heath got to a safe location.

They only encountered two maintenance techs in the service corridors, and a quick bribe from Bishop ensured their silence. A short time later they opened a door into the concourse near the restaurant, and they returned to Bishop's establishment.

"Why, Captain March," said Anne, grinning at him from behind the bar. "Looks like you and Bishop found some new friends."

"We did," said Bishop, gently guiding Roanna and Heath forward. "These are friends of mine. Let's call them the Lady and the Officer. Make them comfortable in the storeroom, will you? Captain March and I need to discuss a few things." He offered a genial smile to Roanna and Heath. "Please, make yourselves at home. Once the captain and I have made some plans, we can discuss how to proceed."

"I should help," said Heath.

Anne looked back and forth between Roanna and Heath, a bright smile on her face, but March saw the calculation in her pretty eyes.

"Not yet, Officer," said Bishop. "I'm afraid you don't have any local knowledge of Rustbelt Station, which I have, nor extensive experience in doing dirty work, which is what Captain March has."

"But..." said Heath.

"I'm sure you'll agree," said Bishop, "that the Lady's safety must be our first priority. My storeroom is the safest place for her until we can find a more secure location."

Heath sighed. "Agreed."

"Captain March," said Roanna, passing March a piece of folded paper. "A copy of the letter I received on Tamlin's World."

"Thank you," said March.

"Right this way, please," said Anne, and she led Heath and Roanna into the storeroom behind the bar. Bishop claimed two cups of coffee, and he and March sat at a booth in the corner, out of earshot of any of the patrons.

"Well, Jack," said Bishop. "What do you think?"

March took a drink of the coffee, felt it burn against his tongue, and swallowed.

"A damned mess," said March.

Bishop snorted. "I thought you might say that."

"A damned mess, and we don't know nearly as much as we need to," said March. "Let me read this, and then we can decide what to do."

Bishop nodded, opening a little packet of sugar and dumping it into the coffee. March unfolded the letter and read it. The technique of cutting up letters from different publications and pasting them to a sheet was ancient, but it was still effective. The letter said that Thomas Vindex was held captive by a cell of Machinist sympathizers. Lady Roanna was to meet them at Ore Complex 5 on Rustbelt Station at a specific date at 02:00 in the morning. If she brought sufficient funds, Thomas would be released to her unharmed, and they would go their separate ways.

If not, he would be killed.

March passed the letter to Bishop, who read it in silence.

"Seems simple enough," said Bishop.

"That means it isn't," said March, watching the restaurant and the crowds passing through the concourse outside.

"Ore Complex 5 is abandoned," said Bishop. "Has been

before I even set up shop out here. Most of the equipment is still there, but no one has touched it in decades. It would be the perfect place for someone to set up shop for a quiet prisoner exchange."

"Three things that bother me about this," said March.

Bishop gestured with his coffee cup.

"First," said March, "I'd wonder if the Machinists were involved at all. Wouldn't be the first time some petty criminals used the Machinists as cover. Except the involvement of Lorre proves this is a Machinist operation. Why are they holding Thomas for ransom and then trying to assassinate his sister when she comes to pay the ransom?"

Bishop shrugged. "Your guess is as good as mine."

"Second," said March. "Why have the sister deliver the ransom?"

"She wants to avoid a scandal," said Bishop. "Fat chance of that, though. Too many people know at this point."

"But why the sister?" said March. "You know as well as I do how dangerous it is out here. A young woman traveling alone is a tempting target for all kinds of scum. If she's unlucky, she'll wind up chained to the wall in the rec room of a pirate ship or sold to some Kezredite warlord or banker with a taste for slave girls."

"Maybe the Machinists want her out here for some reason," said Bishop.

"What reason?" said March, and Bishop shrugged. "A third problem. Are we going to have to shoot Samuel Heath?"

"You don't trust him?" said Bishop.

"No," said March. "A naval officer going without leave to help a woman with a sob story? It's not believable."

"It's very believable," said Bishop. "I've spent more time

with young naval officers than you have, my friend. They have this chivalrous streak. The older ones are wiser, but the young ones like to think of themselves as dashing knights fighting to defend King and Calaskar from the dangers of the galaxy. A pretty girl like Roanna? A man like Lieutenant Heath would fall for her, and fall hard."

March grunted. "Any way to check his claims?"

Bishop shrugged. "In time. I don't have a database of active naval personnel. I could send in a records request, but it might take three or four weeks to get an answer."

March shook his head. "Don't bother. In three days, we'll know the truth one way or another. It is still a suspicious story."

"You have no romance in your soul, my friend," said Bishop with a laugh.

"It was surgically removed years ago," said March. "Fine. We can both agree Heath is a romantic young fool. What do you think of Lady Roanna?"

"That," said Bishop, taking another sip of coffee, "is a very dangerous young woman."

"Agreed," said March.

"She's got Heath twisted around her little finger," said Bishop, "and I don't think she even had to sleep with him to do it. The best part? I doubt she's even completely realized what she's doing. She's had servants all her life. Likely she's used to thinking that everyone will put her wishes first."

"I think she knows exactly what she is doing," said March. He saw Anne emerge from the storeroom and return to the bar. "There's a way to find out. Let's ask Anne what she thinks."

"Why?" said Bishop, following suit as March stood.

"Women notice things about each other that men do not."

Bishop started to argue, but then shrugged. "That's not a bad idea."

March crossed to the bar, and Anne flashed a smile at him.

"Captain March," she said. "Got any new friends for me? Or do you want to get to know me better?"

"What do you think about the woman in the storeroom?" said March.

Anne laughed. "Seriously?"

"It would be helpful, Anne," said Bishop. "You know my business gets complicated sometimes, and the young lady is one of those complications."

"All right," said Anne with a shrug. "She's trouble, boss."

"What makes you say that?" said Bishop.

"You can always tell the type," said Anne. "That boy with her? She's got his head all twisted around. If she told him to shoot himself, he'd probably do it before the words were out of her mouth. She doesn't feel for him the way he feels for her, I can tell you that much." Anne hesitated. "But I don't think she's a bad sort, not really. She was polite to me." Her mouth twisted. "You can always tell a lot about people by how they treat the waitresses and bartenders. Some of the nobles think people like me are dirt. If your noblewoman thought that, she was too polite to say it." She shrugged once more. "Mostly, she just seems scared. Rustbelt Station will do that on the first visit."

"Thank you," said March.

"We could talk more about it later," said Anne.

"Perhaps," said March. "Thank you again." He walked with Bishop back to their table.

"You should talk about it with her later," said Bishop. "I'm sure she has other things on her mind than just talking."

March grimaced. "I'm working. And she knows I'm a privateer. Likely she just wants a ride off this rock."

"Nothing wrong with that," said Bishop. "It wouldn't hurt you to have a little fun. If a man gets his head too messed up about women, he could do something stupid like go AWOL because a noblewoman told him a sad story."

March gave him a flat look.

Bishop only smiled and spread his thick hands. "It is obviously a sore spot. I would not keep picking at it otherwise."

"I suggest," said March, "we focus on finding a way to keep Lady Roanna and her brother alive. You can devote your attention to finding me a woman after we have finished."

Bishop laughed. "Very well. What did you have in mind?"

"As I see it, we have three tasks before us," said March, ticking off the points on the fingers of his right hand. "First, we need to keep Lady Roanna alive until we have ransomed her brother. Second, we need to do what we can to gain additional information. Third, if the Machinists have not yet arrived to take control of Ore Complex 5, we can prepare the battlefield to our liking."

"It wouldn't be best to keep Roanna here," said Bishop. "Too many people have seen you come here, and at least some people know that I have connections to the Silent Order. This would be the obvious place to keep her."

"Your friend's bar, perhaps?" said March.

Bishop laughed. "And we could have Roanna dance on the stage? It might be worth it just to see Heath's expression. No, no. The scum of the station tends to gather there, and I wouldn't leave a five-credit note unattended there, let alone a potentially valuable hostage like Roanna Vindex."

"The *Tiger*, then," said March. "We'll keep her and Heath on my ship. Vigil can watch for threats, and Lorre and his men won't get onto the *Tiger* without heavy weaponry." He thought for a moment. "We need a way to get them unseen onto the ship, though."

"Maintenance tug," said Bishop at once. "They occasionally do circuits of the landing bays, watching for the development of fault lines on the surface of the asteroid. A small bribe will suffice to get our guests aboard one. The tug can set down in your bay, and we can get our guests aboard the *Tiger* without notice."

"That should work," said March. "After that, I'll take a look around Ore Complex 5. If the Machinists are setting up there, perhaps we can sabotage them. While I do that, you should check the records of any incoming ships. If Thomas Vindex is already at the station, we can grab him. If he's arriving and we can puzzle out what ship he's on, we can lie in wait for him."

"All right," said Bishop. "What time is it?"

"18:00 hours," said March. "Local station time."

"Already?" said Bishop with a frown, and then he yawned. "Well, it has been an eventful day, hasn't it? The next maintenance tug should go out at 20:00 hours. I'll make some calls, and we'll have you and your friends shipped over to the *Tiger*. I suggest you go with them. If assassins come after Roanna, you have the best chance of keeping them alive."

"Agreed," said March, and he finished his coffee.

≈

AFTER THE ADVENTURES of the day, reaching the *Tiger* proved surprisingly easy.

Bishop led them through the service corridors until they reached a utility hangar. The tug pilot, a surly middle-aged man Bishop had paid to be blind, deaf, and mute, led them to his craft, a boxy ship painted a dull yellow. March, Roanna, and Heath strapped in, and the tug took off, circling the pockmarked surface of Rustbelt Station until it hovered over Bay 93. March called Vigil, and the ship's computer opened the *Tiger's* dorsal airlock, letting the tug dock.

March led the way into the ship, followed by Roanna. Heath trailed after the noblewoman, grunting as he maneuvered their travel bags. He was carrying both his bag and Roanna's. March didn't offer to help.

"This is a Mercator Foundry Yards Class 12 light freighter, is it not?" said Roanna, looking around the gray metal corridor.

"Class 9," said March. Heath got the bags onto the deck.

"Ah," said Roanna. "I've inspected a lot of ships during their departure ceremonies, but never a Class 9 freighter."

"Your cabin is there," said March, pointing at one of the doors in the dorsal corridor, "and yours, Lieutenant Heath, is there." They would be Spartan compared to what someone like Roanna would be used to, but thanks to the ship's maintenance drones, at least it would be clean. "Vigil?"

"Yes, Captain March?" came the pseudointelligence's voice over the speakers.

"This is Lady Roanna Vindex and Lieutenant Samuel Heath," said March. "They are guests. Give them guest access level three."

"Of course, Captain March," said Vigil.

That would give them access to the cabins and the galley, and it would permit them to exit the ship, though

Vigil would send a notification to March if they did. If Roanna and Heath tried to access the flight cabin, the engine room, the cargo hold, the armory, or any of the vital systems, Vigil would lock them out and notify March.

"I suggest you get some sleep," said March. "It was a long day, and the next few days are likely to be longer. If you need me, speak to Vigil, and she will call me."

"Yes, of course," said Roanna. "Thank you, Captain March, for all your assistance. Good night."

March inclined his head. "Good night."

"Good night, Sam," said Roanna. She smiled, picked up her travel bag, and disappeared into the cabin, the door sliding shut behind her. Heath hesitated, looking at the closed door as if he expected her to invite him in after her. Then he shook his head, picked up his bag, and vanished into the other cabin.

March went to the flight cabin and dropped into the pilot's chair, bringing up the diagnostic displays. All systems were functional and on standby. March scrolled through the sensor logs and camera feeds, but Vigil had recorded no signs of sabotage. No one had even approached the *Tiger*, save for the bay drones that had hooked up the fuel lines to replenish the ship's dark matter reactor and repaired some minor damage to the ship's armor plating.

At least March had gotten some value for his bribe money.

He exited the ship and did a visual inspection of the hull and landing struts, but found no trace of bombs or sabotage. So far, at least, Lorre's bag of dirty tricks had not extended to attacking the *Tiger*. March had no doubt that would change.

He returned to the ship and sealed the airlock behind him, instructing Vigil to keep watch for any saboteurs. March knew he ought to go to sleep, but he found himself restless. Mostly it was because he did not yet understand the enemy's plan. Too many things did not add up and did not make sense. March wanted to go for a walk, but leaving Roanna and Heath unattended aboard the *Tiger* would be a bad idea.

Instead, March went to his cabin, donned a T-shirt, loose pants, and exercise shoes, and went to the ship's gym.

He started off with a two-mile sprint on the treadmill, getting his heart rate up. Once that was finished, he climbed down and walked to the weight rack.

"Vigil," said March, wiping some sweat from his forehead. "One hundred and fifty percent gravity, please."

"Exercise at this hour of the night is inadvisable," said Vigil. "Sleep is more conducive to optimal health, Captain March."

"Noted, thank you," said March.

The lights dimmed at a little, and the gravitics increased in strength. March grunted, bracing himself against the increased weight, then nodded and began his standard strength training routine. After he finished his deadlifts, his shirt was soaked with sweat, so he peeled it off, hung it on the side of the treadmill, and started his military presses. As ever, lifting weights required careful concentration. His left arm was vastly more powerful than his right, but he wanted to make his right arm as strong as possible. That meant carefully adjusting the weight load on his left arm while letting his right arm do as much of the work as possible.

March set the bar back into the rack, the bench cold against the skin of his back, and the door hissed open.

He looked to the left as Roanna stepped into the room, and her eyes went wide at the enhanced gravity, a gasp of pain escaping from her lips.

"Vigil!" snapped March, getting to his feet. "Normal gravity!"

The lights went brighter, and the gym resumed normal gravity. As ever, for a moment March suddenly felt as if he was flying from the sudden reduction of weight, but he raced across the gym and caught Roanna's arm before she fell.

"Thank you," said Roanna, breathing hard. "I...don't know what happened..."

"The gravity was heightened," said March. "If you're not ready for it, you could snap your ankle like a twig." He scowled at her. "What the hell are you doing in here?"

She blanched at his anger. "I couldn't sleep. I asked your computer, and she said the ship has a gym. I figured a run would clear my head, so..."

"Fine," said March.

His brain caught up with his alarm, and he noticed that she had changed to exercise clothes, a tank top and a pair of shorts. The garments were snug, and they fit her well. He was holding her left arm with his right hand, and the skin felt smooth and warm beneath his fingers. Belatedly he remembered that he had taken his shirt off.

A wave of chagrin went through him. March hated for anyone to see him in any state of undress. It wasn't out of modesty, or self-consciousness, or shame.

It was for a far more obvious reason.

Roanna's eyes went wide, blue and stark against her pale face.

"What happened to you?" whispered Roanna.

Whenever he was in any state of undress, his scars were visible, and he hated to look at them.

His left arm was metal, but his shoulder was a mixture of metal and flesh and bone, the skin where the metal arm joined the flesh gnarled with old scars. A larger Y-shaped scar went down both sides of his chest and his stomach, stopping an inch or so below his navel. He had seen enough dead men to know that autopsied corpses had exactly that scar on their torsos. The surgeons of the Final Consciousness were efficient and far more skilled than any other surgeons among the starfaring human nations, but they were not concerned about aesthetics.

"Use the treadmill if you want," said March, releasing her arm. "Just be sure to knock next time. My superiors sent me to fly you back to Antioch Station, not to break your damned ankle."

He had let go of her arm, but her left hand came to rest on his right forearm, and March froze.

"What happened to you?" said Roanna again.

March stared at her, trying to read her expression. She only looked sad. Was she trying to seduce him? To gain an advantage over him? At the moment, she only looked like a frightened, saddened young woman.

"What do you think?" said March, his voice rougher than he would have liked. "I was an Iron Hand. They don't wear uniforms. The changes go...deeper. Surgery. Cybernetics. Nanotech."

"Did you choose it?" said Roanna.

She stepped a little closer to him, staring up at his face.

"Choose what?" March said.

"To become an Iron Hand," said Roanna. "To join the Final Consciousness. To do...this to yourself."

Her other hand strayed down his chest, brushing the scars, and her touch sent fire through him.

"Choose this?" said March, his voice thick again. "No. I was chosen. The Machinists destroyed Calixtus, crushed its civilization. I grew up in a labor camp. My mother died when I was young. The Overseers came through and tested us. Only about every one in five people can join the Final Consciousness. No one knows why. The eighty percent who cannot are used as slave labor until they die, and then their bodies are fed into protein reclamation plants. Me, I was one of the lucky ones. They took me and determined I was suitable to be a soldier. Not just a solider, an Iron Hand."

"What...what was it like?" said Roanna. Her eyes were wide. She looked fascinated, but in a horrified sort of way, like a young soldier seeing a corpse for the first time.

"The Final Consciousness?" said March. "It is hell, but you don't know it at the time. You hear the voice of the hive in your thoughts...and it's so strong. You agree with it. You're drowned in it. You lose yourself. You become part of the machine, and you don't even realize that it has happened. You..."

He shook his head, pushing aside the memories. His throat ached a little. He wasn't used to speaking for so long.

"That is why you hate them so much," said Roanna.

"The Final Consciousness thinks itself a god," said March. "The Machinists think they have built a replacement for God. They haven't. They've built a devil, and it will kill and kill until it is stopped, all because they think they can perfect humanity..."

He blinked, realizing how much he had said.

"I'm sorry," said Roanna.

"Why are you here?" said March.

"I wanted to go running," said Roanna.

"And you got me talking about myself," said March. "A lot of things about this situation do not make sense, but they make far more sense if you are a Machinist agent."

"No," said Roanna. "I just thought...I would talk with

you." She brushed his arm. "Maybe try to understand you better. Maybe..."

Gently, he reached up and put the fingers of his left hand on her cheek, his thumb curling beneath her jaw. Roanna flinched at the cool feel of the metal against her skin. March had only to squeeze, and her head would shatter like a melon beneath the wheels of a car. He wouldn't even need to squeeze that hard.

"Are you a Machinist?" said March.

"No," said Roanna, meeting his gaze. "I'm not. I'm a fool, and an idiot and I've made a lot of bad decisions." He saw her pulse in her neck. "I hate the Machinists. Not like you. I don't have the right. But one of my friends died at the Orbital Shipyard bombing. That was why I was so angry with Thomas when he fell in with those dissidents. He should have known better."

"Fine. You're not a Machinist agent," said March. "You might have come here to run, but you thought I was here. Then what do you want?"

She pushed against his metal hand, gently, and he had no choice to release her or inflict injury upon her.

Roanna's fingers slid across his back, and she kissed him on the mouth.

Soft, her mouth was soft, and her tongue slipped beneath his lips. It had been a long time since he had had a woman. It had been a long time since anyone had touched him.

March put his hands on her shoulders and eased her away.

"What?" said Roanna.

"Did you give this speech to Lieutenant Heath as well?" said March.

She flinched but didn't look away from him. "I...no. But I

deserved that. We haven't slept together. He hasn't touched me..."

"But you let him think he might," said March, "and so he's followed you all the way out here."

"I needed help," said Roanna.

"Then go knock on his door," said March. "He'll fall on his knees and worship you. Probably bring you breakfast every morning and compose poems for you every night."

"No," said Roanna. "Sam is...kind, good-hearted, but he's a boy in many ways. I need a man."

"A man?" said March. "Go talk to Bishop. He can probably find one you to rent by the hour."

Anger flashed over her face. "Is that what you think of me?"

"I haven't decided what I think of you," said March. "But you're giving me evidence to make up my mind."

"Yes. I...suppose I am," said Roanna. "You must think me quite the wanton. But I am a long way from home, and I am frightened out of my mind. I am the only one who can save my brother. Don't you see? Thomas is like Sam. He's a boy, and he rushed into something over his head. I need to save him. But I can't do it alone. I need a...a man, a fighter. Someone like you."

"A wreck of scars and cybernetics?" said March.

She gave him a little smile. "There are a lot of muscles under those scars. You might be more attractive than you think."

"A Calaskaran noblewoman should not be sleeping with former Iron Hands," said March.

"A lover or two before I find a proper husband would not be the end of the world," said Roanna. "It's quite common."

"No," said March, letting go of her and stepping back.

It cost him more than he would have expected.

For a moment pain went over her face, then she made herself smile. "You're lying. You want to do this." Her eyes flicked below his waistband, where the loose exercise pants made it impossible to conceal his physical arousal.

"What I want is immaterial," said March. "I have my duty. My orders are to get you and your brother to Antioch Station, and that's what I'm going to do." He stepped away from her, picked up his shirt from the treadmill, and pulled it on. The chill of the sweat-sodden shirt helped cool his ardor.

She stared at him for a moment. "I believe you. I don't think I've ever met anyone quite like you."

"Best thank God for that," said March.

"Do you believe me?" said Roanna.

"I think so," said March, stepping past her towards the door. "I'll find out in three days, won't I?" He looked back at her. "Enjoy the treadmill."

March stepped back into the dorsal corridor, the door to the gym sliding shut behind him.

A moment later he heard the dull, rapid thud of her footsteps upon the treadmill.

"Jesus," muttered March.

He went to his cabin, used the sanitation booth to clean himself off, and went to sleep.

MARCH HAD NOT BEEN able to finish his workout because of Roanna's interruption, but he slept better than he expected. At 05:30 he awoke and checked in with Vigil, despite the lack of notifications. There had been no unusual activity in the night, and no one had approached the ship. March rose, dressed, and walked down the dorsal corridor to the galley.

The galley was a small rectangular room, dominated by a steel table and a pair of benches. One counter held a variety of food-making equipment, and a flatscreen display hung on one wall.

Samuel Heath sat at the table, staring into his coffee.

"Lieutenant," said March, stepping past him to head for the coffeemaker.

"I heard you and Lady Roanna last night," said Heath without preamble.

March poured himself a cup of coffee, wondering if Heath would draw his gun. "Do you often make a practice of eavesdropping?"

"No," said Heath, still staring into his coffee. "I...was on the intercom. I heard her get up and go to your gym, and I turned on the intercom, hoping to talk to her. I heard you instead."

March grunted. That had been an error on his part. The intercom system was nothing but speakers and wires and microphones, and Vigil wouldn't have turned it off unless he had instructed her to do so.

"I heard everything," said Heath.

"For God's sake," said March.

"Why didn't you sleep with her?" said Heath.

"For God's sake!" said March, his temper slipping. Heath looked up from his coffee, momentarily frightened out of his brooding. "This is a matter of life and death, and I am burdened with two children who have more hormones than brains. People are going to get killed, and you two are preoccupied with your damned soap opera."

He rebuked himself, restraining his temper. That little outburst had accomplished nothing. Truth be told, he was not annoyed with Heath. March was annoyed with himself, for letting Roanna get to him, for letting himself be attracted to her.

"That...is not undeserved," said Heath.

March sighed and sat across the table from the younger man.

"If you must know," said March, "I didn't sleep with her because it would have been an extraordinarily bad idea. Perhaps that is advice that you should take."

Heath snorted. "I know you and Bishop think that I am a fool."

March almost said yes, but he stopped himself.

"What has brought you to that conclusion?" he said instead.

"Because I have acted like a fool," said Heath. "I abandoned my post and helped Lady Roanna to Rustbelt Station on this mad errand. And, yes, I have fallen in love with her."

"I am awaiting the part," said March, "where you explain that you are not a fool."

"It wasn't just about her," said Heath. "Are you familiar with the twisting fever?"

"It's a viral disease native to Calaskar," said March. "It causes uncontrollable muscle contractions and organ failure. Every few years there is an outbreak, and it always takes some time before the doctors can formulate a vaccine for the latest variant of the disease."

"My family has always worked as gas miners," said Heath. "We lived in the swamps of Toridex Peninsula on Calaskar, and the fever always festers in the swamps. When I was a boy, the fever broke out among us in a bad way. We would have died, but the Earl of Sundrex spent a fortune forcing the vaccine development along faster. His wife was from the Peninsula, and he had an interest in it that many of the other nobles did not. A lot of people would have died of the twisting fever if not for the Earl's help."

"Roanna's father," said March.

"Yes," said Heath. "I should have been an enlisted man in the Royal Calaskaran Navy, but I got into the Academy on a scholarship from Lord Sebastian. When I heard that Lady Roanna Vindex would inspect the RCS *Raymond* before we set out on our tour, I was excited. Then when she told me about her troubles, I thought I had a chance to repay Lord Sebastian, even if he would never know that he had helped me." Heath let out a long breath. "I'm afraid..."

"You fell in love with her on the trip," said March.

"Yes," admitted Heath.

"Can't blame you," said March. "She's a beautiful young woman. She's also very used to getting her way."

"Yes," said Heath again. "When I heard her talking to you...it ripped me up. Then you refused her...God, in your place I wouldn't have lasted a second."

"I'm not so besotted with her that I went AWOL from the Royal Calaskaran Navy to follow her," said March.

Heath opened his mouth, closed it, and then sighed.

"Look," said March, resisting the urge to rub his temples. "I'm not good with clever words, so this is going to sound harsh. But what the hell do you think is going to happen? That she'll see how helpful you were and fall in love with you? That she'll abandon her position and family to marry you? Her father would disown her for that."

"He might not," said Heath.

"Maybe," said March. "But you'd still be thrown out of the Navy, and you'd be the disgraced son-in-law. No. You might have a dalliance with her, but once she gets back to Calaskar, she will probably cut you out of her life very gently and politely. If we live through this, she's going to marry either a powerful nobleman or a wealthy man. That's a very determined young woman, and she's good at getting what she wants."

Heath scowled. "You make her sound like some... conniving seductress."

"Do I?" said March. "I doubt she's ever been with a man. Else she would have slept with you already to get you under her thumb. She's a determined young woman who loves her family. That's why she's out here, to save her brother. She likes you, but she loves her family, and they matter more to her than you do." March shrugged. "Nothing wrong with that. Just the way it is."

"You were right," said Heath. "That was harsh."

March shrugged and took a long drink of his coffee. It was too early for this kind of crap. "It's the truth. Take it or leave it."

"It is nothing that I have not said to myself a dozen times in the last week," said Heath. He sighed again and rubbed his face. "I've been a romantic fool."

"Yeah," said March.

"You have a gift for blunt speech," said Heath.

"Gift or not, it's how I talk," said March.

"What are you going to do now?" said Heath.

"Investigate Ore Complex 5," said March. "If the exchange is supposed to take place there, we might learn something useful. Or we might have the chance to set an ambush for the kidnappers."

"Let me help," said Heath. "At least I can do something useful. I was a security officer aboard the *Raymond*, so I know how to handle myself in shipboard combat."

March started to refuse, and then changed his mind. Heath had a point. It never hurt to have someone to watch your back, and March would be able to determine in moments if Heath actually knew how to handle himself. March could have asked Bishop to watch his back, but Bishop would be more useful at the Emperor's Rest.

And it would get Heath away from Roanna. That would only be a good thing. Maybe March was going soft...but he had to admit that this seemed the best plan for now.

"All right," said March. "I need to call Bishop, and make sure that Roanna stays on the ship. Get your weapons and get ready to go."

ANNOTATIONS ON SILENT ORDER: IRON HAND CHAPTER 6

March and Heath scout Ore Complex 5 on Rustbelt Station where the prisoner exchange is to take place. There they find a mercenary gang lying in wait, most likely holding Thomas Vindex hostage. March and Bishop decide to try and break out Thomas, and Bishop uses his influence over Administrator Heitz to induce him to help.

With Heitz's forces, March leads an attack on the mercenary camp that overwhelms the enemy and takes them prisoner, but there is no sign of Thomas.

In this chapter, the story structure encounters another unexpected complication when March plans to rescue Thomas Vindex, only to find that he isn't in the mercenary camp.

SILENT ORDER IRON HAND CHAPTER 6: AMBUSHES

March walked down the silent corridor, Heath following him, the few lights in the ceiling throwing a flickering, dim light over the rough rock walls.

Rustbelt Station's maintenance standards were not high, but the abandoned levels and domes that housed the ore processing facilities had fallen into total disrepair. Wires hung loosely from the ceiling and the walls, and doors stood half-open, revealing rooms of rusted equipment. Dead maintenance drones squatted against the walls, their repair and cleaning arms askew. The residents of Rustbelt Station had begun using the abandoned ore complexes to dispose of trash, and piles of junk and bags of garbage rested against the walls. Evidently dumping things here was cheaper than paying the fee for the station's recyclers and organic decompilers. March suspected that sooner or later they would find a corpse or two tucked into a quiet corner.

The air was stale and smelled as if no one had been down here for some time. March had been surprised to learn that the life support and gravitics were still working.

Bishop said that Rustbelt Station's life support equipment was antiquated and that Heitz and the station administrators could not turn off life support to any individual portion of the station without crashing the entire system.

This did not fill March with confidence, so he carried a breath mask at his belt, and had a radiation sensor clipped to his collar. So far, though, the atmosphere hadn't failed, and the sensor hadn't detected any dangerous radiation, which surprised him.

Samuel Heath's competence also surprised him.

The naval lieutenant knew his business, and he had been trained well. He did not waste time with unnecessary questions or chatter. What was more, he moved with the fluidity of experience instead of the rigid predictability of a newly-trained man. March could tell that Heath had been in a few firefights, and away from the emotional influence of Roanna Vindex, he became collected and competent. He moved with the smooth motions of a professional accustomed to violence. Based on his behavior around Roanna, March had expected Heath to be a babbling fool. Clearly, that assessment had not been completely accurate.

His earpiece beeped. March looked around and beckoned to Heath, and the younger man followed him to a side room. The room looked as if it had once been a break room for the ore workers. Metal tables were bolted to the floor alongside benches, and a row of empty vending machine and dead cooking devices filled one wall.

"Watch the corridor," said March, and Heath nodded, stepping into guard position. March reached up and tapped his earpiece. "This is March."

"Jack," said Bishop. "I've pulled the last few years' worth of work orders and construction permits. No one has touched Ore Complex 5 in decades. Of course, this is Rust-belt Station..."

"If someone is hiding out in Ore Complex 5, they're doing it off the books," said March.

"Undoubtedly," said Bishop. "Lady Roanna has been kind enough to go through the ship departure and arrival records." March had suggested that as a task to keep Roanna busy, safe aboard the *Tiger*, and out of their hair. He had set her up with a laptop in the galley, and Bishop had transferred the appropriate records to Vigil.

"Has she found anything interesting?" said March.

"As it happens, yes," said Roanna, her voice cool and calm. It sounded very different from the young woman who had tried to seduce him last night, and March stifled a laugh. "There are no freighters or any other craft scheduled to arrive at Rustbelt Station for the next five days."

"It is possible Lord Thomas's captors lied to Lady Roanna," said Bishop.

"It is," said March. It was also possible that Thomas had wished to go over to the Machinists entirely, and concocted a ruse with a ransom as a way to disappear. It was also possible that Thomas had tried to escape and gotten killed and dumped into space somewhere. If that was the case, they would never learn what had happened to Thomas, and this entire thing had been a waste of time. The systems explored by the starfaring nations were vast, but they were only a tiny percentage of the galaxy's hundred billion stars, and it was very easy for one man to disappear.

On the other hand, it was also possible that the ship carrying Thomas Vindex had not filed a flight plan. March hadn't, and there was no reason Thomas's captors could not do the same.

"There is something else," said Roanna. "Four days

before Captain March arrived, a bulk freighter docked and departed again the same day after unloading its equipment."

"What was it carrying?" said March.

"Machine tools," said Roanna.

"That's not uncommon," said Bishop. "There is some manufacturing here."

"The specific kind of machine tools," said Roanna, "were plasma drills, disintegrators rated for rocks, heavy-duty carts, and magnetic resonance detectors."

"Mining equipment," said March.

"Except there has been no mining on this asteroid in decades," said Bishop. "Given all the illicit activity here, the one activity that has not been pursued illegally is mining. The station seismographs still work, and Ronstadt Corporation and Heitz would chase off any illegal miners. It would be too easy to rip the asteroid apart."

"Then the manifest was falsified," said March.

"It's entirely possible," said Bishop. "Not that hard to do, either."

"Then you think Thomas might have been smuggled onto the station already?" said March, impressed. He hadn't expected anything useful from Roanna. Still, she was an intelligent young woman, and perhaps he shouldn't have been surprised.

"It might be," said Bishop. "That's how I would do it. If they've been here for five days already, they've had lots of time to set up. Plenty of time to plan nasty surprises, too."

"Hell," said March. Heath gave him a startled glance, and then returned his attention to the corridor. "Which means we could be walking into the Machinists' hired muscle."

"Maybe," said Bishop. "Be careful."

"I'm always careful."

"An Operative ought to be a better liar," said Bishop. "I'll let you know if we find anything useful."

He ended the call.

"Bad news?" said Heath, still watching the corridor.

"Probably," said March. "Your girlfriend went through the shipping records. Five days ago, a ship loaded with mining equipment arrived."

"Except there hasn't been mining here for years," said Heath. "You think the Machinists might have smuggled Lord Thomas onto the station already?"

"It's possible," said March.

"Then we're walking into a trap?" said Heath.

"Maybe," said March, stepping to the door. "On the other hand, they might have Thomas here already. If we move fast, we might have a chance of snatching him away from his captors and getting the hell out of here before they react."

Heath frowned. "Is that even feasible?"

March shrugged. "We won't know until we try, will we?" He glanced at his phone, refreshing his memory of the map of Ore Complex 5. "Follow me."

Heath nodded and fell in behind March. Together they walked down the corridor and turned a corner. Twenty meters away loomed a massive set of double doors, the dull metal gleaming in the sputtering lights. March saw his own distorted reflection in the metal, twisted and monstrous.

"Behind those doors is the main smelting chamber for Ore Complex 5," said March. "When they dug the ore out of the asteroid, they smelted it right there and dumped the slag into space on a vector that would take it away from the station."

"Is it pressurized?" said Heath.

"Probably," said March. "Unless there's a leak." He looked around at the walls, noting the position of the power conduits. "You've got those night vision goggles I gave you before we left the *Tiger*?" Heath nodded. "Get ready to put them on."

March walked to the wall, followed the line of the power conduits, and pried open a metal junction box. Inside were a row of circuit breakers, and he flipped them all at once.

The corridor plunged into darkness as the lights went off.

"Ah," said Heath. "You didn't want any light going through the door when you opened it."

"Right," said March, reaching into his pocket and pulling his own night-vision goggles over his eyes, the strap digging into the back of his head. The ghostly green image of the corridor appeared before his eyes. He saw Heath don his own goggles, the eyepieces glinting with ghostly green light.

"How are you going to get the door open without power?" said Heath.

March pulled the glove off his left hand. "Cover me."

"I see," said Heath. He stepped back, his pistol trained in the direction of the doors, and March stepped forward.

The fingers of his metal hand plunged into the gap between the doors, and March adjusted his position, set his footing, and strained with all his strength. A shiver went through his metal arm as it brought its full power to bear upon the doors, and March braced his muscles. If he wasn't careful, the metal arm could tear itself free from his flesh, breaking half the bones in his chest and leaving him to bleed to death in short order.

But he knew his limitations. The right door slid open a few feet with a faint rasp, and dim light spilled into the corridor from the vast chamber beyond. March reached up and flipped his goggles onto his forehead, blinking as his eyes adjusted. Through the half-opened door, he saw a vast chamber carved into the heart of the asteroid, easily large enough to hold the *Fisher* or a ship of similar size. Eight massive cylindrical machines stood against the walls, and March recognized them as the smelting furnaces used to extract the metal from the ore. Metal tracks had been installed on the floor, and here and there empty carts stood abandoned. The air was cold and smelled stale, and yet March smelled something else on the breeze.

He thought it was a vacuum-sealed meal getting reheated.

March raised his hand, and Heath nodded, settling into a guard position. In the distance, March saw a flicker of electric light in the gloom between two of the blast furnaces. He reached into his coat, drew out a pair of electronic binoculars, and snapped them open. As he did, he hit the record button on top of the binoculars. The device would send a video recording to his phone, which would, in turn, send it to Vigil.

He focused the binoculars on the space between the two blast furnaces, zooming to a higher magnification level. An impromptu camp had been set up between the cold furnaces, complete with a small prefabricated building and a pair of cylindrical security drones that rolled back and forth on heavy treads. March spotted six men standing outside the prefab building, some of them talking to each other, others standing guard with assault rifles in hand. The men wore tactical vests over gray jumpsuits, and on the right shoulder of the jumpsuits, March saw a patch that showed a gray wolf's head.

It was identical to the symbol on the ship that had attacked him.

It seemed the Graywolves mercenary gang had arrived on the station along with Roanna's faked machine tools.

March tapped a control on the binoculars, activating the device's infrared sensors. He focused on the squat rectangular prefab building. His binoculars detected a half-dozen people within the building, though it could not give any details about them. More Graywolves, most likely.

Was Thomas Vindex a prisoner in that building?

March didn't know. But it was possible.

He moved the binoculars slowly and systematically over the entire cavern, trying to look at every corner of the chamber. As far as he could tell, save for the prefab building and the Graywolves, there was no one else in the cavern. March would have liked to move closer and look around, but that seemed risky. The guards were watching the cavern, and the security drones would never waver in their vigilance. If Thomas was in the prefab building, March might be able to snatch him away right now.

He might also get himself killed.

Once he was satisfied, he closed the binoculars, slipped them back into his pocket, and gestured to Heath. The younger man nodded, and together they moved back into the corridor.

"What did you find?" said Heath once they were far enough away not to be overheard.

"Graywolves," said March. "You know them?"

"One of the Machinists' pet mercenary gangs, aren't they?" said Heath. "We saw some of their ships near Tamlin's World."

"They are," said March. "One of their ships attacked me on the way here. There are a dozen Graywolves in the smelting cavern, and they've got a little prefab barracks between two of the furnaces."

"The perfect place to hold a prisoner," said Heath.

"My thoughts exactly," said March. "Let's have a talk with Bishop and see if we can hire some reinforcements."

"YOU KNOW," said Bishop as they stepped into Bay 93, "I thought your ship was a piece of junk, but now that I see it up close again, I see that my memory was generous."

"The *Tiger* is fast and well-armed," said March, unlocking the cargo airlock. Though he had to admit that some of the armor plating could be replaced. "Aesthetic concerns are of no importance."

"And that is why you don't have a woman in your life," said Bishop. Heath gave them both a look halfway between surprise and embarrassment.

March suppressed a sigh. "You have a one-track mind, Constantine."

"I have a healthy mind with an appropriate appreciation for the opposite sex," said Bishop.

"And you don't even run a brothel," said March, waiting as the airlock cycled open.

"I'm far too classy of a businessman for that."

March tapped his earpiece. "Vigil. Status?"

"I have detected no unusual activity since your departure, Captain March," came the cool voice. "No one has approached the ship, and there have been no incoming transmissions."

"Thank you," said March. They entered the cargo bay, climbed the ladder to the dorsal corridor, and went to the galley. Lady Roanna awaited them there, seated at the table with a laptop computer in front of her. Bishop offered her a gallant bow and seated himself, while March simply sat. Heath looked at Roanna, hesitated, and then remained standing on March's side on the table. For an instant Roanna looked hurt, but then her cool mask fell back into place.

"All right," said March. "We've found a secret encampment of Graywolves in Ore Complex 5. The Graywolves are a mercenary company the Machinists like to use for covert ops, and we think they crept aboard the station in that shipment of fake 'mining equipment' that you found. They've got a prefabricated barracks set up down there, and it is possible they've got your brother inside it."

Roanna blinked. "Could...could we break him out?"

"Maybe," said March, pulling his phone from his pocket. "Vigil, the most recent video file, please. Let's have a look and see what we can figure out."

The flatscreen on the wall flickered, and the recording from March's binoculars appeared on the display. They watched in silence, though Bishop grunted a few times. The video finished, and Bishop asked March to play it again, which he did.

"What do you think?" said Roanna once the video finished for the second time. "Is Thomas in there?"

"Possibly," said March. "It may even be likely. But if I had kidnapped your brother and was holding him for ransom, I wouldn't keep him at the meeting location. I would send you the location, and once you had arrived, I would take you somewhere else to make the exchange. Less chance for you to make trouble or arrange an ambush."

"Then Thomas isn't in that building?" said Roanna with some exasperation.

"We don't know," said Bishop, "and there is no way to know unless we go inside and have a look."

"Can we do that?" said Roanna. "Could you...break into the building and look around? Or send in a drone with a camera?"

"We could," said Bishop, "but if anything goes wrong, they'll realize we're on to them."

"Better to take them all at once and keep them from sending a warning to their friends," said March.

"What do you mean?" said Roanna.

"What Captain March means," said Heath, "is that he wants to attack the Graywolves, overwhelm them before they can report to their masters, take as many prisoners as possible, and interrogate Lord Thomas's location out of them."

Again, March found himself impressed. Heath might have been a fool with women, but in military matters his thinking was clear.

"Would...would that work?" said Roanna, some fear leaking through her calm mask.

"It might," said March. "It might not. A billion things could go wrong. But it's worth the risk. They might have your brother in that prefab building. If they don't, they'll know where he is. If we really get lucky, we might catch Simon Lorre. He's either the mastermind behind this, or he's in charge of the entire operation. And if we don't find Lorre or your brother, we can capture some of the Graywolves and get useful information about them. There might be data inside the prefab building as well."

"That is all very logical," said Roanna, "but there are just four of us, and while I am not prone to self-deprecation, I doubt I would be much use in a fight."

"I'm afraid it might be some time to apply some bribe

money," said Bishop. "Have you had the pleasure of meeting Station Administrator Heitz?"

"I have not," said Roanna, "but I heard the captain of the *Fisher* paying him while we were landing. Is he that corrupt?"

"And more," said Bishop. "Ronstadt Private Security Corporation has the law enforcement and public order contract for the station, and Heitz regularly feeds them bribe money. It should be relatively cheap to hire them for an assault on the Graywolves."

Heath frowned. "If these Ronstadt mercenaries are corrupt, will they not turn on us?"

"Probably not," said Bishop. "Heitz is corrupt, but he's a survivor of the battle at Martel's World, so he hates the Machinists and will go out of his way to screw with them so long as it doesn't put himself at risk. Ronstadt dabbles in corruption, but they wouldn't dare work with the Machinists since they have too many contracts with governments opposed to the Final Consciousness."

"Can the Ronstadt mercenaries handle the Graywolves in battle?" said Roanna.

"I would say they are both equally inept," said Bishop, "but with proper preparation, we should be able to win." He looked at March, eyebrows raised.

"We'd have to jam any radio signals in Ore Complex 5," said March. "If they get word to their friends, this entire thing will have been for nothing. They were wearing armored tactical harnesses, but no body armor or powered combat armor. No gas masks. If we gas them, that will take out quite a few of them, and we can overwhelm any who remain awake."

"That sounds like a reasonable plan," said Bishop. He sighed. "The bribes will not be cheap."

"No one joins the Silent Order to get rich," said March.

"A fact of which I am reminded every day," said Bishop. "All right. Let me make some phone calls, and we'll see what Heitz can do for us."

ADMINISTRATOR HEITZ WALKED into Bishop's restaurant at noon, flanked by four Ronstadt security officers. The officers wore their black jumpsuits and scowled at everything in sight. They were muscle-bound and looked dangerous, but March took one look at them and thought of a dozen ways he could neutralize them in the space of three seconds.

Perhaps asking their help wasn't such a good idea.

"Administrator Heitz," said Bishop, walking around the bar with a wide smile on his bearded face. "Welcome, welcome. A beer on the house?" He lifted a cold bottle.

"Thank you," said Heitz, taking the bottle and opening it. He took a drink, paused to admire the backside of a passing waitress, and then turned his attention to March. "Well, well. Captain March of the *Tiger*."

"Administrator," said March, keeping his voice calm. He did not like corrupt officials, even if they were useful to the mission of the Silent Order.

"I thought you were trouble the moment you stepped off that ship," said Heitz. "I can always tell."

"I was hoping for a moment of your time," said Bishop. "Captain March and I wish to speak to you about a business matter."

Heitz smiled. "As Station Administrator, I am always delighted to talk about business."

"Shall we have a drink in my office?" said Bishop.

"Certainly," said Heitz. He looked at his bodyguards.

"Wait here. I assume your friend Captain March will join us?"

"If you do not object," said Bishop.

Heitz only grunted, and March followed them through the storeroom and into Bishop's office. Bishop dropped into his desk chair, and Heitz sat in the guest chair. March leaned against the wall and folded his arms over his chest, watching them.

"All right," said Heitz, dropping the genial mask and lifting his beer. "Let me guess. This is Silent Order business?"

March frowned. "You know about the Silent Order?"

Heitz snorted. "Of course I know about the Silent Order. I'm not an idiot. And I like working with the Silent Order. You know how to play ball, and you hate the Machinists, too." He took a drink of his beer. "That, and you don't mind a man turning a profit under the table so long as he's loyal. Mention that to a Navy man, and he won't shut up about it."

"Then you admit you're corrupt?" said March.

"Obviously I'm corrupt," said Heitz. "A man has to look after his own interests. But I'm a patriot. I hate the Final Consciousness just as much as any of you spies. All three of my brothers fought in the battle at Martel's World, and those bastards killed them." He took another drink of beer and set down the bottle on Bishop's desk with a little more force than necessary. "Well. We've got Machinist trouble?"

"Our friends the Graywolves," said Bishop.

Heitz scowled. "I've banned them from Rustbelt Station."

"I suspect they don't care," said Bishop. "Recently a group sneaked onto the station using a freighter with a forged manifest. They've set up in Ore Complex 5, and I think they've got a hostage with them."

Heitz scowled, picked up his beer, and took another drink. "Who's this hostage?"

"Someone important," said Bishop. "Frankly, you'll be happier not knowing. The Graywolves are working for a specific Machinist agent named Simon Lorre. They plan on ransoming their prisoner back to the Kingdom of Calaskar for a large sum."

"So what?" said Heitz. "It sounds like some noble twit hung around with the wrong people and got in over his head. It's not my problem."

March reflected that Heitz may have been smarter than he looked.

"It is actually your problem and a serious problem at that," said Bishop. "One, if the Graywolves get a foothold here, if they can come and go as they please, they'll take over the station and get rid of you. Two, if the prisoner gets killed here, there's going to be a serious investigation. The Silent Order can play ball with you. The Calaskaran Ministry of Security and the Royal Calaskaran Navy take bribery a bit more seriously." Heitz grimaced at that. "And three...you hate the Machinists, Heitz. This is a way for you to screw them over and make a profit at the same time. What's the downside?"

Heitz rubbed his jaw for a moment. "What did you have in mind?"

Bishop looked up from his desk. "Captain March?"

March looked at the fat administrator. "We start by jamming all their transmissions. Best that they don't call for help from their friends. While we do that, we'll need men ready to take out their security drones. Once that's done, we should hit their prefab building with gas grenades, something nonlethal to knock them out. We then hit them hard and fast with stun weapons, take as many prisoners as possible, and free their hostage from their building."

Heitz frowned. "And if this noble moron of yours isn't their camp?"

"Then we have lots of prisoners to question," said March.

Heitz let out a nasty laugh. "They won't want to talk to you."

Bishop smiled. "My friends and I can be very persuasive."

Heitz snorted. "You'll cut little bits off them until they talk, is that it? Well, I told the Graywolves not to poke around Rustbelt Station, so it's time they suffered some consequences. But if we're going to do this, we can't do it officially. If we do it officially, I'll be expected to hand over some arrested suspects to the Ministry of Security. They tend to frown on extrajudicial executions."

"I can promise you," said Bishop, "any captured Graywolves will never trouble you again. Bureaucratically or otherwise."

That was a polite way of saying the Graywolves would be executed and dumped into space. It was a brutal way of doing business, but March had no sympathy for those who sold themselves to the Final Consciousness. That said, if the Graywolves cooperated, there was no reason not to let them go quietly on a neutral world somewhere. Former enemies could become future allies. But there was no reason to trouble Heitz's mind with that.

"All right," said Heitz, leaning forward. "The employees of Ronstadt Corporation are not above doing dirty jobs on the side for the right amount of money. All that remains to determine is the correct sum of money."

Bishop smiled. "I assume you will be taking a percentage?"

"A man has to turn a profit," said Heitz, and he named a ridiculous sum.

After that, it was all over but the haggling.

March let Bishop handle the negotiations, and he listened with half an ear as Bishop and Heitz argued for half an hour. Eventually, Heitz settled on a more reasonable price, and the two men shook hands.

"Excellent," said Bishop, getting to his feet. "For the practical portions of the operation, I shall turn things over to Captain March."

"I knew you were trouble," said Heitz.

"I've had a lot of practice at it," said March. "Let's get started at once. I want to move before the Graywolves realize that we're on to them."

BY MUTUAL AGREEMENT, March, Bishop, and Heath decided to leave Lady Roanna on the *Tiger*. March had become confident enough in Heath's abilities to invite him along, but he was also entirely certain that bringing Roanna Vindex anywhere near a firefight would be a bad idea. Fortunately, Bishop persuaded her to remain on the *Tiger* by giving her access to the communications channel they would use during the attack, allowing her to listen to the progress of the battle. He also promised that if Lord Thomas wasn't in the prefab building, she could listen to the interrogation of any captured Graywolves. March wasn't sure of the wisdom of that, but he knew he could not have persuaded Roanna to remain on the ship. Fortunately, Bishop was eloquent when necessary.

An hour later Heitz returned with twenty men in the black jumpsuits of Ronstadt Private Security Corporation. March looked them over with a critical eye. They were the usual assortment that turned up in a private mercenary force. Some of them looked little better than thugs, and others had the brittle bluster he associated with men who had been unable to make the cut for one military force or another. Nevertheless, a few of them looked like veterans, though they had likely ended up with Ronstadt due to a dishonorable discharge.

Their commander, however, seemed competent. He was a middle-aged man with graying brown hair and a pronounced paunch, but March watched as he surveyed the room for potential threats, and his weapons looked simple and effective, rather than the ostentatious pistols and rifles preferred by less reliable mercenaries. Unless March missed his guess, the man had once been a member of the Calaskaran Royal Marines. His cold brown eyes flicked over Heath, and then March, and one of his eyebrows rose as he considered March's gloved left hand.

The Ronstadt men sat down to lunch, which March noted that Bishop did not provide for free. Bishop, Heitz, March, Heath and the commander took a table in the corner. Anne approached with a tray of sandwiches, winked at March, and then returned to the bar.

"Think the girl likes you, March," said Heitz, helping himself to two sandwiches.

"Then she's got poor taste in men," said March. "Who's your friend?"

"This is Site Supervisor Karlman," said Heitz, gesturing at the commander. "He's in charge of the Ronstadt personnel on Rustbelt Station." He took a bite of a sandwich, and then waved it in March's general direction. "Karlman, this is Captain March of the *Tiger* and his associate Mr. Heath." Heath bristled a little at the omission of his rank but he knew enough not to protest.

"He looks like a Navy boy," said Karlman. "He's the one who's supposed to be in charge?"

"No," said Bishop. "That's Captain March."

Karlman considered March for a moment. "That a Machinist prosthesis under that glove, Captain?"

"Yep," said March.

Karlman grunted. "Fought some Iron Hands once. Hell of battle. I wouldn't like to do that again." He looked at Bishop. "You sure you can trust him?"

"I have personally seen him kill several Machinist agents with that prosthesis," said Bishop.

Karlman laughed. "In our line of work, I suppose that qualifies as a credential." He stuck out his right hand. "Robert Karlman, site supervisor for Rustbelt Station." March shook his hand, as did Heath. "Administrator Heitz says we have some troublemakers that need to disappear quietly."

"Graywolves mercenaries," said March. "A dozen of them. They're doing dirty work for the Machinists, and I think they have a high-value hostage. We need to eliminate them, rescue the hostage, and take as many prisoners as possible."

Karlman rubbed his chin. "For interrogation in case we can't find the hostage?"

"Right," said March. "If they play ball, I'll drop them off someplace neutral. If they don't cooperate, they disappear."

Karlman did not seem to find this disagreeable. "How many are we talking?"

"A dozen," said March. "They're holed up in Ore Complex 5. I can send you the video. They've got a pair of security drones, are armed with plasma guns and fully auto-matic firearms. I want to jam them so they can't warn their friends, and then gas them."

"Video?" said Karlman.

March drew out his phone, and Karlman produced a chunky tablet from his belt. March sent the video file of Ore Complex 5, along with a map, and Karlman spent a few moments reviewing the data. Heath watched him with tense eagerness. March busied himself by eating a sandwich. For spaceport food, it wasn't bad.

"It should be doable if we have surprise," said Karlman. "I've got a man named Trevor who's good with signals equipment. He should be able to jam their transmissions. I've also got access to knockout gas for riot control. It won't last long, and it will dissipate quickly, but it will last long enough for us to get some prisoners."

"What's the delivery mechanism?" said March.

"Grenades," said Karlman. He squinted at his tablet's screen. "Heavier than air, so we'll fire it at the wall right over their heads. I've got two men who are decent with rifles at a distance, so we'll take out the security drones at the same time. Hit them hard and hit them fast."

"You trust your men?" said March.

"Not particularly," said Karlman. "We'll need to do this fast before someone can spill the beans. I'll have to pick someone to spearhead the attack once the gas goes in."

"I'll do it," said March.

"You?" said Heitz, lifting his eyebrows as he chewed on a bite of sandwich. "You can do that all by yourself?"

"Yes," said March, meeting his gaze.

Heitz and Karlman stared at him for a moment.

At last Karlman shrugged. "If he gets himself killed, do we still get paid?"

"Yeah," said Heitz.

"Suit yourself," said Karlman, setting down his tablet and reaching for a sandwich.

"I'll cover you," said Heath.

"You might do better taking out the security drones," said March.

Karlman started to speak, but Heath answered first.

"No," said Heath. "Supervisor Karlman will want his own men to cover the security drones. The gas won't affect those things, and if they get loose, they're dangerous. He won't want a stranger covering the drones."

"He doesn't," agreed Karlman.

"I did get my marksman certification in the Navy," said Heath.

"All right," said March. He was reasonably sure Heath would not accidentally shoot him. It also gave Heath something useful to do that would keep him away from Lady Roanna.

"Gentlemen, I believe we have a plan," said Karlman. "When do you want to roll?"

"Now," said March, getting to his feet "Have your men waiting outside Ore Complex 5 in one hour's time with their equipment. Mr. Heath and I will meet you there."

MARCH AND HEATH stopped by the *Tiger* long enough to tell the plan to Lady Roanna and to arm themselves from the ship's store of personal weapons.

"Good God," said Heath, blinking as March opened the door to the armory. "How many guns do you have?"

"Not enough," said March.

The armory was a small room just off the dorsal

corridor from the flight cabin, which would let March quickly retrieve armaments if the ship was ever boarded. Metal shelves lined the walls, and handguns, rifles, grenades, ammunition, knives, mines, and still more ammunition filled the shelves, all of it labeled and organized.

"You could arm a Royal Army battalion with just the stuff in here," said Heath.

"I'm a Silent Order operative, so I need weapons," said March, taking a tactical harness from the wall and handing it to Heath. "My cover story is that I'm a privateer operating in the wild systems at the fringes of the Kingdom and the other major interstellar powers. To maintain my cover story, I need lots of weapons."

"Flawless logic," said Heath. "You don't have any powered armor, do you?"

"No," said March. "The maintenance workshop for the damned things would take up half the cargo bay."

He took off his coat, pulled on a tactical harness, and started arming himself. A handgun went on each hip, knives up each of his sleeves, and a set of grenades clipped to his harness. For his main weapon, he took a plasma rifle, its capacitator rated for a hundred and sixty rounds, and it would fire single-shot, semi-automatic, and full automatic. He also claimed a stun pistol, a compact boxy thing that looked like a small black plastic brick on a handgun grip. It had a shorter range than he would have liked, but the energy bolt it discharged would temporarily scramble a human nervous system, which would prove useful for taking prisoners.

"What should I take?" said Heath, eyeing the weapons.

"Help yourself," said March, stepping back.

Heath only took one pistol, one knife, and a pair of

grenades. He lifted a Royal Armaments Shadow-class sniper rifle from the rack and looked it over.

"You know how to use one of those things?" said March.

In answer, Heath ejected the power cartridge, opened the maintenance ports, and checked the power coil, the particle accelerator, and the waste energy discharge vane.

"Guess so," said Heath.

"Ever kill anyone with one of those?" said March.

Heath hesitated. "Couple of times, yeah. Once when we were boarded by pirates on my first tour. Another time when we were skirmishing with some Machinist trouble-makers." He smiled. "No Iron Hands in that battle. Just the usual drone soldiers. But this isn't my first action."

"Good," said March. He reached onto a shelf and handed another stun pistol to Heath. "Take one of these, too. You'll be doing distance attacks, but you never know when things can go wrong. Range is only thirty or forty feet, but if Lord Thomas isn't with the Graywolves, we'll need to beat it out of the prisoners."

Heath took the pistol without protest. "We should say goodbye to Lady Roanna before we go."

March grunted. "You sure?"

"You don't like her very much," said Heath.

"I like her just fine," said March, thinking of the kiss. He pushed it out of his head. "I also like alcohol just fine. Too much of it makes trouble."

"Did you just compare a noblewoman of Calaskar to...a strong drink?" said Heath.

"You tell me," said March. "I'm not the one who went AWOL for her."

Heath grimaced but conceded the point with a nod.

"Let's check in," said March. "We'll need to make sure she's on the communications channel anyway."

Heath nodded and followed March from the armory, their boots clanking on the deck. The galley door was open, and Roanna sat at the table, typing at a laptop computer. She had claimed an additional monitor out of the *Tiger*'s engine room and plugged it into the computer. An array of cargo manifests scrolled past on the display. Roanna rose as they entered, her eyes wide. A pistol rested at her hip. March had given her one in case the enemy boarded the *Tiger*.

"It's time?" she said.

"Yes," said March. He glanced at the computer. "You're keyed into our communications channel for the battle. Don't interrupt us unless it's necessary. Vigil will keep an eye on the exterior of the ship." It had occurred to him that Lorre might use the distraction of the battle to try and kidnap Roanna. At the moment, the *Tiger* was the safest place on Rustbelt Station for Roanna Vindex. Vigil would monitor the exterior of the ship continuously, and if any attackers approached, the pseudointelligence could raise the kinetic and the radiation shields and use the laser turrets to fight back.

"I will remain on the ship until you return," said Roanna. "If...you don't return..."

"If I don't return," said March, "either Heath or Bishop will come for you, or if we're all killed, whoever Bishop had designated as his successor as head for this branch of the Silent Order." That might have been a little harsh, because she went pale. "But one of us should return."

Roanna nodded and recovered the poise of a Calaskaran noblewoman. "Good luck, Captain March." Her eyes shifted to Heath, and she smiled a little. "And you, Lieutenant Heath."

He hesitated and offered her a bow. "Thank you, my lady."

That seemed to hurt her a little, but she didn't push it. Perhaps she had realized that she had led him on, or how much a conviction for going AWOL would damage his life.

"God be with you," said Roanna, and she seated herself at the computer, staring at the displays.

Heath looked at her, took a deep breath, and then turned. "I'm ready," he said.

"Good," said March. "Let's move."

He led the way from the ship, sealed the ramp behind him, and they headed for Ore Complex 5.

MARCH AND HEATH arrived in the gloomy main corridor of Ore Complex 5 first, and Karlman and his troops showed up a few moments later.

The Ronstadt men had donned body armor over their black jumpsuits, layered plates of ceramic and metal that could absorb a few plasma bolts or high-caliber rounds before disintegrating. All the men carried automatic plasma rifles of roughly the same configuration as March's, though a few of the men had more specialized equipment – grenade launchers, radio jammers, and high-end sniper rifles. To March's relief, the Ronstadt men moved with a reasonable modicum of stealth. He would have preferred that they were quieter since sound carried a long way in these asteroid tunnels (assuming they were properly pressurized), but they were quieter than he would have expected.

"Captain March," said Karlman. "I'm glad we could join you. What's the situation?"

"We just got here," said March "I'm going to go have a look around, see if anything has changed. I suggest you set up your equipment and get ready. I'll be back in a few minutes. Heath, stay here." Heath nodded and moved near one of the walls as the Ronstadt men began setting up their signal jammer.

March walked back to the double doors leading to the main chamber holding the dead smelting furnaces. He had wrenched open the doors during his last visit here, and they had not moved since. March paused long enough to check the doors for traps or any security tripwires but found nothing.

Sloppy. The Graywolves should have patrolled the complex again by now. Then again, reputable mercenary companies would not work for the Machinists. March slipped through the doors and into the vast, gloomy chamber. Nothing had changed since his last visit. The Graywolves still stood guard around the prefab building, nearly a dozen of them. The security drones had not moved. March took a moment to scan the vast chamber, looking for hidden traps and cameras, but nothing seemed out of place.

Either the Graywolves had gotten complacent, or this was an excellent trap.

There was only one way to find out.

He slipped back through the doors and into the corridor. The Ronstadt men had finished setting up their equipment and were ready for action. The mercenaries had donned gas masks and goggles, giving their faces an insect-like look. One of the men was operating a jamming device, typing commands into an attached laptop computer, while two of the mercenaries held launchers loaded with gas grenades.

"Better sync your earpiece to our frequency," said Karlman, his voice rendered metallic by his mask. "Our jammer blocks the entire radio spectrum, but it does have a rotating window of variable frequencies that allows us to communicate."

"Right," said March. "Heath, do it too." Heath nodded and donned his own gas mask and goggles, syncing his earpiece to the jammer, and March followed suit. The gas mask and its attached cylindrical respirator felt tight against his mouth and nose, the straps digging into the back of his neck, and the goggles were heavy. He had a feeling of asphyxiation, and then the goggles flicked on as he took a breath of odorless, dry air. Enhanced images scrolled across the goggles, along with environmental and targeting information.

"Ready?" said Karlman.

"Ready," said March. "Have your men set up, and for God's sake keep it quiet."

They slipped through the doors one by one, working with reasonable silence. The snipers set up, putting their rifles on tripods and calibrating their scopes. The men with the grenade launchers aimed the weapons at the prefab building. The rest of the Ronstadt men filed through, save for those assigned to guard the man operating the jamming machine. Heath slipped through the doors and put his back to the wall next to the Ronstadt snipers, adjusting his own rifle.

"All right," said March in a quiet voice. "I'm going to get into position. Switch on the jammer when I send word, and then fire the gas grenades. I'll neutralize as many of the guards as I can. Remember to use non-lethal force if possible."

"It's your money," said Karlman with placid calm. "Or Bishop's, anyway. Good luck, Captain March."

"You too," said March. He nodded to Heath, put his rifle

in its harness across his back, drew his stun pistol, and glided forward.

March moved with absolute silence through the vast chamber, using the abandoned machines and carts as cover. The stealth training of the Final Consciousness had been brutal and efficient, with punishments administered for every failure, and the skill would remain with him until his death. It pleased him to know that he was now using the skills the Machinists had given him to hinder their purposes.

Step by silent step he moved closer through the old mining equipment, and then ducked under a conveyor belt that had once carried chunks of ore quarried from the asteroid's heart into the smelting furnaces. He crawled through the rock dust and then got back to his feet, crouching behind another cart.

He was only about thirty meters from the prefab building. Any closer and the security drones would almost certainly detect him. In fact, they could have already detected him but might have lacked the necessary logic capabilities to conclude he was a threat until he took a hostile action. A dozen Graywolves stood in clumps before the squat rectangle of the prefab building, speaking to each other in low voices. They were not paying attention, no doubt trusting in the security drones to alert them of danger.

It was as close as he was going to get.

He tapped his earpiece.

"I'm in," he whispered. "Karlman, start the jamming."

"Acknowledged," said Karlman.

There was a burst of static in his ear, and then Karlman's voice came a moment later, with an odd resonance from the modulation program.

"Snipers and grenadiers in position," said Karlman. "Firing in five, four, three, two, one...firing!"

A lot of things happened at once.

The Ronstadt snipers knew their business. There was a flash of plasma bolts, and suddenly both security drones twitched, charred craters appearing in their centers of mass. The Graywolves started to turn, frowning in confusion, and the grenadiers fired. Both grenades exploded with a flash and a bang over their heads, but nothing else happened. The gas contained within the grenades was invisible.

But it was fast-acting. Four of the Graywolves dropped at once, their eyes rolling into their heads as they collapsed. Four more reeled on their feet, staggering. They must have only gotten a partial dose, but the gas would take effect before much longer.

Four of the Graywolves had avoided the gas entirely and had enough presence of mind to snap masks to their faces, raising their rifles as they did.

March was already moving.

He seized the side of the mining cart with his left hand, using its cybernetic strength to heave himself over the vehicle. March hit the ground running, taking aim with the stun pistol as he did so.

The Graywolves, panicked by the sudden attack, did not see him coming until he was ten meters away and firing. A flash of blue light from the stun pistol and one of the Graywolves collapsed. The remaining three men started shooting at him, and March ducked, throwing himself to the side of the prefab building. Plasma bolts passed him, tearing chunks from the prefab wall and molten chips from the stone floor.

March dropped his stun pistol, yanked the rifle from his

harness, flipped the selector to full auto, and spun around the corner.

They had enough prisoners.

He squeezed the trigger, the emitter flashing as the accelerator hurled charged plasma particles. The bolts hit two of the Graywolves, sending their corpses to the ground. The third Graywolf mercenary jumped around the corner, rifle flashing. March dodged, his left hand seizing the barrel of his enemy's rifle and slamming it against the wall hard enough to shatter both the weapon and the mercenary's wrist. His right hand hit the mercenary in the head three times. On the third blow, the mercenary collapsed.

March stepped away from the wall and dropped the ruined rifle just as the Ronstadt men rushed to the prefab building. At Karlman's command, they produced handcuffs and started securing the stunned Graywolves, binding their hands and taking their equipment.

"Good God, man," said Karlman, striding forward with a rifle in hand. "Four of them at once?"

"I was in a hurry," said March, striding to the prefab building's door.

He hit the lock four times with his left hand, and it shattered. His metal fingers gripped the door and ripped it aside, and he strode into the building, leading with his rifle as he checked the corners.

The building was one room, long and rectangular. There was a computer desk in one corner, and racks of rifles lined the walls. A chemical commode occupied another corner, and crates of supplies stood on the wall opposite the rifle racks.

There was absolutely no sign of Thomas Vindex.

ANNOTATIONS ON SILENT ORDER: IRON HAND CHAPTER 7

Heitz's men begin interrogating the mercenaries, who are more than willing to share what they know in exchange for leniency. From the prisoners, March learns that Thomas Vindex is being held in Dome 12 on Rustbelt Station. However, March realizes that the mercenaries have been infected with Machinist nanobots, which then kill them and transform their corpses into infiltrator drones. (We mentioned those earlier in this book in the chapter on descriptions.) March, Bishop, Heath, Heitz, and Roanna barely manage to escape from the infiltrator drones with their lives.

After their escape, Simon Lorre contacts March, telling him it is time they had a little chat.

This chapter is an excellent example of both rising action and unexpected complications. March didn't expect the mercenaries to be infected with infiltrator nanobots and was nearly killed as a result.

SILENT ORDER IRON HAND CHAPTER 7: INTERROGATION

To March's complete lack of surprise, Administrator Heitz had a black site for dealing with undesirables.

He had encountered this before when dealing with security forces on the fringes of the great starfaring powers, where laws were lax, authority was distant, and the local officials could get away with a lot so long as they kept it quiet. Local officials in backwaters like Rustbelt Station tended towards the thuggish, and invariably had black sites where they could imprison undesirables, conduct interrogations, and do business under the table.

Administrator Heitz was no exception.

His black site was an abandoned hydroponics bay about forty kilometers from any of Rustbelt Station's landing bays, making it harder for any prisoners to escape. The Ronstadt men had bound and hooded the surviving Graywolves mercenaries, and packaged them up for transportation to the hydroponics station. March and Heath rode with them on the station's cargo lift system, guns trained on the prisoners. The cargo lift took them to the hydroponic station in ten minutes, shooting through the tunnels on magnetic rails, and the Ronstadt men unloaded the hooded and shackled prisoners, urging them none too gently into the hydroponics bay.

March left the cargo lift and looked around the bay, his weapons ready. It was a long rectangular room carved from the rock of the asteroid, with harsh white lights shining overhead. Hydroponics tubs stood in orderly rows, empty and cold, and a maze of tubes and cables covered the walls and ceiling. Heitz and Ronstadt Corporation had modified the bay, and a row of cells with heavy steel doors stood on one side of the room.

"How often do you have that many prisoners?" said March to Karlman.

"Hardly ever," said Karlman. "But it does come in handy when we need it." Each Graywolf mercenary was shoved into a cell and cuffed to the walls, the hoods and handcuffs still in place. He pointed at a balcony that ran the length of the room, with doors opening into small rooms on the side. "Heitz is waiting for you in room five."

"Thanks," said March. He walked to a grillwork stair and climbed to the balcony. The doors on the wall looked like they led to offices and administration rooms once used by the hydroponic workers. March opened the fifth door and stepped into a conference room. Once it had been opulent, but now the carpet was faded and worn, and the table looked dingy and battered. Heitz sat at the table, smoking a cigar, a battered laptop computer before him.

"Well, well," said Heitz. "Captain March. I knew you were trouble, but I'm glad you aimed the trouble at the other side."

"That's my job," said March.

Heitz grinned around his cigar and blew out a cloud of smoke. "Graywolf prisoners to interrogate and not a single Ronstadt man lost. If we avoid having to pay any death bonuses this year, we'll be able to negotiate a lower rate on the security contract for next year."

"No sign of the hostage," said March.

Heitz shrugged. March knew he didn't care that much, so long as none of the blame for Thomas Vindex's misadventures landed on his shoulders. "Well, we've got nine prisoners. We'll beat it out of one of them." His phone chirped, and he pulled it out of his jacket pocket. "Bishop's on his way down." He glanced at Heath. "Bringing your girlfriend, too."

"She's not my girlfriend," said Heath.

"Bad idea, getting women mixed up in this," said Heitz, taking another draw of his cigar. "When it comes to interrogation, women either have no stomach for it, or they're way too vicious."

"It wasn't my idea," said March. "I'll meet her and Bishop and bring them here."

"Do that," said Heitz. He waved a thick hand at the window behind him. "I'll have Karlman set up for interrogations next door. We can watch from the conference room. Sooner or later, we'll figure out what happened to your hostage."

March nodded and went through the door, Heath following him. Four Ronstadt men approached, escorting one of the Graywolf prisoners, and March and Heath stepped aside to let them pass. They disappeared into the office next to the conference room. Bishop and Roanna hadn't arrived yet, so March leaned against the railing, looking over the derelict hydroponics bay. Once it had grown food, and now it was a deserted room full of failed machinery, which put him in mind of his childhood home. The thought made him grim, so he put it aside.

"Are they going to torture the Graywolves?" said Heath.

"Probably not," said March, not looking at the younger man. "Doubt there will be a need. See how they're cooperating? They haven't tried any trouble yet. They know the game. They'll tell us what we need to know, and then we'll dump them on a neutral world somewhere."

"And if they don't cooperate?" said Heath.

March shrugged. "Then I'll get it out of them myself."

"Torture is illegal in Calaskar," said Heath.

March let out a short laugh. "Yes. So are several other things we've done in the last few days. Out here, there aren't really any laws. You can do what you want, so long as you can endure the consequences. A place like Rustbelt Station is where you see what a man really is. Out here, your only guide is your conscience and your duty."

They stood in silence for a while.

"You're a hard man, Captain," said Heath.

March grunted. "Yes, I am. Can't deny that. But someone has to do what needs to be done." He flexed his metal fingers beneath the glove. "I'm better equipped for it than most people. Might as well be me."

"Why?" said Heath.

"Why what?" said March.

"Why did you join the Silent Order?" said Heath.

March almost told him to shut up. Yet, to his surprise, he found himself talking. No one could overhear them here, for one. Heath had handled himself well during the fight, so maybe he deserved to know. Or perhaps the hydroponics bay had put March into a melancholy mood.

"I was born on Calixtus," said March. "Suppose you

know what happened there. Poor colony world and the Machinists came in and took over. It became one of the slave worlds of the Final Consciousness. I grew up in a labor camp. Eventually, I was tested for compatibility, and then I was joined to the Final Consciousness."

"And you became an Iron Hand," said Heath.

"Yeah," said March. "I did. For years I was an Iron Hand. I did the Machinists' dirty work, and I heard the Final Consciousness in my thoughts the entire time."

"What's it like?" said Heath. "Being part of the Final Consciousness, I mean. They...say it's like slavery, like you're a puppet with strings on your arms."

"It is," said March, voice distant. "But you don't know it at the time. You don't realize it. Imagine everyone you ever knew, everyone you ever cared about. Imagine they all are talking in your head at the same time, and they all agree, and they all want you to do something. That's what being part of a hive mind is like. You're still an individual, but it's like you've got God in your head, and he's there telling you what to do."

"It's...like social pressure, is that it?" said Heath.

"Sort of," said March. "If you want to look at it like that, social pressure is like aspirin. The Final Consciousness is the finest nanotech-refined morphine."

"Why did you leave?" said Heath.

"Martel's World," said March.

Heath hesitated. "You...were part of the bombing?"

March snorted. "No. I missed it. That was why I left."

He fell silent. Heath waited. March sighed and kept talking.

"When the Machinists occupied Martel's World, I was part of the occupation force," said March. "During one of the riots, I was wounded and separated from my unit. When

I woke up, I was in one of the slum apartments. I thought they would kill me. Instead, the family that lived there cared for me until the nanotech regenerated enough for me to walk."

"Why?" said Heath.

March stared at the far wall. "They said they were members of the Royal Calaskaran Church, that God commanded them to look after everyone who needed help, even their enemies. Like the parable of the Good Samaritan. You know what happened then. The Royal Calaskaran Navy took the system, and rather than let the Kingdom have Martel's World, the Machinists bombed it from orbit. Killed every last man, woman, and child. After that, I knew I was done. I left the Machinists, killed a bunch of them in the process, and joined the Silent Order. Been pretending to be a privateer ever since."

They stood in silence for a while.

"Hell of a story," said Heath.

"Mmm. Most of it is technically classified. Tell anyone, and I'll have to kill you."

Heath laughed. "I might be an idiot around women, but I'm a loyal Kingdom man." He sighed. "Even if I am going to get a dishonorable discharge."

"Depends on how this turns out," said March. "We come back with the Vindex twins, the Earl of Sundrex would probably put in a good word for you. I might, too."

"You would?" said Heath.

"Depends on how this turns out."

Heath laughed again. "Fair enough."

March heard the whirring noise as the lift slowed. "Speaking of things that make men into idiots, your girlfriend's here."

"For God's sake," said Heath. "She's not my girlfriend. She threw herself at you, not me."

March supposed it was a good sign that Heath could joke about that.

He watched as the lift door opened and Bishop and Lady Roanna stepped out of the car. Bishop strolled into the hydroponics bay with confidence, but Roanna hesitated for a half-step. She had likely realized that she was the only woman in a room full of men comfortable with violence and breaking the law. Then the cool mask fell back over her features, and she followed Bishop.

March kept himself from laughing. Whatever else Roanna Vindex was, she was no coward.

He waved to them, and Bishop and Roanna climbed up to the balcony, the grillwork clanking beneath their boots.

"Charming place, isn't it?" said Bishop.

"If you get bored," said Heath, "you can try to grow some food down there. Save on costs at your restaurant."

Bishop laughed. "Freighter crewers don't have terribly discriminating palettes."

"Captain March," said Roanna. "Do any of these men have knowledge of the whereabouts of my brother?"

"Don't know," said March, "but we're going to find out. This way." He hesitated. "Sure you want to see this? Might get messy."

She met his eye. "I've come this far."

March nodded and led the way into the conference room. Heitz and Karlman sat at the table, facing one of the mirrored windows. Beyond the glass, March saw a room about the size of Bishop's office. A chair rested in the center of the room, and in the chair sat one of the Graywolf mercenaries. The mercenary had been stripped to his underwear, but he looked uninjured, and he seemed to be talking freely to the three Ronstadt men surrounding him.

"Ah, good," said Heitz. "Listen to this."

Roanna hesitated a little at the sight of the stripped man, but sat down and folded her hands on the table. Bishop sat next to her, but March and Heath remained standing. Heitz hit a sequence on his keyboard, and voices crackled over the speakers in the ceiling.

"Tell me more," said one of the Ronstadt men. "Cooperate and it will..."

"Yeah, yeah, I know the drill," said the Graywolf. "I didn't get paid enough to die. Drop me off on a neutral world, and I'll tell you whatever you want to know."

"Very good," said the Ronstadt interrogator. He was middle-aged, brusquely efficient, and his nameplate read WILSON. "So what do you think I want to know, Mr. Rockwell?"

Rockwell, presumably the name of the Graywolf mercenary, smirked. "You want to know about that Calaskaran noble, right?"

Roanna sat up a little straighter.

"Why don't you tell us all about him?" said Wilson.

"It's like this," said Rockwell. "You might have guessed we do a little dirty work for the Machinists on the side from time to time. It's illegal in the Kingdom of Calaskar and a bunch of other starfaring nations, but we're operating out of neutral space, so it's totally legal." Wilson ignored that hole in Rockwell's argument but let the Graywolf keep speaking. "Anyway, we got hired by this Machinist agent. Ugly bastard with a scar on his face, but he had money."

Wilson touched his tablet and turned it towards Rockwell, and March caught a glimpse of Simon Lorre's scarred face from the images that he had provided to Heitz and Karlman. "Was this him?"

"Yep," said Rockwell. "Like I said, ugly bastard. But his money was good, and he paid well, so the captain said we'd take his job. We flew out to Tamlin's World and picked up the noble. Arrogant little shit, let me tell you. Kept blathering on about his rank and position and how his daddy would make us regret this." He let out a nasty laugh. "Lucky for him the Machinists wanted him in once piece. Else we would have beat some respect into him."

Roanna looked appalled. Though given some of Thomas Vindex's poor choices, perhaps a beating would have been good for him.

"Where is he?" said Wilson.

"Suppose that's what you really want to know," said Rockwell. "All right, I'll play. The plan was to get a big ransom for him from his sister, right? Well, the Machinist agent figured the sister would show up. Then we'd take her, take the ransom, keep the brother, and then sell them both to the highest bidder."

Roanna said nothing, but March saw the knuckles shine white against her folded hands.

"A little treacherous, isn't it?" said Wilson.

Rockwell shrugged. "It's business. The Machinist bastard paid well enough, so he called the shots. We smuggled ourselves aboard the station, set up a temporary barracks in Ore Complex 5, and waited for the noble bitch to show up with her money."

"Once you had her, what were your instructions?" said Wilson.

"We were to take her to one of the old residence domes, one of the abandoned ones," said Rockwell.

"Which one?" said Wilson.

"Dome 12," said Rockwell. "The Machinist agent is waiting there." March felt the fingers of his left hand curl into a metal fist. "He's got a ship tucked away there, a little gunship that we carried on board our freighter when we sneaked onto this hole of a station. Figure he'll load up the nobles, pay us, and fly off." He snorted. "At least that was the plan."

"We'll have to confirm that, you realize," said Wilson.

"Yeah, yeah," said Rockwell. "You can give the others the same treatment, they'll all tell you the same thing. Maybe with more swearing."

"Very well," said Wilson, and he stepped off to the side with the other Ronstadt men, speaking in low voices.

"We've got him, then," said Heitz with satisfaction.

"You know where this Dome 12 is, then?" said Roanna.

Heitz scowled and started to say something acerbic, then thought better of it and spoke in a calmer voice. "It's one of the oldest residential domes on the station, left over from the first mines. No one's been in there for years. At least no one's supposed to have been in there for years."

"We'll need to confirm this," said Bishop.

"No problem," said Karlman. "We can keep the Gray-wolves confined for a few days if necessary. If their information turns out to be accurate, we can dump them on the next ship heading for a neutral world. Getting home is their problem after that."

"I can confirm it," said March. "I'll take a look, and from there we can decide what to do."

Bishop grunted and looked at Heitz. "We might need to hire your men again."

Heitz smiled. "Of course. It will cost you, though."

Bishop sighed. "Of course."

They started haggling. March paced around the back wall of the conference room, lost in thought as he considered his next course of action. It was entirely possible that Simon Lorre was holed up in Dome 12 alone, or with only a few guards. Perhaps March could slip in, rescue Thomas Vindex, and then escape with the nobleman.

Or perhaps he could slip into the dome, shoot Lorre in the head, and then escape with Thomas.

That seemed like the better course of action, if possible.

Lorre had caused a great deal of trouble for the Silent Order, and March did not spare Machinist agents if he could help it...

He frowned.

There was something wrong with the wall.

The wall had been carved from the rock of the asteroid, but pipes and ducts ran along its surface. The metal of the pipes and ducts had been...corroded, somehow, with dozens of tiny holes dotting their surface like the holes in expensive cheese. It didn't look like rust or chemical damage, or any sort of corrosive effect. The edges of the holes were smooth as a river-rounded rock.

The bits of metal had just disappeared.

"What is it?" said Heath, watching March.

"I've seen this before," said March.

"Ductwork?" said Heath, puzzled.

"No," said March, pointing at the pipe.

"It's corroded," said Heath, scowling. "This entire station is a deathtrap." He tapped the pipe with a finger, expecting it to collapse, and then blinked as nothing happened. "Huh. It's in better shape than it looked."

"I've seen that kind of damage before," said March, a cold fist gripping his chest. Maybe the damage was isolated.

Maybe someone else had used this old hydroponics bay as a base before Heitz had taken it over.

But if not...

March crossed to the window. Rockwell sat in his chair, looking bored, while Wilson and the other Ronstadt men continued their discussion. Right away March spotted what he was looking for. The interrogation room had metal paneling – and some of the panels were dotted with more of the small rounded holes.

"Hell," muttered March.

"Something amiss, Captain March?" said Heitz with irritation.

"Yes," said March. "Did you record the interrogation?"

"We did," said Karlman.

"Go back to the beginning," said March. "Now. Right now."

Heitz scowled. "You don't give me..."

"Do as he says," said Bishop.

Heitz looked ready to protest, but Karlman reached over and tapped some keys on Heitz's laptop. March stooped over and looked at the screen. The timestamp in the lower right-hand corner of the video was from thirty-five minutes ago... and the metal panels in the interrogation room were still intact.

The small holes had only appeared in the last half hour.

"We have to go," said March, straightening up and lifting his rifle from its harness. "Now. Right now. We're about to come under attack from the Machinists. Karlman, get all your men to the lift, now. We need to get the hell out of here before it's too late."

"Wait, wait, wait," said Heitz, scrambling to his feet, his eyes on March's rifle. "Have you lost your mind? We need to finish interrogating the Graywolves."

"Leave them," said March. "They're already dead."

"What are you talking about?" said Karlman. "Speak plainly, man."

"Infiltrator nanobots," said March. "Lorre dosed his men with infiltrator nanobots."

Roanna, Heath, Heitz, and Karlman only looked confused. But Bishop surged to his feet, drawing his pistol, his eyes wide with sudden alarm.

"He's right," said Bishop. "We have to go now. Karlman, call..."

"What the hell?" came Wilson's voice from the speaker.

March looked through the window just as Rockwell's head fell off his shoulders and hit the floor.

There was no blood. When a man's head fell off, there ought to have been blood, but no blood came from either Rockwell's head or from the stump of his neck, only a little bubbling of thick black slime that wasn't actually slime, but the mineral-based byproduct of certain chemical reactions.

"What the hell?" said Wilson, taking a step back.

"Shoot him!" said March. He couldn't tell if Wilson and the Ronstadt men in the interrogation room could hear him. Both Heitz and Karlman were shouting. Likely they thought that someone had shot Rockwell, but March knew better. "Shoot him in the head and in the spine, and do it now! Now!"

The Ronstadt men didn't react. Or, rather, they reacted in exactly the wrong way. They moved to the walls, weapons drawn from the holsters as they scanned the doorway and the ceiling for whatever had just killed Rockwell.

"Sir!" said Wilson, his voice crackling over the speakers. "Sir, we have a situation! It..."

"Listen to me!" shouted March. "Shoot him in the head and in the spinal column!"

Right about then Roanna screamed as the headless corpse of Rockwell stood up.

As it did, the severed head rocked on the floor and then flipped over, metal legs like those of a spider sprouting from the neck. The head skittered back and forth on its metal legs, while the headless corpse ripped free of its restraints. The shredded handcuffs tore deep gashes on Rockwell's wrists and ankles, but again no blood came from the wounds, only a thick black slime.

"What the hell?" said Wilson.

"Shoot it in the spine!" said March. "Damn it, listen..."

The headless corpse moved in a blur, seizing the metal chair from the floor and swinging it like a club. The thick metal legs hit one of the Ronstadt men in the head with a sickening thump, and the soldier collapsed. Wilson managed to shoot Rockwell's corpse in the stomach, but the thing kept moving. It reached out and seized the neck of a second Ronstadt soldier and twisted, and the man fell dead to the floor. Wilson managed to shoot the headless corpse in the chest twice more, but it was useless. Rockwell's corpse grabbed Wilson's neck and killed him.

It had managed to dispose of all three Ronstadt men in the space of about forty seconds.

March's brain flashed through the tactical situation. There had been eight more Graywolves in the hydroponics bay proper, and he had to assume that they had all been compromised.

That meant the tactical situation was bad. Very, very bad.

Even as the thought crossed his mind, he heard screams and the sounds of gunfire from the hydroponics bay.

"Tell me what the hell is happening!" said Heitz. He had

produced a pistol from somewhere and was pointing it at nothing in particular.

"Machinist infiltrator drones," said March.

Something clanged on the balcony outside.

"Heath!" said March. "Secure the door! Quickly!"

"If there are more of those things outside my men will be trying to get in here," said Karlman.

"Your men are already dead," said March, "and we're next."

Heath ran to the door and locked it, and not a moment too soon. A half-second later there was a booming clang. A fist-shaped dent appeared, followed soon after by another.

The infiltrator drones were about to bash down the door.

Though March was more concerned about the one on the other side of the interrogation window.

"Somebody had better tell me what the hell is going on!" said Heitz.

March started to answer, but to his surprise, Heath spoke first.

"Infiltrator drones," said Heath. "Machinist technology. Someone dosed those Graywolves with infiltrator nanobots before we took them captive. They're one of the lowest levels of cybernetic drones the Final Consciousness deploys."

"That's where all those holes in the wall came from," said March, watching Rockwell's corpse move back and forth. The headless body was moving almost at random, but the head on its metal spider legs was staring right at the window. "The nanobots collect metal molecules to build cybernetic implants in the host bodies, and once they were ready, they killed their hosts and rewrote their DNA. They use the head as a scout and the body as light infantry. Brain and spinal cord serve as CPUs for the cybernetic systems."

Rockwell's body backed away from the window. "That's about to come through the window."

"What?" said Heitz, backing away to the far wall. If he had dared, March suspected that he would have used Roanna as a human shield. Heath, Bishop, and Karlman all leveled their weapons at the window.

"It's going to come through the window and kill us if it can," said March. "Aim for the head and the spinal column. If we destroy the brain and the spinal cord, the cybernetic components will lose their CPUs and go inert. Get..."

The body surged forward and smashed into the window with crushing force. The window had been made out of transparent metal, and the impact knocked it from the frame and into the conference room with a ringing clang. The body vaulted through the window and landed between March and the table, while the head skittered up and perched on the window frame, blank white eyes looking over the room.

March shot the head with his rifle, turning the brain into a smoking black crater. He knew the drones had developed a local network among themselves as soon as the conversion process had finished, which meant they could look out each other's' eyes. More to the point, it meant that Rockwell's head could not guide Rockwell's body.

Nevertheless, the body found March with ease.

Rockwell's right arm swung towards March's face with the force of an iron bar. His left arm snapped up and blocked the blow, and even through the cybernetic interface, he felt the impact. Yet the headless body overbalanced, and March sidestepped, hammering his boot heel into the back of the corpse's leg. The infiltrator drone stumbled and landed flat on its stomach, and March twisted, snapped his rifle up, and held down the trigger.

His first two shots slammed into Rockwell's back before the corpse reacted. It started to rise, but enough of the spinal column had been destroyed that the drone's responses time was down. March sprayed three more shots into its back, and the drone went motionless. He supposed he hadn't technically killed it, but it wouldn't be getting up ever again.

More banging came from the door to the balcony.

"Good shooting," said Karlman.

"Thanks," said March, looking at the door. "But another eight of those things are about to come at us." He looked at Heitz. "Is there another way out of this room? The ducts, maybe?"

"I...no, I don't think so," said Heitz. He had recovered himself, though he looked on the edge of terror. "This hydroponics bay was cut out of solid rock. The ducts aren't big enough for the girl, let alone the rest of us. There's no other way out."

Another dent appeared in the door, accompanied by the shriek of stressed metal. Sooner or later the pounding would rip the door right off its hinges, and then they would be swarmed. March could take three or four infiltrator drones in a straight fight, more if he destroyed their heads first. Eight at once would be a quick and painful death.

The door made a useful bottleneck. Against human opponents, that might have been decisive. Against the infiltrator drones of the Final Consciousness, it would be less of an advantage. It would take three to five hits to the spinal column to stop one of the infiltrator drones, and the only other way to shut down one of those machines of meat was to inflict enough physical damage that it could no longer move.

March's eyes flicked around the room, taking inventory

of their weapons. He knew what he carried, and what Heath carried. Heitz and Bishop both had pistols, as did Roanna, but he doubted Roanna had ever fired a weapon in anger. Karlman had a more impressive loadout of weaponry, and...

"Are those shaped grenades?" said March.

"Yes," said Karlman, his rifle pointed at the door. "Three of them. You can set the blast geometry..."

"Give them to me," said March, holding out his hand.

Karlman, to his credit, did not hesitate. March took all three grenades and set the controls, configuring them for a conical blast and a five-second fuse. He placed the grenades on the door, the metal quivering as the infiltrator drones hammered at it.

"I'm going to blast the door and go through it," said March. "When I do, run for the lift car. The blast will distract the drones, and I'll distract them even more. If I don't make it, get out of here."

"But..." said Roanna.

"Captain March knows what he is doing," said Bishop.

"Ready," said Karlman, pointing his rifle at the door.

March armed the grenades and stepped back, cradling his own rifle. He hoped the grenades were not defective. Otherwise, he was going to get a fatal blast of shrapnel in about three seconds...

The grenades went off with a roar and a flare of fire, and the explosion ripped the door and most of its frame from the wall and hurled them across the balcony, through the railing, and to the hydroponics bay below. The debris ripped through two infiltrator drones, tearing them to a pulp, and threw another two back, one falling to the floor, the other slamming into the damaged railing.

Their heads climbed up the walls, metal legs clinking against the stone.

"Go!" shouted March, and he leaped through the door, his rifle set to full auto.

The infiltrator drones on their feet were the priority, and March started with them. He shot two in short order, the end of his rifle spitting bolts of superheated plasma. A third infiltrator drone staggered towards him, and March kicked it in the leg, spun it around, and stitched up its back with a volley of plasma bolts.

Behind him, the balcony clanged as Heath, Bishop, Heitz, and Karlman ran for the stairs to the lift car, Heath helping Roanna along. One of the infiltrator drones lunged at them, but Heath shifted his sniper-rifle one handed and shot it three times through the spine. The infiltrator drone flipped over the railing and crashed into a row of hydroponic equipment.

Some part of March's mind noted that had been a hell of a shot.

The rest of him focused on staying alive.

He whirled and ran backward, spraying fire as he retreated. The explosion had done a lot of damage to the infiltrator drones, but most of them were on their feet, and nearly all of the head-spiders had survived. March shot two of the head-spiders, plasma bolts turning their skulls to charred debris, and took down another headless corpse. His rifle beeped empty as the capacitors went dry, and March yanked a grenade from his harness, turned, and ran.

The stairs to the lower level had come into sight when the grenade went off. The explosion echoed through the room, and March seized the railing, vaulted over it, and jumped. The arc of his leap carried him towards the wall, and he drove his left hand forward, his metal fingers scraping down the stone and slowing his descent enough that his legs absorbed the landing without shattering his knees and his ankles.

As he straightened up, he scanned the pipes running along the wall below the balcony, spotted the one he wanted, drew his pistol, and fired three times. The pipe ruptured on the third shot, and a thick cloud of greenish gas started to spew into the room.

The infiltrator drones scrambled towards him, ignoring the toxic gas spouting from the pipe.

"That stuff's toxic!" shouted Heitz as March ran towards the lift doors. Heath, Roanna, Bishop, Heitz, and Karlman had retreated into the lift car, and March was pleased to see that six of the Ronstadt security men had escaped as well. At least this wouldn't be a total slaughter.

"Yes," said March, stepping into the car and yanking a grenade from his harness. He set the fuse for five seconds. "Also flammable. Get out of here!"

Heath hit the car controls, and the doors slid shut two seconds before the headless corpses reached them. As the doors clanged shut, March armed the grenade and flicked it through the doors.

The lift car shot away down its tube, the engines whining to life.

About three seconds later March saw the flare of fiery light through the windows and felt the vibrating roar of the explosion as the hydroponics bay disappeared in a fireball. He feared that he had miscalculated, and that the explosion would disable to the lift car or damage the track, but the car did not slow, and soon the light and the vibration passed.

No one spoke for a while. March busied himself by returning his pistol to its holster and reloading his rifle.

"Oh my God," said Roanna, sinking into a seat. "Oh my

God. That was horrible. That was the worst thing I've ever seen in my life."

"You're only twenty-three," said March. "You'll have plenty of time to see worse things."

She gave him a stricken look.

"How did you know?" said Karlman. "If you hadn't warned us, we'd have been wiped out to a man."

"The holes in the metal," said March, letting out a long breath. "Lorre must have dosed the Graywolves with infiltrator nanobots. They lie dormant in the bloodstream until activated. Once they do, they gather metal from their environment, build cybernetic implants, and then kill their host. They turn their victims into sort of...machines of meat, with the hijacked brains and nervous systems acting as a computer. It's one of the Machinists' favorite tricks for covert ops. Dose some people with infiltrator nanobots, active the bots, and you have instant saboteurs."

"That's horrible," said Roanna.

"That isn't even the nastiest trick the Machinists have," said March. His voice was harsher than he would have liked, but he was not feeling generous. Her idiot brother had decided to run off and play politics with a Machinist cell, and a lot of men had gotten killed as a result. "That was nothing compared to what they can do. That was nothing, and it still killed eighteen men, maybe more. That's what the Machinists are really like. World after world of people enslaved or killed and turned into meat machines. That is..."

"Captain March," said Bishop in a quiet voice.

Roanna was on the edge of tears and the Ronstadt men themselves looked shocked. Not surprising, given that they had just seen several of their colleagues butchered. March rebuked himself. Losing his temper would accomplish nothing, and might endanger the mission.

"At least we know where the hostage is," said March. "Dome 12."

"You'll have our help when you go after this Lorre asshole," said Karlman.

"It'll cost you," said Heitz, scowling at the wall.

"You can charge him if you want, Heitz," snapped Karlman, "but the Machinists have killed Ronstadt men, and we don't forgive that."

"Thank you," said March. "My task is to rescue the hostage. If you want Lorre once we've rescued the hostage, you can have him, so long as he's dead when you're finished with him."

"All right, fine," said Heitz. "I won't stand in the way. Do whatever the hell you want. Just don't damage the station too much."

"Thank you for your approval, Administrator," said Karlman. He managed to keep the sarcasm out of his tone.

"We had better move at once," said Bishop. "Mr. Lorre hired the Graywolves, and once he realizes his trick with the nanobots failed to kill us, he..."

March's phone started chiming. He frowned and looked at the display. It was an urgent call from Vigil.

"What?" said March, tapping his earpiece.

"Captain March," said Vigil. "There is an encrypted call from an unknown location coming to the *Tiger*. There is an image with a recent timestamp attached to the call. Given its nature, I concluded that you should be informed at once."

March looked at his phone's screen again and swore.

"What is it?" said Bishop.

"You had better see this," said March, turning the screen towards them.

Roanna's hands flew to her mouth.

The picture showed Thomas Vindex sitting in a dusty room, a gag in his mouth, his wrists and ankles shackled to the chair. Blood trickled from his nose and lip, and his right eye was swollen shut.

March tapped his phone and accepted the call. "I'm listening."

"Captain March," said Simon Lorre. "I think it's time that we talked, don't you?"

ANNOTATIONS ON SILENT ORDER:
IRON HAND CHAPTER 8

Lorre presents March with an ultimatum – come alone with Roanna to Dome 12, or else he will kill Thomas. March agrees and leaves for Dome 12 with Roanna but prepares for treachery. He sends Heath to the Tiger and tells him to fly the ship around the station and take position outside of the dome. If there is any trouble, Heath will fire the Tiger's railgun on the dome.

March and Roanna proceed to Dome 12 and find Simon Lorre and Thomas Vindex. Unfortunately, Thomas has sided with Lorre, and points a gun at Roanna and tells her to surrender. Before Lorre jams their communications, March tells Heath to fire the Tiger's railgun in exactly ten minutes.

Chapter 8 is the final chapter of rising action and complications before we arrive at the climax. March faces one final nasty complication. Thomas Vindex isn't a hostage but a willing participant in Lorre's mysterious plan.

SILENT ORDER IRON HAND CHAPTER 8: NEGOTIATIONS

"That depends," said March. "What do you want to talk about?"

The others stared at him. He considered putting the phone on speaker but decided against it. Both Roanna and Heitz were worked up enough to interject themselves into the conversation, and March wanted to deal with Lorre alone. Besides, Vigil would record the conversation and March could play it for them later.

"We have matters of business to discuss, Captain March," said Lorre. "We are, after all, two professionals, so I imagine we have a great deal to talk about."

"Really," said March. "That's optimistic."

Roanna leaned forward. "I want to talk to Thomas."

Bishop hushed her, and Heath put his hand on her shoulder and eased her back.

"Ah, is that Lady Roanna Vindex?" said Lorre. "Such a lovely young woman. Family piety is a noble quality, wouldn't you say? Though the Final Consciousness shall make all such things obsolete when the revolution comes to Calaskar."

"Spare me the sermon," said March.

"Yes, you've heard them all and rejected them," said Lorre. "How you could be part of the Final Consciousness and then reject it...I am baffled. I am truly baffled."

March barked out a laugh. "You're a true believer? You seemed too cynical for that."

"And you are a true believer in the Kingdom of Calaskar and its Royal Church?" said Lorre. "I would have thought you too cynical for that, Captain March, but we both know that such cynicism is facile. We are both believers and soldiers in our causes. Some men fight with fleets of starships and plasma rifles. We fight with the tools of spycraft."

"Do you always talk so much?" said March.

"I do," said Lorre. "It is a failing of mine, but I only indulge it when I have the upper hand."

"You think you have the upper hand?" said March. Lorre might like to make speeches, but the man was too clever to indulge a passion for rhetoric if it might endanger himself. He was up to something.

"That is one of the matters we must discuss," said Lorre.

"Actually, there is one only thing to talk about," said March.

"Oh? Do enlighten me, Captain."

"Thomas Vindex," said March. "We know where you are. All your Graywolves are dead, and your trick with the infiltrator drones failed. Ronstadt Private Security Corporation wants your head for the men your drones killed, so I have all the troops I need to defeat you. So, you're going to let Vindex go. If you do it now and run to your ship, you might be able to escape before the station shoots you down."

"All that you say is true," said Lorre. "There is, however, one factor that you have overlooked."

"And that is?" said March.

"I have a gun to Lord Thomas's head," said Lorre, "and I fear my trigger finger is twitchy."

"A bad habit," said March. "Fire discipline is important."

"True," said Lorre, "but I haven't gotten to shoot anyone for days."

"You kill Vindex, and this will all have been for nothing," said March. "No ransom, nothing."

"Now, now, Captain March," said Lorre. "You've been in this business long enough to know that an operation can have levels of success. A ransom would have been nice, yes. But even if I shoot Vindex, I will have killed a nobleman of the Kingdom of Calaskar and kept an Alpha Operative of the Silent Order from more important tasks. A small victory, true. But wars are not won in a day, but with a thousand such small victories."

"So killing a young man will help bring about the victory of the Final Consciousness?" said March. "How noble."

"Sacrifices are necessary for the revolution," said Lorre, "necessary to create a unified and superior humanity free of class and rank and economics and religion."

"Good for you," said March.

"This is what you are going to do, Captain March," said Lorre. "You are going to take Lady Roanna, and you are going to come alone with her to Dome 12. You will order your allies and your men to hold back for thirty minutes. My sensors here are quite good, and if I detect anyone other than you and Lady Roanna approaching, I will kill Lord Thomas. Lady Roanna, of course, will bring the ransom with her."

"Those are unreasonable terms," said March. "Why should I agree to them?"

He already knew the answer.

"Because," said Lorre, "if you do not arrive within forty-five minutes of the end of this conversation, I shall kill Lord Thomas and depart. If I detect anyone other than you and Lady Roanna approaching, I shall kill Lord Thomas and depart. If I detect the station's weapon systems near Dome 12 coming online, I shall kill Lord Thomas and depart."

"Forty-five minutes?" said March. "That's tight. Our lift car won't even get back to the spaceport concourse for another four or five minutes."

"Well, then," said Lorre. "You had better hustle, hadn't you? Tick-tock, Captain March, tick-tock."

He ended the call.

March looked at his phone, swore in vexation, and shoved it back into his coat.

"Well?" said Bishop.

"That was Lorre," said March. "We've got forty-five minutes. If Lady Roanna, myself, and the ransom don't show up at Dome 12 before time runs out, he shoots the hostage." Roanna closed her eyes. "If anyone other than the two of us shows up, he shoots the hostage. If the station's defensive systems go online, he shoots the hostage. Probably wants to make sure he can launch and get to hyperspace before Heitz's people blow him out of the sky."

"He won't have time to calculate a proper hyperspace tunnel before the missiles come online," snarled Heitz.

"He won't need to," said Heath. "He can just do a short-distance jump, exit his tunnel a few tenths of a light-minute from the system, and calculate a proper jump from there. He probably has his navigation computer pre-programmed for the jump."

"And he's ready to jump," said Heitz, scowling at his phone. "An alert just came over the internal sensors. Dark matter radiation was detected in Dome 12. Lorre has a ship there, and its dark matter reactor is warming up. He'll be ready to go..."

"Long before forty-five minutes," said March.

"What are we going to do?" said Roanna.

They all looked at March. The expressions on the faces of the men were expectant. Roanna's face was pleading. She wanted March to find a way to save her brother.

"Cut our losses and blast Dome 12," growled Karlman.

"No!" said Roanna.

"I'm sorry, but the hostage...a relative of yours, I assume? The hostage is already dead," said Karlman. "Lorre probably killed him weeks ago. We know Lorre's ship is there, and Dome 12 is unused. Shoot five or six missiles into the dome and send him and his ship to hell."

"I'm not having you blast a hole in the station's infrastructure," said Heitz.

Karlman scowled. "I don't need your authorization. Ronstadt employees have been killed, and we will take revenge."

"Do that, and you might lose the contract for Rustbelt Station," snarled Heitz. "We..."

"Shut up, all of you," said March. "There's only one thing to do. Lady Roanna and I will go to Dome 12 with the ransom."

"That is walking into a trap," said Bishop. "You will probably get yourself killed."

"And you cannot put Lady Roanna at risk like this," said Heath. "She..."

"I put myself at risk, Sam," said Roanna in a quiet voice, staring at the deck. "I put myself at risk when I decided to come out here, and I convinced you to put yourself at risk as well. At least this way only Captain March and I will put ourselves in danger."

"But..." said Heath.

"There is something you can do," said March. "Can you fly a Mercator Foundry Yards Class 9 light freighter with some engine and thruster modifications?"

Heath looked at him. "I can fly anything."

March nodded and hit his earpiece. "Vigil?"

"Captain March," said the pseudointelligence.

"Lieutenant Heath will be coming to the *Tiger*," said March. "You're to permit him full flight and weapons control."

"Acknowledged, Captain March," said Vigil.

"You're letting me fly your ship?" said Heath.

"Yup," said March. "Launch and stay close to the surface of the asteroid, but get a weapons lock on Dome 12 with the railgun. I'll keep an open call to you. If I give the word, fire at the apex of the dome. Understand?"

Heath gave a slow nod. "I do."

"Won't Lorre detect the launch?" said Bishop.

"Not necessarily," said Heitz. "So long as you don't start the dark matter reactor, and so long as you stay within fifty meters of the asteroid's surface, whatever sensors Lorre has on his ship won't register you as a threat. Probably peg you as a maintenance drone."

"Good," said March. He looked back at Heath. "You can run the ion thrusters and the railgun's coil off the fusion reactor. Get a target lock on Dome 12, and fire if I tell you to do it."

"What's that railgun of yours fire?" said Karlman.

"A five-meter tungsten rod at a hundredth of the speed of light," said March.

"Good God, man," said Heitz. "That will peel open the dome like a goddamn onion."

"Guess that will give the connecting airlocks a good test,"

said March. He tapped the emergency breath mask on his belt. "This will give fifteen minutes of emergency oxygen. Karlman, can she borrow one of your masks?" Karlman nodded and pulled the mask from his own belt and tossed it to Roanna, and she caught it with surprising deftness. "Give me a second one. Might need it for the hostage." One of the Ronstadt men handed March a mask, and he took it. "Lady Roanna. You have the ransom?"

"Here," she said, patting one of the pockets on her jumpsuit. "A credit drive that will transfer funds to any Mercator-compatible bank. Anonymously."

"The sort preferred by all good covert agents," said Bishop. "What is your plan?"

"To improvise," said March. "Any questions?"

There were none.

A SHORT TIME LATER, the lift car returned to the spaceport complex, and Heath, Heitz, Karlman, Bishop, and the remaining Ronstadt men left the car. Heath headed for the *Tiger's* docking bay at a run. Karlman departed with his men, and March suspected that the Ronstadt supervisor might have his own plan for vengeance.

Lorre might escape with the ransom, but he wouldn't get very far.

"Good luck, Captain March," said Heitz. "You're an idiot, but good luck."

"Thanks," said March. He turned to Bishop. "You had better head back to the restaurant. If those goes sour someone will need to know what happened."

"Good luck," said Bishop. "Come back, and you'll have a free meal on the house."

March laughed once. "There's a reason to live."

"Anne would be glad to see you," said Bishop with a wink.

"I'm sure," said March. He looked at Roanna, who stood with her arms wrapped around herself, face tight with fear. "Come on."

He walked back into the lift car with Roanna, set it for Dome 12, and closed the doors. The display panel informed him that the journey would take twelve minutes, and then the car shivered into motion.

"Anne," said Roanna at last

"What about her?" said March.

"She's the woman at Mr. Bishop's restaurant," said Roanna. "The one in the tight skirt."

"She said you were polite to her," said March.

"I was raised to be polite," said Roanna, staring at the wall. "Is she..." She thought about it for a moment. "Is she your girlfriend?"

"No," said March.

"Then she's not the reason that you..."

Her voice trailed off.

"The reason that I what?" said March.

"That you turned me down," she said in a quiet voice.

"No," said March.

She laughed a little. "I would have felt better if it was. A girl doesn't like to be rejected, even if the man rejecting her is keeping his head, and she is not."

"This isn't the time to discuss such things," said March.

"Lorre might kill us both," said Roanna. "There might never be a time to discuss anything ever again."

"Which means it is especially not the time to discuss it," said March.

"This is my fault, isn't it?" she said.

"What?" said March.

At last, she looked at him, her blue eyes full of pain. "I got all those men killed, didn't I?"

"No," said March. "You didn't."

She blinked, puzzled. "You're just trying to make me feel better."

"Do I really seem like the kind of man who makes women feel better?" said March.

She blinked again, then laughed, sobbed a little, laughed again, and pulled herself together.

"No," said Roanna. "No, I think no one in my life has ever spoken as bluntly to me as you have. Maybe I would be a better person if more people were so blunt to me. Maybe I wouldn't have gotten those men killed."

"You didn't get them killed," said March. "Lorre did. He's the one who dosed them with infiltrator drones, and the infiltrator drones are the ones who killed the Ronstadt men."

Roanna shook her head, black hair lashing around her face. "They were only there because of me."

"No," said March. "They were there because of your brother."

She stared at him.

"Your brother dabbled in dangerous things and got himself into trouble," said March.

"He did," said Roanna.

"And you came out here to rescue him," said March.

"You must think that was stupid," said Roanna, looking down again.

"Yes," said March. She flinched. "Stupid, but noble."

Roanna laughed a little again. "High praise."

"There are worse things in life than stupid and noble," said March. "No, if anyone is to blame for this, it's Lorre. Or, to be blunt, your brother. He did something stupid and a lot of people suffered for it." He shook his head. "I hope he's worth it."

"He is!" said Roanna. "He's a good man, I swear, he…he really is. He just got in over his head. He wanted to do something big with his life, something grand…"

"He should have stayed home and attended to his duty," said March.

They looked at each other.

"Yes," said Roanna. "Maybe I should have, too. I should have stayed home." She took a ragged breath. "But I had to help Thomas. I had to. Can you understand that?"

"I can," said March. "What's done is done. We have to be ready. You still have your pistol?"

She took one more deep breath and nodded, touching the gun at her hip.

"Keep it ready and in your hand," said March. "And follow my lead. If I tell you to get inside an airlock, do it."

"Because you will have told Heath to blow up the dome," said Roanna.

"If he aims right, the rod should go right through the dome and rip open the top," said March. "We should have a few seconds to get behind an airlock before the dome depressurizes. If not, that's what the masks are for." He shrugged. "We don't have to worry about being blown up."

"That's…comforting," said Roanna.

March grunted and checked his rifle again. "We just have worry about what Lorre might do."

"That's less comforting," said Roanna.

"Yes," said March. "There's not time to put together a good plan. We will just have to improvise."

They rode in silence for a few minutes.

"Captain March?" said Roanna.

"Yes?" said March.

"Thank you for all of this," said Roanna.

March shrugged. "It's my job."

"Even so," said Roanna. "I know you hate yourself, but you shouldn't. You've gone above and beyond the call of duty."

March snorted. "I don't hate myself."

"Men who don't hate themselves don't get annoyed when someone sees them with their shirt off," said Roanna.

"Men of sense don't appear half-undressed in front of unmarried young noblewomen," said March.

She laughed. "If nothing else, Captain March, you are a man of sense."

March said nothing. If he was a man of sense, he would have killed Lorre on Antioch Station and saved himself a world of trouble. And if he was a man of sense, maybe he wouldn't be rushing to this confrontation.

Roanna might have a point.

March pushed aside the thoughts. What was done was done. Regret was useless, and it was time to focus on the task at hand.

The car slowed as it approached Dome 12.

"Let me go first," said March. "Draw your pistol, but don't fire unless I say."

Roanna nodded and drew her gun.

"Also, please don't shoot me in the back," said March.

She almost smiled. "I promise."

The car stopped, and the door hissed open, stale air washing into the lift. March snapped up his rifle, looking through the door, but he saw nothing but a dim corridor, the only illumination from emergency lights along the floor.

"Come on," said March. He stepped into the corridor, leading the way, and Roanna trailed after him. She made more noise than he would have liked, but she was still quieter than he would have expected.

The corridor opened into Dome 12, the musty smell sharper. The dome overhead was about a hundred meters across, built of transparent metal braced with thick gray beams, the stars blazing overhead. The buildings below the dome were laid out in a round mall around a courtyard. Once a hydroponic garden had dominated the center of the courtyard, but now it was nothing more rusting equipment.

"Where is he?" whispered Roanna, her voice tight with strain.

March came to a decision. Any moment Lorre would detect them. Almost certainly he would take lethal action as soon as he felt safe to do so. March needed a distraction, and he needed it soon.

"Heath," he whispered, tapping his earpiece. "Fire in exactly ten minutes."

"Acknowledged," came Heath's voice.

"Are you sure?" whispered Roanna.

"No," said March.

Roanna digested this. "Where do you think Thomas is?"

"That building, likely," said March, looking at a two-story building on the other side of Dome 12. "Smallest windows. Most defensible place here, and it probably has an airlock connected to his ship. If I was hiding out, I would..."

A burst of static went over his earpiece. Their communications were being jammed.

Then static crackled from somewhere in the dome, and March spotted the speaker mounted over the door of the two-story building.

"Captain March, Lady Roanna, welcome," boomed Lorre's voice.

"Do you think he can hear us?" said Roanna.

"I can hear you just fine, Lady Roanna," said Lorre. "Please divest yourself of your weapons and come inside. I'm afraid, for the sake of your brother's health, that you must come unarmed. It would be a pity if a stray plasma bolt impacted his chest or skull."

"Do as he says," said March.

Roanna grimaced but dropped her pistol on the ground.

March had a lot of weapons, and he took his time removing them, stacking them upon the ground one by one. He kept a running count in his head as he did. Ten minutes came to six hundred seconds, and the training of an Iron Hand ensured he could keep an accurate count in his head.

That meant he had an operational plan. He had to locate Lorre and Thomas Vindex. Once he did, he to stall for the remainder of the time until Heath fired the railgun. And once Heath fired the railgun, March would need to neutralize Lorre and make sure Roanna and Thomas survived.

Right now, that meant stalling.

March divested himself of his weapons as slowly as he could, which took seventy-five seconds. Roanna watched him with a puzzled expression, but March could not share his plan with her with Lorre listening.

"All right," he called. "Weapons gone."

"Though an Iron Hand is never unarmed, is he not?" said Lorre. "Come into the building, please. Captain March first."

"Follow me," said March.

Ninety-six seconds had passed.

March crossed the mall and walked to the door. It swung open at his approach, revealing a darkened lobby illuminated only by a few emergency lights. A row of old chairs stood against one wall, and a receptionist's desk again another. A door behind the receptionist's desk led into a corridor lined with offices, and a flight of stairs led up to the second floor.

One hundred and sixteen seconds had passed.

Simon Lorre stood next to the office hallway, a plasma pistol in his hand and pointed at March. He looked just as he had on Antioch Station, big and scar-faced, but this time he was smiling, and his gun did not waver. March was fast, but there was no way he could cross the lobby before Lorre pulled the trigger.

"Face to face again, eh?" said Lorre. "Rare in our line of work, isn't it?"

"Conversation isn't in our line of work," said March. "We have the ransom, and we're here for Lord Thomas."

"Right to the point," said Lorre. "I appreciate that." He turned his gaze towards Roanna, though his gun remained pointed at March. His eyes flicked up and down Roanna's body in a proprietary manner. Roanna remained stony-faced. "Do you have the ransom, Lady Roanna?"

She held up the credit drive. "Where is my brother?"

"I think we can begin now," said Lorre. "Lord Thomas! Please join us."

One hundred and forty-seven seconds had passed.

A door opened in the offices, and a young man in a ship crewer's jumpsuit emerged. He had a lean build with thick black hair and deep blue eyes, and the family resemblance to Roanna was obvious. Roanna often wore a cool mask, but an arrogant sneer was Thomas Vindex's default expression.

He did not look as if he had been mistreated, and he was not restrained.

Thomas stopped at Lorre's right side. He looked at March, dismissed him, and shifted his eyes to Roanna, his sneer intensifying.

The cold suspicion in March's mind hardened into certainty.

"Thomas," said Roanna, relief flooding her voice. "Oh, thank God. Thank God. You're all right." She took a step forward, her arms coming up for a hug.

"Stay right where you are," said Thomas, his voice cracking like a whip.

Roanna froze, puzzlement coming over her face. "What? Thomas? I..."

"I said," said Thomas, drawing a plasma pistol and pointing it at her chest, "to stay right where you are."

Roanna stared at him, bewildered hurt going over her face. "Thomas? What are you doing?"

"I am acting for the greater good," said Thomas, smiling for the first time.

"Ah," said March. "They always say that."

One hundred and eighty seconds had passed.

"Why are you pointing a gun at me?" said Roanna in a small voice.

"Because, sister," said Thomas, "you are going to help me bring the Revolution of the Final Consciousness to Calaskar."

ANNOTATIONS ON SILENT ORDER: IRON HAND CHAPTER 9

T homas gloats over his betrayal of Roanna, boasting that the Final Consciousness is the next stage of human evolution and that he will feed Roanna into a mysterious mind-control machine built by the Machinists. Lorre cautions Thomas against gloating, but before they can proceed, Heath fires the railgun and damages Dome 12. In the resultant confusion, March overpowers Lorre, but the veteran operative escapes. Thomas is about to shoot March, but Roanna kills him first.

This is the climactic chapter, and the conflict is resolved. Roanna is rescued, but Thomas has been revealed as a traitor. The reason for Lorre's plot is the mind-control machine, which March captures after the final confrontation. March has succeeded in his mission, but at a cost – Thomas Vindex is dead, and Lorre escaped to continue plotting elsewhere. Nonetheless, Roanna is safe, and March has uncovered the mind-control machine of the Final Consciousness.

SILENT ORDER IRON HAND CHAPTER 9:
THE GLORY OF THE REVOLUTION

"What?" said Roanna. "No, no, no. Why are you saying those things?"

Thomas laughed with contempt, while Lorre's attention remained on March. "Poor little Roanna. You never were terribly bright, were you? Your whole life is dresses and banquets and stupid little social events. A brood mare for the upper classes of Calaskaran society. That was your entire purpose in life. You ought to thank me for this. You will have a chance to help the Revolution bring Calaskar under the guidance of the Final Consciousness."

"I don't understand," said Roanna. "I brought your ransom. I came here to rescue you. I..."

"This never was a ransom, was it?" interrupted March.

It was a golden opportunity. Thomas Vindex was all but quivering with gloating emotion. If March could keep him talking for another six and a half minutes, then Thomas would still be standing there pontificating when Heath fired the railgun.

Thomas's gaze turned towards March, and the contempt

upon his face intensified as the two hundredth second passed.

"What a pathetic man you are," said Thomas. "You were an Iron Hand, the elite of the Final Consciousness. You were the vanguard of the Revolution, its harbinger and its defender. You were part of the Final Consciousness, the only true god that humanity will ever know. And you threw it all away to join a wretched little kingdom with obsolete social structures and its shabby little secret service."

"It seems the traditional education of a Calaskaran noble," said March, "has given you the ability to dress envy up in pretty words."

Two hundred and thirty-three seconds had passed. Thomas Vindex clearly liked to talk.

"Envy?" said Thomas, incredulous. "Envious of what?"

"Of your father," said March. "Of your older brothers."

Thomas laughed, but there was a shrillness in his laughter that told March the insult had hit the mark. "Of my father? A dusty old fool..."

"Thomas!" said Roanna, but he kept talking.

"And my brothers? Pompous fools strutting about in their Calaskaran uniforms and spouting outdated religious superstitions..."

"Men who did their duty," said March, "and you were too weak to follow in their path. They had all the same chances you did, all the exact same opportunities, but they made something of them, and you screwed them up." Thomas's face darkened. "You screwed them up, and you ran away to the Machinists to have a tantrum, and..."

"Shut up," said Thomas, his voice low and dark.

"You ran away to have a tantrum," said March, "and Lorre's using you because you're too stupid to realize that you're being used."

Two hundred ninety-eight seconds had passed. March just had to stall for five more minutes.

"I said," said Thomas, "to shut up."

"Do you really think you'll get what Lorre promised you?" said March. "That he'll join you to the Final Consciousness? No. They'll feed your body into the organic recyclers or use you as slave labor in the foundries or the fields. Or he'll just shoot you and dump you out of an airlock because you were too stupid to see what..."

"I said to shut up!" roared Thomas, stepping forward.

Lorre laid a hand on Thomas's forearm, and the younger man subsided.

"Comrade Thomas," said Lorre, using the pompous style of address Machinist cells liked to affect among themselves. "I urge restraint."

"But..." said Thomas.

"I also urge you," said Lorre, "not to come within the grasp of an Iron Hand."

Thomas blinked, chagrin going over his expression as he realized the depth of his folly.

"Yes," he said. "Yes, Comrade Simon. You are right. I... almost acted rashly."

"Come along," said Lorre, gesturing with his pistol towards March and Roanna. "Both of you. Into the hallway."

"Aren't you going to tell her why, Comrade Thomas?" said March, putting scorn into the title.

"What?" said Thomas.

Three hundred and thirty seconds.

"She flew out all this way to rescue you," said March. "Aren't you going to tell her why you're going to kill her? Or are you going to let your sister go to her death believing you to be the moronic dupe of a far smarter man..."

"I'm not going to kill her, you idiot," said Thomas.

"Comrade Thomas," said Lorre with a grimace, but Thomas was too angry to care.

"I'm going to put her to use," said Thomas.

"What are you talking about, Thomas?" said Roanna.

"You're going to join us," said Thomas, and Lorre sighed with annoyance. He was too canny an operative to gloat about his plan, but Thomas lacked that kind of discipline.

"Comrade Thomas," said Lorre, "there is no need for your sister to know..."

"She will know!" said Thomas, his voice rising to a shout as he glared at the older man. "Let her know! I want to wipe that stupid smug smile off her face, just as I'm going to wipe the smug smiles off the face of every stupid stinking noble on Calaskar."

Lorre sighed again. "Fine. Just please be quick about it."

"You, sister, are going to join us," said Thomas, calming again.

Three hundred and sixty seconds.

"I will never join the filthy Machinists," said Roanna, making no effort to hide her contempt. "I know the atrocities the Final Consciousness has carried out. And I saw them with my own eyes. I saw what you did to the Graywolves! Your own men and you stabbed them in the back and turned them into those monsters. And for what?"

"To bring you here, of course," said Thomas. "And you will become one of us. Entirely against your will."

"No," said Roanna.

"Yes," said Thomas. "You see, sister, the victory of the Revolution of the Final Consciousness is inevitable. I have seen the future. I have seen the secrets of the Final Consciousness, and the Pulse is coming. It will bring Calaskar to its knees. To prepare the way for the Pulse, we are seeding agents throughout Calaskar. The science of the

Machinists has found a way to forcibly convert someone to our cause."

"What?" said March.

"Oh, the Silent Order doesn't know everything?" said Thomas. "There's a surprise." He laughed as the four hundredth second passed. "I admit I don't understand the science behind it myself. The machine rewrites and reprograms the nervous system, mapping its electrical impulses and reshaping them. With the device, we can turn anyone into a covert agent for our cause without their knowledge. It actually is rather brilliant. Agents of the Final Consciousness tend to have red flags in their background like I do now, or have obvious cybernetic and nanotech alterations as does your poor pet Iron Hand here. The device will create undetectable agents."

"Then that's what this was about," said March. "This wasn't a ransom. This was never a kidnapping. It wasn't even an assassination attempt. This was always a trap. You and Lorre wanted to lure your sister out here so you could use this machine of yours to convert her into a Machinist agent."

"Yes," said Thomas. "Once you are dead and we have finished, my sister and I will return to Calaskar with the machine. No one will suspect us. I will renounce my past sins and throw myself into my work with enthusiasm, all while feeding information to the Machinists. And I will convert my siblings one by one. I especially look forward to seeing my father's expression when I strap him into the machine."

"Why would you do this?" said Roanna, on the verge of tears. "We love you, Thomas. I love you. I..."

"What a useless word," said Thomas. "You love me? You and all my family only loved me so long as I smiled and saluted the King and went to church and said all the right things. What useless, hollow creatures you are…and you are all the more appalling because you stand in the way of progress. You stand in the way of human evolution. The Final Consciousness is God, Roanna. Mankind will evolve to become God, and all shall be one together in the unity of the Final Consciousness for the duration of the universe."

"I'm sure the people in the Machinist slave camps," said March, "are feeling all kinds of unity."

Thomas laughed. "When mankind becomes God, the unworthy will have to be purged."

"You're a monster," whispered Roanna. "You're a monster, and you're a murderer. I defended you! I stood up for you for years, every time you got drunk and made a scene! I came here to rescue you." Her face quivered with grief. "I thought you were a better man than this."

Five hundred seconds had passed. March just had to keep this conversation going for another minute and a half, and then he could act.

"I am a better man than you thought," said Thomas. "I am one of the vanguard of the Revolution." March was watching Lorre, so he caught the brief flicker of contempt that crossed the Machinist agent's face, a flicker that soon vanished behind his professional, sardonic mask. "I will help overthrow the obsolete and reactionary Kingdom of Calaskar and bring it into the fold of the Final Consciousness. History will remember me as a hero."

"I threw away my life to save you," whispered Roanna, "and they were right about you."

"What?" said Thomas, his face darkening. "What did you say? What did they say about me?"

"They said you were a coward and a drunkard, too much of a spoiled child to take a man's duties," said Roanna, "but I see that they were too kind. You are a coward and a murderer, tearing down the work of better men to salve your pride..."

"You dare!" said Thomas, starting towards her, drawing back his hand to strike her. Roanna did not move but only glared at him with shriveling contempt.

"Comrade Thomas," said Lorre. "Comrade Thomas!" He grabbed Thomas's arm, and the younger man stilled, glaring at Lorre.

"What?" said Thomas.

Five hundred and forty-seven seconds had passed.

"You've said your piece, and further delay is dangerous, comrade," said Lorre, his attention on Thomas, though his gun remained pointed at March. "Might I remind you that both Administrator Heitz and Ronstadt Corporation know exactly where we are located? The sooner we are gone from here, the better."

"Yes," said Thomas, getting control of himself with an effort. "Yes, you are right. Maybe we had better load the machine onto the ship."

"No," said Lorre. "That would defeat the purpose of this entire operation if you were caught with me. No, the procedure on Lady Roanna should take no more than five minutes. Once that is done, I will depart. Eventually, the Ronstadt thugs and the local branch of the Silent Order will arrive, and you and your sister can spin a tale of how Captain March sacrificed himself heroically to save you both, though the sinister Machinist agent escaped in the chaos."

"So, what are we going to do with March?" said Thomas.

Five hundred and eighty seconds had passed.

"This, of course," said Lorre, and he pointed his pistol at March and squeezed the trigger.

There was a flare of a plasma bolt, but March had seen it

coming, and he had been ready. His left arm snapped up, his metal hand coiling into a fist as it tried to shield his chest.

The plasma bolt drilled into his left arm and turned his hand to vapor.

It didn't hurt, not precisely. His left arm never felt pain the way his flesh did. Nonetheless, it was not a pleasant sensation, and the feeling of damage shot up his cybernetic arm as his brain tried to interpret the input.

But in the heat of the moment, there was no way for Lorre to know that March's arm had blocked the bolt.

March threw himself backward, feigning a grunt of pain, and collapsed upon his back, breathing hard. Roanna screamed and started towards him, but Thomas pointed his gun at her again, and she froze.

"Is he dead?" said Thomas.

"Not yet," said Lorre, taking one step forward and leveling his gun at March's face. "But he's going to be. Take her back there and strap her into the machine, and start the precheck. We'll begin the procedure as soon as I..."

Six hundred seconds had passed.

For another second, nothing happened.

March felt the vibration in the floor before he heard the explosion.

Lorre froze, looking around in alarm, and then the sound reached them as Heath's railgun shot ripped off the top of Dome 12. A howling gale rushed through the reception room, followed by the furious bleating of vacuum alarms. More alarms went off as the air started to retreat, followed by a metallic hiss as an emergency door came down over the entrance.

"What the hell?" snarled Lorre, stepping back, his gun sweeping back and forth as he tried to cover every possible angle at once.

"What's happening?" said Thomas, his eyes wide as he backed towards the wall.

"A breach," snapped Lorre. "An attack. An ambush..."

He realized his danger at the last minute and swung back towards March, but by then March was already moving.

He leaped off the floor, his damaged left arm serving as a lever, and flung himself at Lorre. The Machinist agent cursed and fired again, but March anticipated the movement and ducked. He felt a flare of pain in his left shoulder as the plasma bolt passed close enough to vaporize a patch of his jacket, and then his shoulder slammed into Lorre's gut. The Machinist agent fell with a grunt, and March hammered his damaged left arm down like a club. The stump of his wrist clipped the pistol and sent it clattering to the floor. March drew back his right arm to strike, but Lorre reacted faster and grabbed something from his belt.

It was a stun gun.

March twisted as Lorre fired, and the stunning blast only clipped him. Nevertheless, it was enough to make the muscles of March's left leg seize up, and he stumbled and landed hard on his back as the alarms continued wailing. Lorre whirled and sprinted down the corridor, and a second later March heard the clang of a cycling airlock. Likely that airlock led to Lorre's gunship.

Simon Lorre was clever enough to know when a situation had gone bad and it was time to cut his losses.

March cursed in fury, trying to force his twitching legs to obey him, and Thomas Vindex stepped before him.

His gun was pointed at March's face.

"It's over, Thomas," said March.

"No, it's not," said Thomas, his voice glacially calm. All the rage had drained from him, leaving cold clarity in its wake. "If I kill you, I can say Lorre did it. There's still time to put Roanna in the machine and finish before your friends arrive to rescue you." He smiled. "Then the plan will still work, and I get all the credit."

"Then you'll do this to your sister?" said March. "To your family?"

"With a smile on my face," said Thomas, "because they deserve it. Just as I'm going to kill you with a smile on my face."

He smiled, pointed the gun at March's chest, and a plasma bolt flared in the gloom.

Thomas stiffened, his eyes going wide, and smoke rose from the crater that had just been blasted into the back of his head.

He collapsed, dead before he hit the floor.

Roanna stood behind him, Lorre's gun in her hands. She dropped the weapon, walked to her brother's side, and fell to her knees next to him.

She bowed her head and sobbed.

ANNOTATIONS ON SILENT ORDER: IRON HAND CHAPTER 10

In the final chapter, we wrap up the story with the resolution. March takes Roanna and Heath to safety on a Calaskaran space station. Heath is recruited into the Silent Order in exchange for keeping his naval career, and March has a new assignment from Censor – deliver the mind-control machine to scientists who will study it.

The mind-control machine acts as a plot hook for the next book in the series, SILENT ORDER: WRAITH HAND. Chapter 10 allowed me to wrap up the plot of SILENT ORDER: IRON HAND, resolving all the conflicts while leaving threads to continue the story in SILENT ORDER: WRAITH HAND.

SILENT ORDER IRON HAND CHAPTER 10: THE SILENT ORDER

Between the stun blast, the near-hit from the plasma bolt, and his damaged arm, March didn't feel all that good, but there was work to be done.

"I'll be right back," said March.

Roanna didn't seem to hear him, her shoulders hunched and shaking as she wept. March started to head down the hallway and then realized that leaving a distraught woman alone with two guns was probably not the smartest thing to do. He picked up both pistols with his right hand.

Roanna didn't seem to notice.

March headed into the hallway, tucking one pistol into his pocket and holding the other with his right hand. He walked to the end of the corridor and peered through the narrow windows in the airlock door. Beyond he saw the barren surface of the asteroid, with recent scorch marks from a takeoff. No doubt Lorre's ship had left the scorch marks when he made his hasty escape.

That was disappointing. He had really wanted to kill Lorre.

In the last office before the airlock, he found the

jamming device. It was a standard broad-spectrum radio jammer, similar to a hundred other March had seen, and he switched it off. Next to the jammer rested something that looked like a dentist's chair, and attached to the head of the chair was a machine that March had never seen before.

A metal visor rested against the back of the chair, adjustable to the size of the victim's head. Electrodes ringed the visor, a bundle of wires connecting to a small cylindrical computer about the size of a can of soup. The computer was connected to...

March blinked.

He didn't know what the computer was connected to.

It was a bundle of alien-looking electronics about the size of his head, glowing with an eerie green light. Part of it looked like fiber-optic cabling, and if he had to guess he would say that some of the components were capacitors and transmitters of some kind. At its heart was a strange thing that looked vaguely like a metallic green beetle the size of his thumb, and March had no idea what it did.

He felt a growing pressure in his damaged left arm. He would have to attend to that soon.

His earpiece crackled. "March? March, you there?"

"Yeah," said March, gazing at the machine. "Good shot, Heath. Came right in time."

"What's your status?" said Heath.

"A little scorched, but otherwise well," said March. "Lady Roanna is unhurt." He grimaced. "Lorre escaped, and Thomas Vindex is dead."

"Dear God," said Heath. "What happened?"

March looked up and saw Roanna standing in the doorway, her face twisted with pain.

"Lorre tried to kill Roanna to cover his escape," said March. "Thomas threw himself in front of the shot, and

Lorre got away before I could get him. I don't suppose his ship got shot down?"

"No," said Heath. "The station fired a half-dozen missiles at him, but he opened a hyperspace tunnel about three seconds before they would have taken him."

"Damn it," said March. "Bring the Tiger to Dome 12 and dock at the airlock. We'll come aboard and decide what to do from there."

"Acknowledged," said Heath, and the call ended.

Roanna looked at him in silence, and March grimaced and pressed the stump of his left hand against the interior wall of the office.

The pressure in his arm got worse.

"Is that what we're going to tell everyone?" Roanna said at last. "That he died heroically saving me from Lorre?"

"Yes," said March. "Unless you would rather tell everyone the truth."

"The truth that I murdered my brother?" said Roanna.

"You saved my life," said March. "Also, killing isn't murder if it's in self-defense."

Tiny holes appeared in the wall around the stump of his arm, like the holes in expensive cheese.

"He wouldn't have killed me," said Roanna.

"No," said March, nodding towards the machine. "He would have done something worse."

"What...what is that thing?" said Roanna.

"I have no idea," said March. "At a guess, I think that it would turn you into an agent of the Final Consciousness, maybe even without you knowing. It can't be nanobots or cybernetics. Those show up on most scans. It must be some kind of...neurological reprogramming. I don't know."

"We should destroy it," said Roanna.

"No," said March. "We need to take it back with us. The

Silent Order has to know about this thing, whatever it is. You heard your brother. He planned to use the machine on your entire family. I would bet this isn't the first time the Machinists have done this."

The pressure in his arm got worse.

"Oh, God," said Roanna. "Oh, God. Thomas, how could you have done this?" She rubbed her face. "I'm always going to hate myself for this. Always, always, always."

"You shouldn't," said March. Wisps of smoke rose from the wall. "You saw what he helped to do. He confessed it in front of you. He would have done much worse."

"Is...that how you live with what you've done?" said Roanna in a small voice.

"Sometimes," said March.

"Does it get easier?" said Roanna.

"No," said March.

They lapsed into silence. Roanna cried for a little while, the silent, ugly tears of someone who could not stop themselves. At last, she pulled herself together and sniffled a few times.

"What are you doing to the wall?" she said.

The pressure in his arm reached a crescendo. "This."

He wrenched his stump loose, and Roanna yelped and took a step away from him.

A mass of molten metal glowed at the end of his arm, rippling and folding as the nanobots did their work.

"The wall," said Roanna. "It...it looks like the wall in the hydroponics bay."

"It does," said March. "I was an Iron Hand. This is a Machinist cybernetic prosthesis." The pressure grew, and he clenched his new left hand, the fingers molten and glowing. "It knows how to rebuild itself. The nanobots in my arm harvested metal from the walls and started repairing the hand."

Roanna stared at his glowing fingers with a mixture of fascination and revulsion. "Like...like the infiltrator drones."

"The exact same technology," said March, forcing the fingers to clench again. It would take a while before the new hand was calibrated. The pressure in his arm had eased, but his shoulder hurt, and he felt light-headed and ravenous. Rebuilding damage to his cybernetic parts always threw his metabolism into overdrive.

They waited in silence. March occupied himself by searching the remaining offices. He found the room where Thomas had been staying, with a cot and a laptop computer. The computer he would take with him. Perhaps the Silent Order could find something useful on it.

"Captain March?" said Roanna at last.

"Yes?" said March, looking at her.

"Thank you for trying to save my brother," said Roanna. March inclined his head.

"I think I would like to go home now," said Roanna.

"We can do that," said March.

Light flared outside the airlock window as Heath brought the Tiger in to dock.

AFTER HEATH DOCKED, Roanna went straight to her cabin and locked herself in, no doubt to cry. March let her go, and then helped Heath get Lorre's machine and Thomas's laptop into the strong room. With March's hand still molten, Heath had to do most of the work, but the young man was eager as ever.

"Then Lorre killed Lord Thomas?" said Heath once March had finished giving him the altered version of events.

"I'm afraid so," said March. "Shot him in the back of the head. The entire thing was a trap, and Thomas was the bait. Once Lorre realized it had gone to hell, he shot Thomas to cover his escape."

"Damn it," said Heath. "Then this was all for nothing."

"Not necessarily," said March. "That machine of Lorre's...whatever it is, it's important. It might be more important than any of our lives. The Silent Order and the Admiralty have to know about it."

"Maybe," said Heath.

"And we did save Roanna's life," said March. "Or saved her from Lorre feeding her into that machine."

"Yes," said Heath, brightening a bit. "That is something. That is more than something."

"Go back to the flight cabin and get Vigil started on preflight checks," said March. "We'll have to leave in a hurry."

Heath nodded and left the cargo bay, climbing up the ladder to the dorsal corridor. March waited until he was out of earshot, then pulled out his phone and called Bishop.

"Well," said Bishop, "how did it go?"

"Thomas Vindex is dead," said March. He gave Bishop the real version of what had happened in Dome 12, along with the proposed cover story. "What do Heitz and Karlman think?"

"They're both furious," said Bishop. "Karlman is out for blood, and Heitz is annoyed that he'll have to repair Dome 12. Our Lieutenant Heath is a good shot. It will work out, though. Heitz and Ronstadt Private Security Corporation have gotten a bit lax. Next time I ask them to help clear off some Machinist agents, they'll be more willing to cooperate. This device of Lorre's. What do you think it is?"

March looked at the device. "At a guess, I think it's some sort of brainwashing machine. Thomas implied it would turn someone into a Machinist against their will, but that usually involves nanotech. I think it must implant hidden commands in the victim, commands that can be activated later."

"Turning someone into a sleeper agent without their knowledge," said Bishop, voice grim. "And you think the Machinists have done this before?"

"Probably," said March. "Or they're field-testing the prototypes, and this is one of them."

"Either way," said Bishop, "you had better get that thing to Censor as soon as possible. I would suggest leaving at once. Heitz is pissed at you, and if you land in a proper bay, he'll probably have Ronstadt arrest you for questioning."

"What about you?" said March.

"Me?" Bishop laughed. "I'm just a simple restauranteur, Jack. A dashing yet stunningly handsome entrepreneur. A businessman trying to turn an honest profit out here on the edge of civilization. Plus, I know where all the bodies are buried. Who knows? Maybe we'll have the chance to work together again."

"I hope so," said March.

He ended the call, and March headed for the flight cabin.

A short time later the Tiger's dark matter reactor, hyperdrive, and resonator came online, and they left Rustbelt Station behind.

~

Fifteen hyperspace jumps and three and a half days later, the Tiger returned to Antioch Station. The five concentric metal rings still gleamed in space, and the twin Royal Calaskaran Navy destroyers guarded the station. March guided the Tiger to its assigned docking port and then walked with Roanna and Heath onto the station.

Roanna had changed clothing, wearing a rich formal blue dress favored by the noblewomen of Calaskar. March had to admit that it made her look beautiful, though her eyes remained haunted. March rented a drone cart to carry her luggage behind them.

"In the files I received when I left Antioch Station," said March as they walked through the crowded concourse on Ring One, "one of them was a letter of transit from your father. I've sent it to your phone. Show that to the officer of the watch at the Royal Naval office here, and they'll arrange for transportation home."

"I know," said Roanna. "Father always did think of everything." She closed her eyes for a moment. "Except, perhaps, for what to do with Thomas." She offered him a brittle smile. "At least Thomas died well."

"Yes," said March. He supposed that was the truth. Thomas Vindex had gotten what he deserved.

At last, they reached the office suite the Calaskaran Royal Navy used on Antioch Station, a sprawling complex that occupied much of Ring One. Large screens showed videos relating the glorious history of the Calaskaran Royal Navy or explained how Calaskar's system of government avoided the historical excesses of dictatorships, parliamentary democracies, socialism, and republics. Quite a few of the screens were devoted to recruitment videos for the Navy.

"You know," said Roanna. "I never thought I would miss those videos."

"Some things make you appreciate home all the more," said Heath.

"Yes," said Roanna. She took a deep breath. "Lieutenant Heath...Sam...thank you. Thank you for everything. I would have died if not for your help."

Heath offered a formal bow. "It was my honor, my lady."

"I'm so sorry," said Roanna. "I know this ruined your career."

Heath shrugged. "Of all the things a man can sacrifice upon the altar of duty, a career is one of the lesser things."

"I will speak to my father for you," said Roanna. "I hope he can intervene on your behalf."

"That may not be necessary," said March. He still had to call Censor...and he suspected he knew how that conversation would play out.

"And you, Captain March," said Roanna, looking up at him. "Thank you. Both Sam and I would be dead if not for you."

March met her gaze. "I regret that I was not able to save your brother."

He did not regret Thomas's death. The man had allied himself to the Final Consciousness. But he did regret that Roanna had been forced to shoot him. That Thomas had not been the man that Roanna had believed him to be.

And a small part of him regretted not taking Roanna's offer in the Tiger's gym.

"Do not," said Roanna. "You did all any man could do. Goodbye, my friends." She hesitated. "If...you are ever in need of help, come to me, and I will provide it if I can."

"Goodbye, Lady Roanna," said March.

To his surprise, she leaned forward and kissed Heath on the cheek, and then March. With one last smile, she turned and walked into the Naval office, the small drone cart carrying her luggage behind her.

"That," said March a moment later, "is a very dangerous young woman."

"Yes," said Heath.

"Just watch," said March. "In a few decades, she'll be one of those noblewomen arranging half the government of Calaskar from behind the scenes. Whoever she marries will wind up as Minister of Security or Prime Minister or one of the Lords of the Admiralty."

Heath snorted. "I wonder if they'll need a janitor."

"A janitor?" said March.

"Well, I am going to need a new career," said Heath. "If I'm lucky, I won't get imprisoned for going AWOL. But either way, I think my days in the Navy are done."

"We'll see about that," said March. "Come with me."

They went to March's favorite restaurant, and he bought Heath breakfast and then bribed the bartender for the use of the supply room. As Heath ate in one of the booths, March locked the door to the supply room pulled out his phone.

A moment later Censor answered his call.

"Captain March," said Censor in his dry, sardonic voice. "I have just received word that Lady Roanna Vindex walked into the naval office of Antioch Station with a letter of transit."

"She did, sir," said March.

"Care to enlighten me as to the particulars?"

March gave his report. Censor listened in silence for the most part, though he interrupted a few times to request greater details.

"I see," said Censor. "You have done well. We've had reports of machines like this on several outlying and neutral worlds, but we haven't been able to capture one for examination. It would have been good to bring in Thomas Vindex for questioning, but his computer will tell us almost as much about his activities."

"Then we shall say he died protecting his sister?" said March.

"Yes, that will be the official story," said Censor. "It would gall Lord Thomas to no end to know that his death will be used as a propaganda weapon against the Machinists."

"The machine, sir," said March. "What is it?"

"We don't yet know," said Censor. "We suspect it is an instrument designed to suborn people against their will, some sort of brainwashing device. Which is why your next assignment will be to fly the device to a rendezvous with a Royal Calaskaran Navy cruiser, which will then take the machine for examination."

"Thomas mentioned something else, sir," said March. "Something he called the 'Pulse.' Do you know what that is?"

Censor was silent for a moment.

"We do not," he said, "much to my very great annoyance. We've heard talk of it among the Machinist agents, but we do not yet know what it is. The Machinists are up to something, Captain March, and there is a great deal of work for the Silent Order to do. Which is why after you drop off the device, you will proceed immediately to your next assignment."

"Yes, sir," said March. "Before I do, I have a request."

"Concerning young Lieutenant Heath, I assume?" said Censor.

March told him what he had in mind.

"Very well," said Censor. "If the lieutenant is amenable, we shall proceed."

March left the room and found Heath halfway through his breakfast.

"Come with me," said March, and he took Heath to the supply room.

"Lieutenant Samuel Heath," said Censor once March had locked the door and switched his phone to speaker mode. "I am known as Censor, the head of the Silent Order."

"Sir," said Heath, his eyes going wide.

"The Calaskaran Royal Navy is the Kingdom of Calaskar's first line of defense," said Censor. "But as you have seen, there are threats that the Navy cannot defeat. If Lorre had succeeded in using his machine on Lady Roanna, he might have caused untold damage to Calaskar, and no ship of the Navy would have stopped him."

"I saw that firsthand, sir," said Heath.

"A choice lies before you," said Censor. "You may choose to leave the Navy and continue your life elsewhere. If you do, in gratitude for your efforts, we will arrange for the Navy to forego prosecution. However, if you choose to swear to the Silent Order, we will ensure that your naval career continues, though you will have to be demoted to Ensign. An AWOL cannot be entirely excused."

"If I swear to the Silent Order?" said Heath, wary. "I will not betray the Navy or the Kingdom."

"Nor would we ask it of you," said Censor. "The Silent Order is dedicated to the defense of Calaskar, just as the Navy is. But the Navy fights battles in space. We fight battles in the shadows...and you, Samuel Heath, have been called to do both. Many in the Navy do not understand the necessity of the work we do. You do. You have seen the dangers that threaten the Kingdom. A Naval officer who understands the nature of our shadow war and who can protect the Navy from traitors within the fleet would be invaluable. Will you join us?"

"I will, sir," said Heath, and Censor led him through the oath to become a member of the Silent Order.

"Welcome, then," said Censor. "Your first assignment is to report to the naval office and present yourself for duty. Once the matter of the AWOL charge is cleared, you will receive your new assignment...and your first orders from the Order. Captain March, you, too have your tasks."

The call ended.

"Well," said Heath at last. "I guess I'm a spy now."

"You are," said March. "Perhaps we will work together again."

"I would enjoy that," said Heath.

They finished eating breakfast, and then went their separate ways, Heath to the naval office, and March to the Tiger.

He had work to do. Oh, yes, he had work to do.

March had seen firsthand the horrors the Final Consciousness wreaked upon its victims...and he intended to stop them.

33

A FINAL NOTE

I hope the annotations and the chapters of Silent Order: Iron Hand have given you an example of story structure to follow.

Remember to follow the rules of story structure, and you will be able to write compelling books that will hold your readers' attention!

THE END

For more writing advice, visit my website at Jonathan-Moeller.com or my podcast, The Pulp Writer Show.

If you liked the book, please consider leaving a review at your ebook site of choice. To receive immediate notification of new releases, sign up for my newsletter, or watch for news on my Facebook page.

ABOUT THE AUTHOR

USA Today bestselling author Jonathan Moeller has written over 110 novels, including the bestselling FROSTBORN, SEVENFOLD SWORD, DRAGONTIARNA and THE GHOSTS fantasy series, and the SILENT ORDER science fiction series. His books have sold over a million and a half copies worldwide.

Visit his website at:

http://www.jonathanmoeller.com

jmcontact@jonathanmoeller.com

You can sign up for his email newsletter here, or watch for news on his Facebook page or Twitter feed.